Democracy and Revolution

Democracy & Revolution

*From ancient Greece to
modern capitalism*

George Novack

Pathfinder

New York   London   Montreal   Sydney

ISBN 0-87348-191-7 paper; ISBN 0-87348-192-5 cloth
Library of Congress Catalog Card Number 74-143807
Manufactured in the United States of America

First edition, 1971
Fourth printing, 1993

Cover design by Eric Simpson
Cover illustration: 1848 revolution in Paris

Pathfinder
410 West Street, New York, NY 10014, U.S.A.
Fax: (212) 727-0150

Pathfinder distributors around the world:
Australia (and Asia and the Pacific):
	Pathfinder, 19 Terry St., Surry Hills, Sydney, N.S.W. 2010
	Postal address: P.O. Box K879, Haymarket, N.S.W. 2000
Britain (and Europe, Africa except South Africa, and Middle East):
	Pathfinder, 47 The Cut, London, SE1 8LL
Canada:
	Pathfinder, 4581 rue St-Denis, Montreal, Quebec, H2J 2L4
Iceland:
	Pathfinder, Klapparstíg 26, 2d floor, 101 Reykjavík
	Postal address: P. Box 233, 121 Reykjavík
New Zealand:
	Pathfinder, La Gonda Arcade, 203 Karangahape Road, Auckland
	Postal address: P.O. Box 8730, Auckland
Sweden:
	Pathfinder, Vikingagatan 10, S-113 42, Stockholm
United States (and Caribbean, Latin America, and South Africa):
	Pathfinder, 410 West Street, New York, NY 10014

Dedicated to the memory of

Tom Paine

Lover of justice, friend of man, implacable enemy of tyranny, international revolutionary and citizen of the world

Contents

Foreword 9

SECTION I. PRECAPITALIST FORMS OF POLITICAL DEMOCRACY

1. **Success in Greece** *7*
2. **Failure in Rome** *34*
3. **The Democracy of the Medieval Communes** *39*

SECTION II. THE RISE AND DECLINE OF BOURGEOIS DEMOCRACY

4. **Tasks and Forces of the Bourgeois Revolutions** *49*
5. **Achievements and Limitations of the Bourgeois Revolutions** *58*
6. **Bourgeois Democratic Ideology** *102*
7. **The Evolution of Parliamentarism** *127*
8. **Parliamentary Democracy in Crisis** *142*
9. **Bonpartism, Military Dictatorship, and Fascism** *155*

SECTION III. THE DEVELOPMENT OF DEMOCRACY
IN THE UNITED STATES

10. **Two Traditions of American Democracy** *179*

11. **The Realities of American Democracy** *190*

12. **How Can Democracy Be Defended
     and Extended?** *206*

SECTION IV. PROBLEMS AND PROSPECTS OF
POST-CAPITALIST DEMOCRACY

13. **Socialism and Bureaucracy** *223*

14. **The Colonial Struggle for Democracy** *251*

15. **Democratic Prospects for a Socialist
     America** *265*

     Notes *277*

     Bibliography *280*

     Index *283*

George Novack

George Novack (1905-1992) joined the communist movement in the United States in 1933, and remained a member and leader of the Socialist Workers Party until his death.

As national secretary of the American Committee for the Defense of Leon Trotsky, Novack helped organize the 1937 International Commission of Inquiry that investigated the charges fabricated by Stalin's Moscow trials. In the 1940s Novack was national secretary of the Civil Rights Defense Committee, which gathered support for leaders of the SWP and of the Midwest Teamsters' strikes and organizing drive who were framed up and jailed under the witch-hunting Smith Act. He played a prominent role in numerous other civil liberties and civil rights battles over subsequent decades, including the landmark lawsuit against FBI spying and disruption won by the Socialist Workers Party in 1986. He was also active in defense of the Cuban revolution and against the war in Vietnam.

His works include: *An Introduction to the Logic of Marxism; Genocide against the Indians; The Origins of Materialism; Existentialism versus Marxism; Empiricism and Its Evolution; How Can the Jews Survive? A Socialist Answer to Zionism; The Marxist Theory of Alienation; Democracy and Revolution; Understanding History; Humanism and Socialism; The Revolutionary Potential of the Working Class; Pragmatism versus Marxism; America's Revolutionary Heritage;* and *Polemics in Marxist Philosophy.*

FOREWORD

Democracy has different meanings to different people — and to different classes. Some scholars contend that the concept is too vague and variegated to be precisely or adequately defined. Their doubts come from the fact that the content and forms of democracy have changed considerably in the course of its development. New historical conditions and social alignments have brought new types of democracy into being and novel aspects of democracy to consider and be realized.

Despite this diversity, the essential features of this mode of rule can be discerned and formulated. In the first chapter, *political democracy* is discriminated from primitive tribal equality and defined as a special kind of government in class society representing, in reality or in pretension, the supremacy of the many over the few through the mechanism of the territorial state.

The nature of democracy as well as its prospects can best be understood by tracing the main stages of its evolution. Political democracy, like every other social phenomenon, is the child of time. Its preconditions were created in the womb of class society. It came to birth among certain Greek city-states of the first millenium B. C. The term, *democratia,* was coined by the Greeks in the fifth century B. C. After being stamped out in antiquity, urban democracy again rose to find an uneasy seat in the medieval communes of Western Europe. Later on, democratic and republican nation-states which marked the accession of bourgeois forces to power were established through popular revolutions against the monarchy. Capitalist democracy acquired a matured parliamentary form during the nineteenth century.

Most Americans are ignorant of this twenty-five-hundred-

year career of political democracy. As a rule, they lack a
lively sense of history. The background of their most cherished
institutions is to them an unopened book. Thoroughly convinced that they enjoy the utmost in democracy, our citizens
are taught and know very little about its actual record of
development.

Since the mid-nineteenth century, most Americans have taken
an uncritical attitude toward their political system. As Professor Ralph Gabriel observed: "Romantic democracy was a
cluster of ideas which made up a national faith and which,
though unrecognized as such, had the power of a State religion."[1]

Idealized democracy remains the secular creed of the United
States, the ideological cement that binds together the members
of all its classes. It is venerated as a fixture of almost supernatural origin and substance. Like all objects of worship, this
hallowed institution is enshrouded by taboos which prohibit
too close inspection by profane meddlers who might expose
its pretensions, tamper with its sacraments or alter it too radically.

While the American people are receptive to innovations in
most areas, they remain extremely conservative in their views
on politics. The governmental structure of the United States is
the oldest of any in the major industrialized nations. Yet Americans are persuaded that the constitutional foundations of the
Republic laid down in the late eighteenth century, with certain
rights accumulated and revisions made since, provide a universal standard of good government.

They are mistaken in thinking that their system stands at
the apex of political achievement and the future can bring
no better. Democracy is a good thing. More democracy is
still better. Nonetheless, democracy is far from having attained
its fullest and final expression either in the United States or
elsewhere. In fact, this form of government is destined to undergo its most profound transformation in the present epoch of
transition from capitalism to socialism. As Americans participate in this process, they will have to adjust to this prospect, as other nations have already had to do.

The assertion that our democracy is superficial, incomplete
in essentials, and overdue for radical reconstruction horrifies
ultrapatriots. They have put "democracy: made in the U. S. A."
into a package labeled 99 and 44/100 percent pure and advertise it as superior to any other in the world. Actually, the
commodity peddled by the profiteers is not only inferior but

often injurious. One purpose of this book is to warn uninformed and unwary consumers of its misrepresented claims.

This survey of the career of democracy aims to clear away some major misconceptions about this form of government which befog the minds of Americans and hold back their political enlightenment. Democracy in general, and our own plutocratic brand in particular, has to be defetishized. Once it has been stripped of mystifications and its body laid bare, we can see what it really is and foresee what it may become.

There is good precedent for this kind of undertaking. In the late eighteenth century, an overseas monarchy had dominated the population of the Atlantic seaboard for nearly two hundred years. Almost all the colonists looked upon the rule of the mother country as imperishable and irreplaceable. They did not suspect that its usefulness had been exhausted or that conditions were ripening for its replacement by a new and higher form of government.

Then, as now, the minds of men lagged behind the necessities of their economic and social development and had to be shaken up in order to stir them into revolutionary action. The ideological cornerstone of the old order was a deep-seated belief in the sanctity of the British crown, which it was heretical to question and seditious to deny.

The rebel patriots had to invoke explosive arguments against the king's claims to continued sovereignty. Tom Paine, newly arrived from England in 1774, headed the agitators who dynamited the preconceptions of their fellow Americans. In *Common Sense*, that call to action published early in 1776, he first unfurled the banner of antimonarchism, independence and republicanism.

To render crown rule hateful, ridiculous and insupportable and tear down the "divinity that doth hedge about a king," Paine condemned monarchy in principle and castigated George III in person. Monarchy, he said, was contrary to the laws of nature and the mandates of God. It was no less absurd for a satellite to rule over a sun in a planetary system than for an island like Great Britain to dominate the North American continent. According to his revolutionary interpretation of scriptural authority, kingship had nothing divine about it; it was, on the contrary, heathenish, popish and "the invention of the devil."

The reigning George III was a "sceptred savage," a "royal brute," a "breathing automaton." The time had come, Paine announced, for Americans to throw off submission to his royal

tyranny and establish a free and independent republic which
vested sovereignty in the people.

He concluded his demolition of monarchy by exalting the
common man above the crowned head. "Of more worth is
one honest man to society and in the sight of God," he declared,
"than all the crowned ruffians that ever lived."

The irreverent arguments circulated by Tom Paine to deprive the hereditary monarchy of its halo and expose its desue-
tude fell, as we know, upon receptive ears and led on to its
overthrow in the War of Independence. The shattering of this
idol of the old ruling order and the triumph of the doctrine
of the sovereignty of the people which challenged it culminated
in the establishment of a representative republic. These have
been the greatest steps yet taken to introduce more progressive
institutions and reasonable ideas into American politics.

Contrary to popular opinion, they are not to be the last.
Since belief in the divine right of kings has been forever disposed of, another anachronism has taken its place as the ideological cover for an outlived system of upper-class rule. This
is the cult of an exalted abstract democracy which stands as
a major deterrent to the political understanding and advancement of the American people. Today this fetish has to be un-
masked as ruthlessly as Tom Paine struck at the sanctifications
of British crown rule.

Almost two centuries after Paine's trumpet blast against the
"hell of monarchy," a new indictment needs to be issued in
the spirit of *Common Sense*. Only now, such a polemic would
have to be directed, not against foreign domination, but against
a homegrown plutocracy which is accustomed to masquerade
in pilfered democratic costume.

The imperialist regime of big business in the United States
has become as reactionary and insolent as the British sovereignty before it. It does not extend and defend human rights
but undermines and destroys them at home and abroad, hypo-
critically posing all the while as their benevolent protector.

The democracy of the rich versus the poor, the haves versus the have-nots, the white supremacists versus the blacks,
has ineradicable limitations as well as pernicious consequences.
These can be eliminated only by abolishing the inequalities
bound up with capitalist property ownership. The institution
of a superior type of democracy, resting upon public ownership of a planned economy controlled by the working masses,
is the political goal of the revolutionary socialist movement.

The task of replacing the rule of the rich with the supremacy of the majority of the people in all domains of national life is no less urgent for present-day America than was the overthrow of the monarchy and its retinue in the eighteenth century. And it will take an even harder struggle to do it.

The next American revolution will have to be prepared for by a bold and uncompromising examination of long-established political ideas and institutions, much like that performed by Tom Paine and his associates. In this book I have tried to undertake such a criticism in connection with a review of the evolution of democracy in the Western world.

This survey should show that democracy is not static, uniform or fixed but a dynamic, diversified, changing product of socioeconomic development; that the prevailing form of democracy in the United States is not permanent but transitory and has seen its best days; that the overwhelming political power accruing to the representatives of the wealthy is not only incompatible with genuine democracy but an ever-present threat to the continuance of the existing rights of Americans; and that both capitalism and its bourgeois democracy are destined to be superseded by a higher form of economic and political organization guaranteeing far more freedoms to the people.

These conclusions may infuriate upholders of the status quo. They will be scoffed at by those skeptics who refuse to admit that history and politics have had any logical line of development or that the class conflicts of our time can have any determinate and foreseeable revolutionary outcome.

The realization of the perspectives projected above depends, of course, upon a favorable forward movement by the people of the United States and their victory over the forces of reaction. But the class struggle can take a retrogressive turn here as elsewhere if the monopolists and militarists, threatened and at bay, should succeed in scrapping all existing democratic institutions and destroying the rights of the people, as the bestial fascist palace guards of the German and Italian capitalists felt obliged to do between the First and Second World Wars.

The rulers of this country are certainly capable of such a criminal political course at home. The repressions against Afro-Americans, the restrictions upon democratic and labor rights, the reinforcement of the presidency, the growth of the power of the military and the specter of a fascist mobilization in the future all point in that direction.

The anticapitalist forces have to be aroused against these undemocratic trends in American politics in order to take steps to check and reverse them and resolutely lead the country toward the greater democracy promised by a triumphant socialist movement of the working masses. This book is designed to further such objectives.

G. N.
August 1970

SECTION I

PRECAPITALIST FORMS OF

POLITICAL DEMOCRACY

1

SUCCESS IN GREECE

The equality and fraternity which permeated tribal life should be clearly and strictly distinguished from the types of political democracy found in civilized societies.

Primitive Democracy

In its widest sense, democracy is as old as the first forms of human society. The preliterate tribesmen who with their kinsfolk lived and worked under collective conditions were subjected to nature but not to other men. Each was the equal of everyone else. They did not bow down before any external authority and could not be compelled to act against their will or welfare. The decisions of the clan or tribe were made by all adult members of the community or their chosen spokesmen and enforced only by custom or general consent. The rule of unanimity, not the vote of the majority, prevailed. This primeval democracy became eroded by the inequalities of wealth, the first social differentiations and group privileges that followed the development of agriculture, stock-raising, craftsmanship and the temple towns. Barbarian society saw the emergence of rudimentary aristocratic elements: chieftains, kings, nobles, priests, well-to-do traders, slaveholders and their families. But many of the egalitarian ways of the original collectivism and its kinship system persisted. The warrior-chiefs of the Achaean Greeks celebrated in the Homeric poems, the early Romans, the Germanic tribes and the North American Indians could not go against the councils of the elders and the assemblies of the people which retained final powers of decision on vital matters.

Political Democracy

However, these relations and customs of precivilized times are not connected by direct line of descent with present-day democracy. The rise of class society and the state, which is an apparatus for imposing the will of a dominant class with distinctive interests upon the rest of the population, did away with primeval democracy. *Political democracy is a form of state rule* — and the state is a product of the cleavage of society into opposing classes. The modes of democratic functioning characteristic of preclass society were not based upon relations between rulers and ruled. Indeed, the egalitarian Indian tribal structures of North America had to be extirpated in order to clear the ground for the democracy of our class-stratified society based upon private property.

Democracy among the Greeks, for example, passed from primitive egalitarianism through the military democracy depicted by Homer to civic democracy. But these successive stages of their democracy grew out of different social conditions and economic substructures. The first was linked with tribal collectivism, the second with higher barbarism, the third and last with a class-divided society based on slavery and small-scale commodity production. In Athens, as well as Rome, the traditional organization founded on birth and the ties of clan membership (*ethnos*) was replaced in the course of time by a new order based on locality (*demos*, from which the term democracy is derived) and social class defined by property ownership.

Democracy, then, is a special type of government representing the sovereignty of one segment of society over others through the mechanism of the territorial state based upon propertied classes. It was defined by Pericles and Aristotle as the supremacy of the many over the few. According to the theorists of constitutional law, it requires the submission of the minority to the mandate of the majority expressed through representative bodies.

Since its birth, political democracy has not been a stable or permanent form of government. In the history of class society, it has been the exception rather than the rule. The division of the population into antagonistic and contending class formations is more conducive to the consolidation of aristocratic than of democratic regimes. "Apart from some brilliant, but not long-lived, democratic impulses in classical antiquity, the normal government of civilized states, down to quite modern times, has been in the hands of privileged classes, whether royal or aristocratic or both in co-operation," observes L. T. Hobhouse. [1]

Thus under civilization, democracy was preceded by other modes of rule and has many times been overthrown and displaced by more restrictive types of political organization. These narrower types of government through which small minorities directly dominate the majority include theocracy, rule by priesthood; monarchy, rule by a royal family or dynasty; aristocracy, rule by an elite, usually of landed proprietors; oligarchy, rule by a few leading families; plutocracy, rule by the rich, as in some cities of ancient Greece or medieval Italy; autocracy, one-man rule; military dictatorship, rule by an omnipotent commander or the officer corps of the armed forces. Any one of these can coalesce with or give way to another. Some can even be present as an element within the formal framework of a democratic republic, as France under de Gaulle from 1958 to 1969 demonstrated anew.

These forms of government can be replaced by their total negation, anarchy, which is the absence of all rule. However, under class society such a condition can exist only for a fleeting moment at critical turning points in the revolutionary transfer of power from one group to another when one state apparatus has been pulverized and its successor has not yet been set up.

Oriental Monarchy

Democracy as a distinct form of state sovereignty is not much more than twenty-five hundred years old. Although popular assemblies existed in Sumeria and possibly other Mesopotamian and Indian civilizations, they were not predominant. These may have been survivals of precivilized rights and institutions rather than the political conquests of plebeian masses in direct struggle with the upper strata.

The Mesopotamian peoples were at times ruled by oligarchies and tyrants. But the predominant form of sovereignty in the regimes of the ancient Near East was the absolute monarchy, usually of a special type called theocracy, tied in with priesthoods and landed aristocrats. These were headed by god-kings who embodied the fusion of the royal family with a priestly caste. Such theocracies survived in Asia down to our own day in the Dalai Lama of Tibet, the Japanese Sun-God Emperor and the divine ruler of Nepal. These are relics of the

sort of government which held sway over the civilizations of
the Middle East before the Greeks.

The sacred monarchy was the political crown of a particular
stage of historical, economic and social evolution based upon
the intensive agriculture of the Bronze Age in the river val-
leys of the Nile, the Tigris and Euphrates, the Indus, the Oxus,
the Yangtze and the Yellow River. Their irrigation systems
had to be installed and managed by a centralized authority
which concentrated all power in its hands.

The kings, priests, soldiers, landlords, taxgatherers, traders,
financiers and craftsmen in these kingdoms lived upon the
surpluses produced by the peasant cultivators of the soil. These
had low living standards and few rights. The recurrent round
of agriculture dominated their lives. The handicraftsmen did
not produce for a broad external market but mostly for the
needs of their own communities and especially for the upper
classes. Merchants and manufacturers were comparatively un-
influential since trade was restricted largely to articles of luxury
and weapons of war. The weakness of the mercantile forces
and the utter dependence of the peasant population were politically expressed in the unmitigated despotisms of the period.
The prostration of the subject before the almighty godlike
potentate was the manifest sign of this Oriental absolutism.

Although kingdoms and dynasties of the Middle East and
Asia rose and fell over several thousands of years, they remained remarkably stable and uniform in their political constitution because their economic and social substructures remained essentially unchanged. Through all the disturbances
which shook up and effaced these ancient empires, monarchy
as an institution was never overthrown. One monarch or royal
family might succeed or oust another, as one state might conquer another. But other types of rule never permanently dis-
lodged or replaced the monarchy. Even the Hebrew tribes
came to the divine kingship under Saul and David. People
of high and low estate then accepted kingship as the normal
and exclusive form of political life, just as today's Americans
look upon democracy. The Persians have maintained a monarchy continuously for twenty-five hundred years.

The Background of Democracy in Greece

Democracy was not known in Mesopotamian civilization;
it first appeared in the Western world in seventh-century Greece.
The Greeks created many things we value today; democracy

was not least among them. In addition to organizing the first democratic republics, they also made the first scientific study of politics. They baptized democracy as rule of the people and gave enduring names to many other forms of government from theocracy to plutocracy. Sir Ernest Barker has emphasized that "Greek political thought began with democracy, and in the attempt of the many to answer by argument the claims of aristocratic prestige,"[2] just as the revolts against monarchy in the bourgeois era stimulated and produced modern political theories.

It was no accident that political theory was born and flourished among the Greeks. Their society went through profound transformations and convulsions as it evolved from the Homeric Age to Alexander the Great. The changes in the economic conditions and class relations of the Greek city-states were reflected in the establishment of a wide variety of regimes, many more than contemporary Americans are familiar with. The school of Aristotle, the foremost investigator of political phenomena among the Greek thinkers, collected and compared the constitutions of 158 different states. His *Politics* is the most instructive handbook of this branch of the social sciences in antiquity.

However much the advanced Greek states differed amongst themselves, they differed even more from the kind of government known in Babylon, Assyria, Egypt and Persia. The theocratic monarchy on the Oriental pattern was never solidly rooted in Greek soil. The royal palace, which was the center of the cities of the East and of the Minoans and Mycenaeans, was not to be found among the later Greeks, even where they still had kings.

The political evolution of the Greek people started out where that of the Middle East had stopped. Although Greek civilization began with the monarchy (Homer believed in the divine right of kings), this form of sovereignty withered or was uprooted very early. The Greeks went on to a more advanced development.

From the ninth to the fifth centuries B. C., the Greeks passed through a sequence of political structures proceeding from kingship, through aristocracy, oligarchy and tyranny, to the democratic republic. Only wealthy mercantile city-states from Miletus to Athens completed the full cycle from monarchy to democracy.

Even after these cities had climbed up to the democratic heights, the hold of the people on supreme power was precarious. With sharp shifts in the fortunes and class relations of the state, democracy would be toppled over and the city would revert to an antidemocratic form of rule. The democratic republic had the longest run in Athens. There it lasted for almost two centuries from 461 to its suppression by the Macedonian regent Antipater in 322, with only two brief counter-revolutionary interregnums under the oligarchy, starting in 411 and 404 B. C.

The democratic constitution was definitively overthrown in 317 when a local oligarch was made tyrant of Athens with the aid of Macedonian troops. From then on Athens was rarely free of foreign control, and participation in its government was limited to persons of property. Even so, its constitution had endured for a longer time than any contemporary bourgeois democracy.

These advances and relapses in the political life of the Greeks were brought about by underlying changes in the economic circumstances, social structures and military vicissitudes of the different city-states. The kings who emerged from the warrior chiefs and military aristocrats formed the political bridge between barbarism and civilization. They were challenged and displaced by the heads of the leading families, who were enriched by piracy, land ownership, grazing, slaveholding and other means of wealth accumulation. These privileged and powerful aristocrats, patriarchal masters of extensive households, possessors of large flocks and fields tilled by peasants or slaves, owners of precious metals, not only deprived their fellow clansmen of their ancient rights but went on to depose the kings or restrict their functions. The political hegemony of the patrician families was based upon military power as well as their economic possessions since they provided their own arms, armor, horses and retinues for expeditions of war and plunder. They were primitive prototypes of feudal lords.

Sparta: The Aristocratic State

Sparta was the classic home of such a militarized aristocracy in Greece. Under their kings, the Spartan invaders had conquered the native inhabitants of Lacedaemon and reduced them to servitude. Subsequently the landholding oligarchy, through the reforms attributed to Lycurgus, broke up the old kinship organization and cinched its political mastery over Sparta.

This master class lived on the produce of the fields allotted to them, which were tilled by Helots, the conquered slaves.

Between the upper and lower orders were the *Perioeci*, "dwellers
around," who lived in villages or engaged in petty manufacturing but had no citizen rights. There were eight times as many
Helots and four times as many *Perioeci* as members of the
ruling class.

Sparta was a permanent agricultural military encampment.
The Spartans were forbidden to engage in trade or industry;
the use or importation of gold and silver was prohibited and
only iron bars were used for currency. Foreign commerce and
visitors were discouraged. As a result, Sparta had no cities.

Although Sparta retained two kings, their powers were reduced to performing the sacrifices of the state religion, heading
the judiciary and commanding the army in war. They were
subordinated to the Senate or Council of Elders, composed of
men over sixty. Although an assembly composed of all male
citizens over thirty which met monthly was in theory the sovereign power, it merely ratified by acclamation the recommen-
dations of the Elders. The administration was handled by four
Ephors or overseers who, after the Persian Wars, became the
equals and then the superiors of the kings; they could demote
or punish them.

Under this military despotism, the repressive features of the
state were exhibited without disguise and exercised without
restraint. The army and police ruled by naked force. Every
year the Senate passed an official declaration of war between
the Spartans and Helots which gave its officers legal right to
spy upon and slay any Helot at their discretion. To forestall
revolt, the masters had the practice of periodically killing off
outstanding Helots.

Sparta's political system harked back to the barbarian past
in its retention of such institutions as the kingship, the Council
of Elders, the assembly of warriors and the age groups. Its
entire development was arrested by the conservatism of the
ruling order. Although its government went one step beyond
the monarchy, it never passed beyond the boundaries of aristocracy and autocracy.

The Commercial Cities

The more progressive states of Greece outstripped Sparta in
political development because they promoted extensively the
economic activities of commerce, craftsmanship and colonizing
which the latter stunted or prohibited. From the seventh century
on, the seaport towns of the Greeks flourished like the maritime

centers of colonial North America — and with some comparable
revolutionary results.

The influences of the new social forces crowding the commercial cities — merchants, manufacturers, bankers, shipowners,
maritime workers, artisans, shopkeepers, foreigners and chattel
slaves — transformed the life and culture of the Greeks. The new
money economy also invaded the countryside and overturned
the old conditions by enriching landlords and moneylenders
while ruining and dispossessing small farmers.

During the sixth and seventh centuries, the growth of population and trade, the development of production for exchange,
the broad circulation of money, the building of the towns, the
rise of the mercantile classes and the impoverishment of the
peasantry engendered severe class conflicts and political upheavals all the way from Miletus in Asia Minor to Athens on
mainland Greece. In one commercial center after another, the
new merchant plutocracy assailed the political monopoly of the
old nobility, who had drawn their privileges from birth and
blood and their power and wealth from landed property. In
many places the moneyed men succeeded in overturning the
ancient ruling family cliques and setting up an oligarchy or
plutocracy like that of the merchant princes of Venice and the
Hanseatic cities in Germany of the Middle Ages.

The Tyrants

In other cases, and at a subsequent stage of development, a
more complex situation occurred. In order to beat down the
old aristocracy, the new rich had to call upon the plebeian
forces in the city or countryside for sympathy and support.
These poorer or outcast classes — artisans, maritime workers,
foreigners, peasants and shepherds — fought the nobles, raised
their own demands and, in extreme cases, reached out for
power on their own account.

In the course of these struggles, strong men came forward
out of the upper classes, placed themselves at the head of the
popular forces and seized power in the city-states by maneu-
vering among the plebeians, merchants and nobles. These ambitious and wealthy individuals centralized all power in their
hands. They gave certain reforms and concessions, but little
or no say in the government, to the masses who had lifted
them into the saddle.

These dictators who became sovereign by force, and not by
custom or law, have indelibly impressed their titles upon the

vocabulary of politics. They were called tyrants and demagogues, "flatterers of the people." Every tyrant began as a
demagogue but not every demagogue ended up as a tyrant.

The rule of these men (they were all male since women took
no part in Greek politics) was dictatorial but not necessarily
or essentially reactionary. Some of them pushed through democratic reforms, enfranchised aliens, divided up the land, can-
celed debts and helped the poor peasants. They promoted
manufacturing, trading enterprises and colonization and spent
much of their own wealth and that of their regimes in public
works.

However, despite brilliant achievements in a number of the
leading city-states, the tyrannies were inherently insecure and
short-lived. They were caught and ultimately crushed between
two extreme combinations of forces: the aristocrats and oligarchs to their right, and the mercantile elements leagued with
the movements of the lower classes to their left.

The dialectical development of political history in Greece
showed itself in the fact that democracy was preceded and
prepared for by its opposite, the autocracy of the tyrant. The
tyrants who balanced themselves between the upper and the
middle classes set the stage for the next act in the political
progress of the Greeks, the coming of democracy.

(There was to be an analogous development at the end of
the Middle Ages in Western Europe when the absolute monarchy, balanced between the feudal barons and the town bourgeoisie, exhausted its usefulness after creating the centralized
national state and had to give way to ascending bourgeois
forms of rule.)

The Revolutionary Origins of Democracy

Greek history witnessed the rise and fall of numerous democracies. In every case these were instituted by revolutionary
forces and methods, just as they had to be overthrown by
counterrevolutionary violence. In Athens, for example, the first
democratic victory in 508 B. C. was the outcome of a three-
cornered fight for supremacy in which the democratic forces led
by Kleisthenes won out because their opponents were divided.

None of the Greek city-states was democratized by peaceful
and gradual means. How could the rule of the people have
been voted into existence when the institutions and laws of a
democratic regime had yet to be created? Neither in Greece nor
anywhere else was democracy handed down to a grateful cit-

izenry ~~as a gift from~~ benevolent rulers or enlightened upper
classes.

~~Democracy was everywhere the offspring of revolution.~~ "From
the seventh century to the time of the Roman conquest, Greek
history is full of revolutions and counterrevolutions, of mas-
sacres, banishment and confiscations. Party hatred was never
experienced with more ferocity than in the small city-states
where intestine struggles assumed the forms of veritable ven-
dettas." [3]

Democracy came to the Greek city-states, as it did later to
other parts of the world, only through strenuous and prolonged class conflicts which culminated in the destruction of
more restricted regimes. The plebeians had to use force to tear
supreme power from the hands of its previous possessors.
The Greeks learned from their own experience that democracy
originated through direct action by the people and could be
maintained only by unrelaxed vigilance against the enemies
of their rule and rights.

The basic social forces required to initiate and carry through
the struggle for democracy came out of the mercantile, manufacturing, maritime, monetary economy. Heading these movements were energetic, ambitious, class-conscious merchants,
sometimes of patrician origin, enriched by overseas trade, who
felt that their business enterprises and urban advancement
were being thwarted by the hegemony of the hereditary landowners or the special interests of the tyranny. Mobilized behind
them were artisans, smaller tradesmen, and maritime workers.
(Since antiquity, waterfront workers and sailors have supplied
shock troops for revolutionary combats of a democratic character in many maritime centers and states.)

These city classes won backing from the poorer peasants,
shepherds and miners in the country districts. The foreigners,
women and slaves residing in the cities were excluded from
the arena of political action, although sometimes they lent
unofficial weight to the side of the people. Thus the first democratic movements were based on a coalition of the commercial middle classes with the plebeians of the city and country.

The Institutions of Athenian Democracy

In the second quarter of the sixth century, Chios in Ionia
was the first Greek city to tread the path to democracy. But
the scores of democratic republics were best typified by Athens,

the rival of Sparta and its opposite in economic and political development. In the fifth century, Athens had become the foremost commercial, naval and cultural power in the Mediterranean area.

Athens passed through the gamut of available political forms. It had experienced monarchy, aristocracy, plutocracy and oligarchy before arriving at its democratic apogee. The Athenian city-state had originally been headed by tribal kings who were ousted by an aristocracy of noble landholders. Their rule was in turn supplanted by the sovereignty, first of plutocrats and then of tyrants.

As early as 570 B. C., according to Aristotle, its citizens were divided into three political groupings. These were not formally organized parties in the modern sense but loose amalgamations of elements which tended to combine against opponents on basic issues of concern to Athenians.

One was the Coast party, led by the merchants, which aimed at a moderate middle-class republic. The second was the Plains party, based on the large landholders in the best farming districts, who wanted an oligarchy dominated by a few noble families and rich men. The third and most radical was the Hill party, which mobilized artisans and small shopkeepers, indigent peasants, miners and shepherds behind the more progressive merchants and manufacturers.

This last grouping was the main driving force behind the democratic cause. The incessant contests of the Hill party with the entrenched oligarchic reaction, from 570 B. C. on, eventually culminated in victory for the people.

The democratic republic they created was the historical forerunner of all subsequent democracies in the Western world. In social terms, the democratic revolution of that time consisted in the transfer of supremacy from the landed gentry and the rich to the citizen body headed by the middle classes.

The democratic institutions of Athens, initiated by the reforms of Kleisthenes, were perfected under Pericles, the illustrious statesman who directed the state for thirty years from 460 to 430 B. C. Periclean Athens was a republic administered by elected magistrates and military leaders. It had no single top executive like a mayor, governor or president. Indeed, the Athenians would have considered the exorbitant powers of the U. S. presidency dangerously autocratic.

The legislative functions were carried out by three agencies: the Assembly, the Council of 500 and the Prytany, composed of ten committees of fifty members. The latter two served and were subordinate to the Assembly, the basic governing body which met four times a month.

Formally, all freemen were on an equal footing, whether they lived in the city or country, whether or not they had property, whether they were rich or poor, high- or low-born. Every citizen belonged to the Assembly and was supposed to attend its sessions and participate in its deliberations. The egalitarianism of this democracy was demonstrated by the fact that every citizen could become an officeholder. These were chosen by lot and often by rotation.

The popular Assembly had the final say on all important matters. It chose the administrative officials and had the right to judge and punish them. Athens had a citizen army and navy. Every freeman had the right as well as the responsibility of serving in the armed forces and, in case of war, of being conscripted up to the age of sixty. Athens did not have a full-time standing army, which has been an ever-present threat to all democracies and their gains.

The judiciary, too, was completely democratized. There were no professional judges or lawyers. Cases were decided by juries of citizens on which any citizen could serve and which sometimes numbered in the several hundreds. Their verdicts were given by secret ballot. From the time of Pericles, state officials, jurors and, in part, even military men were paid for their services. This enabled poorer people to shoulder the functions of government. The practice of ostracism was another safeguard against reversion to tyranny. Any individual who was thought to threaten the security or stability of the state could be exiled for ten years through a resolution backed by 6,000 ballots cast in the Assembly.

Under this system democracy flowered in Athens. Its citizens enjoyed a free atmosphere of public discussion and lively debate on all problems of foreign and domestic policy and on all public personalities. They provided a model for all Greece which has been admired from that day to this.

The Defects of Athenian Democracy

However, this pioneer experiment in popular government had serious shortcomings. Females, half the population, had no place in public life. The wives of citizens had a lower status than women in some Moslem countries today. Citizenship was a hereditary privilege. Foreigners and strangers settling in

Athens, even from another Greek city, had no citizenship rights and could be sent away at any time. The slaves, who belonged to the freemen and sustained the urban economy, were barred from politics. Roughly calculating, two-thirds or more of the inhabitants of Athens were excluded from participation in its administration.

Scientifically speaking, Athens was a slave democracy. However paradoxical this combination may appear, it should not be strange to Americans since the pre-Civil War South in our own country set a formally democratic superstructure on a socioeconomic foundation of chattel slavery. Indeed, the ideologists of the southern slave system explicitly and proudly acknowledged their close kinship with the Athenians.

In addition to the disfranchisement of women, foreigners and slaves who made up most of the population, Athenian democracy was restricted in other ways. Within the precincts of its citizen body, the wealthier elements, notables and aristocrats, continued by one means or another to play the decisive role in politics. Behind the forms of majority rule, an upper-class minority became the main administrative officers and policy-makers.

Since not everyone could read and write, the experienced leaders, skilled orators and literate members of the gentry could put many things over on the illiterate mechanics. Moreover, the city-dwellers held the upper hand over the country folk. Athens was divided into three sectors. In the center was the city itself. This was connected by a wall with its seaport, Piraeus, which was about five miles away. Both were surrounded by the country districts inhabited by farmers, herders and miners. All meetings of the Assembly were held within the city, where it was easier for townsfolk to be present. The cultivators had to tend their crops and could not easily get to the city for the sessions.

Athens was the paramount commercial, manufacturing, diplomatic and naval power of Greece, active over a good part of the civilized and uncivilized world of the times. It was the first great city-state which was not economically self-sufficient. The grain which was the principal article of its food supply had to be imported from the Black Sea region. Like Great Britain at the height of its empire, Athens found it absolutely indispensable to protect its lifelines of transport and communications. The whole course of Athenian policy, including its major military and naval engagements, was determined by the need to safeguard its supremacy in the Eastern Mediterranean.

Thus its domestic democracy was counterbalanced and coun-
teracted by its imperialist aims and activities. Athens subjected
other cities to itself, exacted heavy tribute and derived a good
part of its wealth from plundering its vassals. The Athenian
empire incorporated some three hundred states. These conquered populations had the habit of rebelling from time to
time, especially when they were aided and encouraged by such
rivals of Athens as the Persians, Spartans and Corinthians.
Their uprisings were savagely crushed.

The most democratic imperialisms from Athens to the United
States have resorted to the harshest measures in order to defend their material and strategic interests. The Athenians were
among the most civilized and cultured peoples of the ancient
world. Yet their leaders did not shrink from wiping out every
man, woman and child in Melia, a rebellious city of twenty-
five thousand inhabitants.

The economic and social structure of the Athenian republic
and its political customs, such as remunerating citizens for
administering public office, made its democracy dependent upon
the despoliation and oppression of subject peoples. As Pierre
Léveque has stated: "Athenian democracy was not imperialist
by accident, but in its very essence. Its prime aim was to secure
a decent life for even the most depressed citizens. This diffusion
of well-being was only possible by a policy of large-scale works,
subsidized by the tribute, by the search for new markets for
foodstuffs, closely linked to the extension of the *arché* (home-
land), and by the increase in *cleruchies* (colonies), which could
only be established by confiscating the richest lands of the
'allies.' Payment of magistrates, the most reliable basis for
political democracy, presupposed that Athens disposed of considerable resources and these only its empire could provide." [4]

With all these imperfections, the imperial slave state of Athens
was still a genuine democracy. Every Athenian citizen knew
it and was proud of his freedom and equality. He was not a
bondsman or a subject but a dignified member of the Athenian
democracy.

Every social and political institution must be appraised according to its specific position in history and the inescapable
circumstances of its time. The Athenian republic should not be
unfavorably contrasted and condemned by reference to some
ideal democracy. It must be realistically judged in comparison
with what came before it, what prevailed around it and what
came after it. In the context of existing civilization, Athens had
the broadest and freest form of government.

Athenian and Parliamentary Democracy

Athenian democracy differed from the parliamentary democracy of modern capitalism in three main respects. First, it was not the government of a nation but of a city-state, small in territory, population and active citizens. Athens measured a little over 1,000 square miles in extent; under Pericles it had a population of about 400,000, of which no more than 43,000 were citizens.

These proportions offered certain advantages. Athenian democracy was direct. The citizens could participate personally and continuously in the Assembly, the law courts and armed forces. A person who did not fully share in the government was not, in Aristotle's eyes, a citizen at all. The machinery of government was in the hands of the people themselves. The legislative functions were not carried out by elected and uncontrolled representatives, the judicial functions by judges nominated for life, the administration by bureaucrats, or the defense of the state by the officer caste of a standing army.

Third, the republic was not burdened by the permanent officialdoms common to Asiatic despotisms before that time or to the empires which succeeded it. It was not administered by the extensive parasitic bureaucracies which infest contemporary states. The Greek citizens took full charge of all the business of their state and controlled its operations.

However, this democracy was limited to the small city-state and not extended to others. Dependent communities were not incorporated into the Athenian republic and given equal rights but were annexed as subjects.

Athenian democracy has been well characterized by Will Durant as "the narrowest and fullest in history; narrowest in the number of those who share its privileges, fullest in the directness and equality with which all the citizens control legislation, and administer public affairs." 5

Democracy and Dictatorship

The Greek example throws light upon the problem of the relations between democracy and dictatorship. In commonsense thought, especially in the United States, democracy is believed to be one thing and dictatorship another — and never the twain shall meet. They are purely and simply opposite poles of political organization.

The truth is not so simple. In real history, the relations of the two have been far more combined and complex. It has already been pointed out that the autocracy of the tyrants paved the way for democracy in Greece. By breaking up the old political and social order, the tyranny was one of the preconditions for the advent of democracy. That was only the beginning.

The democratic republic itself operated as a social dictatorship. It was the domination of a citizen minority who alone exercised political rights over the noncitizen majority of women, slaves and foreigners. And even within the boundaries of the citizen body, the wealthier elements dominated.

Thus we see that in political actuality a democracy can contain dictatorial forces and features within itself. Of course, democracy and autocracy are logical opposites. But in real life they interpenetrate and are inseparable from each other. *The dialectical interconnection between the political form of democratic sovereignty and social-economic dictatorship has been a constant and common characteristic of all the democratic states in class society.*

This fact will emerge more clearly as the subsequent course of democracy in Western Europe is delineated. The successive stages of democracy fall into three main types: ancient democracy, as in Greece; bourgeois democracy, as in Holland, England and the United States; and finally workers' democracy, as it is realized or restricted in the workers' states of the twentieth century.

The dictatorship of a ruling class has pervaded all these historical forms of political democracy. Ancient democracy was the social dictatorship of slaveholders and the richer merchants. Bourgeois democracy has been and remains the social dictatorship of capitalist proprietors. Socialist democracy is a social dictatorship of the working people.

However, there are basic differences between the forms of democracy based upon the private ownership of the means of production and workers' democracy. Previous forms of democracy from Greece to capitalist times have been based upon exploitative economic relations which gave political supremacy to the owners of the means of production. Workers' democracies are based upon relations of production which are not exploitative in character.

Historical Lessons of Greek Democracy

To sum up:
The first democracies in the Western world were the political

products of a social structure arising out of the transition from the archaic agricultural order to the new economy characterized by elementary commodity production for the market, far-flung trade, colonization, private ownership of land, metal money, the mortgage system and slave labor.

These democratic regimes were the result of the fierce class conflicts and political revolutions engendered by these new economic conditions and the social forces bred by them.

The democratic republics were essentially a form of rule instituted by the urban middle classes and their plebeian allies.

These ancient democracies were limited in extent and depth. They were confined to the small commercial city-states bordering the Mediterranean and involved only a minority of their populations.

They turned out to be unstable and short-lived in the ancient world. The era of democracy among the Greek independent city-states lasted for not more than two hundred years from the sixth to the fourth centuries. Even the most full-blooded democracies of that time were liable to be overthrown every now and then by conspiracies of the oligarchs or tyrants. Miletus, Corinth, Athens and other prominent commercial centers experienced continual fluctuations of political rule during the heydays of their democracies.

The Greek democracies decayed and collapsed when the historical conditions which enabled them to exist and flourish passed away. Their narrow bases were undermined by slavery and fruitless class conflicts from within and by invasion from without. The city-states fell an easy victim to the Macedonian, Alexandrian and Roman conquerors who subjected them to a a new type of imperial monarchy.

In expiring, this first experiment in political democracy could not give birth directly to a higher type of democracy. The next major development along this line had to wait eighteen hundred years until the new bourgeois society in Western Europe brought the necessary economic relations, social forces, revolutionary mass movements and political formations into being.

2

FAILURE IN ROME

Unlike the separate contending Greek city-states, the Latins did establish a single power on Italian soil under the hegemony of one of its members. However, in contrast with the Greeks whom they conquered, the ancient Romans never set up a democratic government for themselves. The achievement of the one was linked with the failure of the other; the conditions which fostered Roman imperialism throttled the development of its democracy.

It seems as farfetched to speak of Roman as of Egyptian democracy — with this proviso. The prodemocratic elements of Rome did fight openly and long for living room under the republic. But they were unable to overcome their aristocratic and plutocratic adversaries and attain political freedoms on the scale enjoyed by the citizens of Athens. Democracy remained stunted in Rome and never passed over from a popular movement to a strong and secure regime.

The Roman Republic and Caesarism

From the ending of Etruscan domination and its kingship in 508 B. C. to the principates of Caesar and Augustus five centuries later, the Roman political structure evolved from the primitive monarchy. to aristocracy and oligarchy and then went through a protracted interregnum of civil strife until it was stabilized in the imperial autocracy of the Caesars. Throughout republican times, the plebeians and their allies conducted many vigorous struggles to wrest more rights and, if possible, sovereign power from the upper classes. As early as 287 B. C. they did secure a popular constitution. Yet they could not thereafter win more than a formal equality with the patricians. The latter at all times retained real supremacy in the state.

The vast metropolis of Rome, capital of a world empire, continued, like the rural market town it had been, to be ruled by a compact oligarchy of a few noble families. The citizen body was accorded sovereignty in theory, had a popular assembly, elected tribunes and was given substantial concessions. But the Senate, drawn exclusively from the aristocracy, remained the dominant and decisive executive organ of government. It controlled foreign affairs, the army, finances, justice and the other levers of power.

The Greek historian Polybius (160 B. C.) praised the "mixed constitution" of Rome because it incorporated the best features of other forms of government while upholding the ascendancy of the old and rich families. It worthily combined, he pointed out, a limited democracy in the legislative sovereignty of the assemblies, an aristocracy in the leadership of the patrician Senate, a Spartan-like "dyarchy" in the brief royal tenure of the consuls and a monarchy in the dictatorships temporarily and constitutionally imposed in times of war or civil stress.

Spokesmen for the lower orders in the republic did not admire this arrangement, which assured the hegemony of the patricians, as much as the Greek commentator did. The rule of the noble clans was opposed and contested at times by coalitions of moneyed men, artisans and proletarians. It was more profoundly and independently defied by insurgent slaves. Up to the slave revolt of Spartacus in 73 B. C., the most formidable challenge to the patrician powers was led by the Gracchi from 133 to 122 B. C. These brothers were tribunes of upper-class origin inspired by Greek democratic ideas. They championed the grievances of the plebeians and peasantry and endeavored to shatter the domination of the patricians, bankers and businessmen who oppressed the poor.

Their programs envisaged the election of tribunes really responsible to the people, the transfer of the decision-making powers from the Senate to the popular assembly, a new agrarian law redistributing public land to the landless, the extension of the Roman franchise to all Latins and the Roman allies, the reform of the jury courts, improvement of conditions in the army and the sale of corn to citizens below the market price. These demands, among others, would, if realized and retained, have effected a revolution in favor of the citizen majority.

However, the recurrent battles waged by the popular democratic forces against the corrupt defenders of the old regime did not result in permanent victory. The Gracchi were executed and the uprisings they headed put down. All the subsequent attempts of the Roman plebeians to defeat and demote the oligarchy and replace it with a democracy on the Athenian model were crushed by counterrevolution and dictatorship after ferocious social war. The final outcome of this prolonged internecine strife between the contending classes was not the triumph of democracy but the establishment of personal and divine dictatorship under the Caesars.

An empire sustained by plunder abroad and slavery at home, with mercenary armies and a productively useless proletariat in its heart, was extremely unfavorable soil for the growth of a powerful and thriving democracy. The composition and balance of its internal social forces combined with the imperatives of imperial rule to prevent the installation of any viable democratic regime under republican Rome.

The plebeian rebels in Rome never organized themselves independently; they remained dependent upon leadership by dissident factions and personages from the upper crust. These ambitious men acquired popularity by demagogic means and then left the masses in the lurch. Lack of self-reliance, a crippling inner weakness from its birth, has resulted in many defeats for plebeian democracy from Greece to our own day. It eventually proved fatal in Rome.

The price paid for unjustified trust in patrician leadership was most graphically demonstrated in the dying hours of the democratic movement. The patrician general Julius Caesar had originally been a favorite of the populace. He took advantage of the exhausting bloodletting and unresolved conflicts between the contending classes to grab state power in his military fist and keep it for his heirs.

Thus tyranny, which had cleared a path for the advent of democracy in Greece, finally shut off its prospects in Rome.

The aborted career of Roman democracy was reflected in the paucity of its theory. The Romans did not contribute anything significantly new either to the development of democratic institutions or democratic ideas. No rounded conception of democratic government came from any noted Roman thinker.

The efforts of the Gracchi as tribunes of the people, the battles of the plebeians against the patricians and plutocrats, as well as the slave uprising of Spartacus, have endured as inspirations to militant democrats and plebeian revolutionists up to the present. But these are remembered not for their achievements but as heroic failures.

Instead of any model for democratic emulation, republican Rome has bequeathed, above all, to later times an outstanding example of the diminishing, denial and destruction of popular liberties under the aegis of imperialist conquest and extortion and domestic exploitation of servile labor. That, too, is a memorable historical lesson.

Early Christianity and Democracy

Primitive Christianity is often credited with initiating and popularizing the conception of the equality of all men, which was rare in antiquity but is an essential component of the democratic ideal. The connection between this Christian doctrine and the origins of the bourgeois-democratic ideology will be discussed in a later chapter. Actually the new religion inherited this idea from various Jewish sects, like the Essenes, and from the universalist Stoic and Epicurean philosophies, which came forward in the cosmopolitan atmosphere and among the polyglot populations of Roman civilization.

To be sure, the early Christian congregations rooted in the masses and persecuted under the emperors did diffuse the sentiment of equality. They did so, not in an active social revolutionary sense, but as a wholly supernatural aspiration, although the Christian teachings did serve to touch off slave revolts in several parts of the empire, notably in North Africa. Christianity taught the equality of all souls in the sight of God; its realization was deferred to an afterlife. In the social and political order of this world, the Christian Church and its officials countenanced and justified slavery along with other forms of social inequality on the pretext that what belonged to Caesar should be rendered unto Caesar. Church serfs were the last to be emancipated in Western Europe.

Throughout Christianity's career, reformers have denounced social and economic inequalities in the name of evangelical charity and called upon true believers to reorganize institutions in accordance with the precepts of Christ and Church. Such exhortations have often sustained protest against prevailing miseries and enkindled revolutionary impulses. But all Christian class formations from Roman times to the present have been incapable of giving the perishable bodies of their members that equality of conditions, rights and opportunities which is so solemnly granted to their immortal souls.

In distinction from unofficial Christianity, which preached

imminent redemption of the world with punishment of the
wicked and wealthy oppressors and exaltation of the humble,
the established church inculcated belief in other-worldly individual reward for submission to the ruling powers and punishment for rebellion against God's order which they maintained.

Democracy as a living political entity reacquired flesh and
blood in Western civilization, not primarily through the preaching of Christian morality and ideology and still less under the
Catholic hierarchy, which was thoroughly authoritarian, but
rather as the result of new economic and social relations of a
commercial character. In feudal times, these made their first
appearance in the most advanced urban communes.

3

THE DEMOCRACY OF
THE MEDIEVAL COMMUNES

In addition to the three main stages of democratic development (slave democracy, bourgeois democracy and workers' democracy), there have been democratic formations of a lesser and transitional sort. The most significant of these in the two-thousand-year hiatus between the last Greek and the first bourgeois democracies grew up in the free communes in the urban republics of medieval Italy, France, the Low Countries and Germany.

However, these democratic regimes occupied a localized and subordinate place in medieval political life and did not acquire predominance in society commensurate with the Greek republics before them or the parliamentary democracies after them. The paramount sovereignties in the feudal society of Western Europe were the monarchy, the papacy and the vassal heads of their principalities. The contests for supremacy among these nondemocratic powers molded the main lines of medieval political history.

The predominance of emperors, princes, popes and prelates issued from the makeup of feudal society, which rested on the demographic, economic, military and political primacy of the country over the towns, and agriculture over commerce and industry. The nobility and church which monopolized the land maintained the laborers on their estates in ignorance and servitude and exercised tyrannical sway over their lives. Although the serfs and peasants were freer than slaves, they had few rights. Democracy could find no foothold in the manorial organization of the feudal agrarian system. The autocracy of church, empire, kingdom and barony was the inescapable prevailing method of rule over the rural toiling masses. North of the Alps there were only a few unimportant peasant communes of single villages or groups of villages.

Communal democracy was a political expression of the pronounced opposition of town and country in the medieval setting. The despotism of the manorial lords, monarchs and prelates corresponded to the inner necessities of the self-sufficient feudal agrarian organization, whereas the democracy of the communes grew out of the elementary commodity production and exchange of the urban population. Democracy was considered the attribute of a citizen, that is, a city-dweller, not the mark of a tiller of the soil, whether serf or peasant.

The economic changes which took place within Western European feudalism through the thirteenth and fourteenth centuries created the material preconditions and social elements for the intrusion of democratic movements. The emergence and growth of towns through the expansion of trade and monetary relations and the development of craft guilds undermined the traditional unrestricted overlordships of the church, emperors and nobility. The new urban social classes of merchants and artisans demanded and secured forms of law and government conforming to their special conditions of life and labor.

The everyday activities of townspeople were incompatible with the requirements of serfdom. They had to have unhampered control over their persons and possessions instead of having them vested in a lord. Their wives and children had to be free-born. They wanted to lease and sell their land and houses and not have these enfeoffed. They insisted on being tried under their own law in their own courts instead of in manorial or clerical courts. They needed to buy and sell freely on the town market and with foreigners.

The economic necessities of their new way of life sought and found political and legal means of satisfaction. The towns that grew out of commerce and colonization became the nurseries of elementary bourgeois freedoms. One way or another, through struggle or mutual agreement, the town dwellers secured from landed proprietors formal charters of liberties which exempted them from servile obligations and manorial dues and guaranteed the enjoyment of privileges denied to the countryfolk. Regardless of social origin, the person who lived in a town unchallenged for a year and a day became a "bourgeois" with a status different from the peasant or serf. "The town air made him free."

These changes in social and legal status, rooted in higher economic relations, became the basis and beginning of bourgeois political liberties. The majority of towns merely acquired the elementary rights needed for carrying on commerce and craftsmanship. Most of the well-to-do merchants and guild-masters who ruled the roost were content with such a state of affairs and did not raise the cry of independence from their sovereigns.

However, some of the more prosperous republics went beyond this point and reached out for some degree of autonomy. The city-states which attained independence were generally called communes.

The communes first appeared in the commercial centers of Italy, such as Venice, Genoa and Pisa, which became independent before the end of the eleventh century. They had extensive rights of self-government. The commune was an association of noble and plebeian townsmen within the city walls sworn to uphold their institutions and extend their collective liberties. Like the Greek democracies, they usually arose as a revolutionary organization that had wrested its freedom by means of insurrection from the ruling prince or bishop.

Laon in northern France typified both the revolutionary origins of the commune charters and their arduous defense by the citizens against the higher authorities. Here is a sketch of its struggles. "A populace always ready for a fight; bishops always encroaching on the royal rights on the one hand and the liberties of the commune on the other; a great and bloody insurrection, a bloodier revenge of the nobles; a great conflagration; a great massacre — such in abridgment are the annals of Laon. Gandri, bishop of Laon, bad successor of a line of bad bishops, who swore to observe the charter which he had sold dear to the citizens, violated it as soon as he could, and in every way possible, and was slaughtered for his reward."[1]

Although free and independent in respect to the lords of the realm, the internal administration of these cities was not democratic. The municipal nobility and plutocracy held mastery inside its walls. These city-states came to be controlled by a few great families enriched by commerce or banking. "The form of government, in these centers of commerce and manufacture, inevitably changed, first from democracy to plutocracy, and then to oligarchy," writes Henri Pirenne. "That the change was inevitable is sufficiently proved by its universality. On the banks of the Scheldt and the Meuse, as at Florence, the *majores*, the *divites,* the "great men," henceforth governed the *minores,* the paupers, the plebei, the 'lesser folk.'"[2]

Thus the townspeople, who had escaped from direct subjugation by a landed aristocracy, fell under the domination of an urban aristocracy, which was often no less cruel, arbitrary and intolerable. After throwing off servitude to prelates and princes, the commune was confronted with the question: how much power was to be allotted to the various categories of its citizens?

The struggles of the lower orders to limit or break the political monopoly of the upper crust that had earlier characterized the Greek city-states and the Roman republic broke out with no less force and ferocity in many of the medieval communes. This class warfare between rich and poor had varying results at different times and in different places. The degree of democracy and measure of liberty enjoyed by the lower orders depended upon the outcome of their contests against the local authorities who abused and exploited them. Each urban political situation was a reflex of the relations established between the contending powers of the notables and plebeians.

The city governments were the product of the social unrest which provoked popular revolts in both city and countryside as the old relations and institutions of feudalism began to decay from the late thirteenth to early fifteenth centuries. During this period, "there was scarcely a county, a province, a city which does not have in its annals the record of some wild outburst of popular turbulence," reports Prof. E. P. Cheyney.[3] Most noteworthy were the insurrection of the "Shepherds" among the rural laborers in northern France (1251) which penetrated Paris and crossed the channel to England; the "Vespers" (1282) when the Sicilians rose against French rule and set up popular governments in Palermo and elsewhere; the peasant "Jacquerie" (1358) in central France; the insurgency of the Parisian "Malletmen" (1382); and the peasant rebellion in England (1381).

Whereas the rural rebellions proved as fruitless as the Roman slave uprisings, here and there the movements of the urban artisans and workmen culminated in the capture of supremacy and the establishment of democratic governments by the lower orders. The most thorough triumphs of the commoners over the plutocratic notables occurred in the Low Countries (Holland and Belgium) and in northern Italy where bourgeois development was most advanced and powerful.

The large manufacturing cities of Flanders, the heart of modern Belgium, formed the epicenter of popular insurrection at its height during the second half of the thirteenth and fourteenth centuries. Four parties contended for control of these wealthy textile and trading centers; the distant French king; his vassal, the Count of Flanders; the upper strata of the merchants, manufacturers, moneylenders, landowners and officials; and the commoners, composed of small tradesmen, artisans, journeymen, members of the lesser guilds, working weavers, dyers, fullers, and shearmen.

Within the cities and the guilds, there were also cleavages and conflicts between the masters and workmen and between affluent master craftsmen and the impoverished semiproletarians. The mass of artisans led a precarious and miserable existence, working long hours, receiving irregular pay and often hit by unemployment. The feelings between the upper and lower classes were further embittered by differences in language and by foreign oppression.

These grievances burst forth in uprisings which were originally directed against French rule and then passed over into social conflicts between the patricians and plebeians. The national democratic movement set off by the "matins of Bruges" (1302) persisted in country and town for the rest of the century. In a number of towns the popular forces wrested control from the Flemish patricians and their overlords and set up plebeian regimes.

The principal movement against the "greater folk" took place in the capital of the principality of Liege. It flared up in the middle of the thirteenth century, continued for more than a century and resulted in complete victory for the "lesser folk." The Liege craftsmen became the exclusive masters in the municipal constitution. They established what the historian Henri Pirenne designates as "the most democratic government that the Low Countries have ever known," which lasted in certain respects until the end of the seventeenth century. There the town council was composed of representatives elected from all thirty-two crafts, each with equal rights. In other places the power was divided among the rich merchants, the larger crafts and the small ones comprising the mass of artisans.

The denouement of medieval democracy was enacted in Florence, the greatest industrial center of Italy, which from 1378 to 1464 passed through a cycle of political development comparable to that of some of the Greek city-states. This aristocratic republic had been chronically disturbed by unrest among its artisans, who finally seized power in 1378 from the patricians through the rebellion of the *ciompi* or common workmen. Their party was led by the cloth-workers who had never been organized into guilds. This revolutionary changeover to a plebeian democracy survived for four years until the aristocracy managed to restore its regime and execute 161 leaders of the *ciompi*.

Torn by inveterate class conflicts and clique feuds engendered by diversified interests, the communes became easy prey for the accession of tyrants to power. The uprisings of the lower orders were often instigated, abetted or joined by noble *frondeurs* at odds with other members of their ruling order. The practice of entrusting the reins of government to one or another of the factional chiefs became the starting point for undermining the plebeian democracy. The leading citizen, who began as principal military or municipal officer, would consolidate sovereignty in his hands, become captain-general for life and then pass the absolute powers he had assumed on to his heirs.

This transformation of plebeian democracy into personal despotism under the hegemony of a wealthy family was most graphically exhibited in the political history of Florence. There, from the fifteenth century on, the merchant banking family of the Medicis, through the connivance of other leading families and the passivity of the citizens, usurped the powers of the republic, subverted the liberties of its democratic constitution and acquired complete control over its government.

The medieval chapter in the evolution of democracy did not flourish for long. Democracy was an anomaly under the feudal regime where it sprung up only under exceptional urban conditions. It was snuffed out by the end of the fourteenth or, at the latest, by the middle of the fifteenth century. The privileges of the communes were gradually withdrawn and their liberties crushed as the European states became centralized under the absolute monarchies during the sixteenth and seventeenth centuries.

The communes suffered shipwreck on the same rocks and reefs as the Greek democratic republics. They were cut off from and often hostile to the mass of peasants around them. As autonomous units, they were separated from one another, as well as divided within themselves, by the exclusive interests of the great families or the guilds. The democratic institutions set up by the craftsmen were undermined and undone by the jealousy with which they guarded their local privileges.

Medieval democracy succumbed to economic processes beyond its control. The agglomerations of small handicraftsmen, confronted with a shrinking market in the countryside as a result of the multiplication of urban centers, tried to halt further development of the productive forces by strict protectionism. These restrictions did not prevent new channels of goods production from being opened up by the establishment of home industries and manufactures in the rural areas, which bypassed the urban guild industry. Rising commercial capital, invigorated by the commercial revolution of the fifteenth and sixteenth centuries, was enabled either to subvert urban democracy or join with the absolute monarchies to crush it.

The disunited urban plebeians could not stand up against the strong-knit alliances of their antagonists. These were the kingly and church powers and nobility who backed and came to the rescue of the great merchants, rentiers and master craftsmen. "During the fifteenth century," concludes Pirenne, "the wave [of plebeian revolts] that had risen during the preceding one fell back upon itself, to break against the inevitable coalition of all the interests it had united against it."

In the sequence of historical formations of democracy, the medieval communes were a bridge between the Greek republics and the parliamentary democracies of the bourgeois epoch. The seat of this transitional mode of government was, as in Greece, the city-state. But it knew no slavery and rested on the higher socioeconomic pedestal of the merchant and craft guilds. On the other hand, the future bourgeois republics were not urban but national in scope and were based upon international competitive capitalist conditions rather than local monopolies.

The traditions of communal democracy did not die out together with their embodiments. They survived in the popular memory under the absolute monarchies and thereafter sprang to life whenever the urban masses in Western Europe rose against their oppressors. On revolutionary occasions the populace spontaneously tended to revive the communal form of government. This was especially true in Paris, the capital of France, where the commune was to have two brilliant resurrections: the first during the height of the bourgeois revolution after 1789 and the second at the dawn of the proletarian revolution in 1871.

SECTION II

THE RISE AND DECLINE OF

BOURGEOIS DEMOCRACY

4

TASKS AND FORCES OF
THE BOURGEOIS REVOLUTIONS

The next step in the progress of democracy was the political product of a globally expanding capitalism which transformed the social structures of the Western world. The emergence of a truly national, as distinct from a localized democratic, movement on the medieval model depended upon the extent of a people's advancement from feudal to capitalist conditions. The new social forces energized by the growth of bourgeois relations could not be contained within the precapitalist framework and sooner or later found themselves at odds with the monarchical-clerical state.

The most militant representatives of the big and little bourgeoisie raised the banner of protest against the plunder and oppression of the feudal autocracy, sponsored and spread democratic demands and led the masses into struggle. Their victory over the old regime brought forth a far more advanced type of democratic government than either the Greek city-states or the medieval communes had known.

The classes which were radicalized by the new economic conditions or the decay of the old were driven toward democracy not by any abstract "love of freedom" but by urgent material interests and cultural needs. They challenged those precapitalist institutions which hampered the growth of their own rights, powers and privileges. Foremost among these obstructions were the ruling bodies rooted in the feudal past.

At first the bourgeois oppositions of high or low estate tried to modify the monarchical-clerical structures to their advantage, preferring reform to the hazards of revolutionary upheaval. The resistance to change by the guardians of the feudal hierarchy compelled the dissidents to switch their methods of action. They had to mount attacks strong enough to batter down the absolutisms arrayed against them. The forces for these could be mobilized and inspired only by arousing sentiments of equality among the common folk and raising demands of immediate concern to them.

Beginning with the class struggles connected with the Reformation, such as the Anabaptist revolt in Germany, every serious stirring of social and political discontent within the bourgeoisified countries tended to acquire a "leveling" coloration and democratic impetus, especially on its left flank. If the oppositional movements which invited or incited the participation of the masses were implicitly antiautocratic and antiaristocratic, their democratic potential was not all at once realized and did not everywhere result in a thoroughgoing overhaul of the state structure. Numerous variants of compromise between the traditional forms of feudal rulership and the cry for reformation were arrived at in the ongoing contest between defenders of the old order and the champions of change. These ranged from a constitutional monarchy to an aristocratic-plutocratic government of the landlords and bourgeoisie.

The historical record shows that none of the important democracies of the bourgeois era came into existence by purely peaceful, legal and gradual means. Bourgeois democracy was actually installed as the accepted method of progressive government through a series of revolutionary victories, which took place over the three hundred years extending from the rise of the Dutch republic in the sixteenth century to the American Civil War of the mid-nineteenth century.

Except for the latter, these revolutions were mainly directed against the dominant powers of the feudal hierarchy: the Church, the monarchy, the nobility and the landlords. What social forces were involved in these democratic movements and what roles did they play in advancing or retarding them? The most timid, vacillating and conservative elements of the new men of money were the merchant princes, bankers and mineowners who held top rank among them. The manufacturers, maritime merchants, shipowners and later the industrialists in the cities and seaports were more audacious and venturesome in their political activities, as they were in their enterprises. They were sometimes joined by the more progressive sections of the agricultural proprietors, such as the English gentry, as well as by plebeian members of the clergy close to their congregations.

These well-to-do strata were backed up, propelled forward and, at climactic points, pushed aside by the lower urban classes — master artisans, mechanics, journeymen and shopkeepers — and by the actual tillers of the soil, the small farmers and peasants who carried the whole nation on their backs. The propertyless wage workers, landless cultivators and diverse pariah groupings in the cities and countryside were usually situated on the fringe of the insurgent forces.

All the bourgeois revolutions were made by broad coalitions of class forces which entered the fray with very different motives and ends in view. It is therefore necessary to distinguish with some care the various social-political components in the antifeudal camp.

The bourgeois "Grandees" had strictly limited objectives which made all except the most intransigent among them reluctant to push too far and too fast in their conflicts with the guardians of autocracy and kept them ready for compromise. The prime accelerators of the revolutionary process, the originators of the more radical actions and far-reaching democratic proposals, came from the middling and lower layers of the budding bourgeois society. Consequently, the plutocratic and plebeian sectors of the bourgeois-democratic movements did not always march in step or see eye-to-eye in their strategy, actions and goals. As the struggle intensified, the original partners in the coalition often pulled apart and, at critical junctures, even moved in opposite directions and clashed head-on.

The split between the Presbyterians and Dissenters and then between the Cromwellians and the Levellers in England, the tests of strength in the successive showdowns between the more moderate and extreme parties during the rise of the French Revolution, the collisions between the patriot leaders and the plebeian masses in the American War of Independence and its aftermath exemplified this phenomenon of fission in the unfolding of the bourgeois revolutions. The extent, depth and outcome of such encounters had much to do with the amount of democracy left in the regime which ultimately issued from the crucible of the class struggles.

The revolutionists of the bourgeois epoch had both a negative and a positive mission. They had to sweep aside obsolescent precapitalist conditions, which in Europe meant the demolition of the feudal organization. In North America the native bourgeoisie and their associates not only had to do away with imported feudal agrarian relations, which had shallow roots in the soil of the British colonies, but also with the more dispersed Indian tribal collectivism and, later on, chattel slavery.

The abolition of precapitalist relations entailed the fostering of bourgeois conditions of life and labor. The positive aim of the revolutionary leadership was to devise ways and means of satisfying the specific demands of the bourgeois strata brought onto the field by the ascending capitalist society.

Although there were variations from century to century and country to country, six feudal institutions held back the advance of the bourgeois forces. First was serfdom, the major precapitalist mode of exploitation; second was the guild system, a precapitalist mode of manufacture; third were the medieval privileges and royal monopolies which hindered the formation and extension of the free market; fourth was the absolute monarchy which first promoted and then impeded bourgeois interests; fifth was the landed nobility upon which it rested and relied; sixth was the Catholic Church which owned one-third of all the land in Europe and was the mainstay of the medieval world.

In order to overcome these institutions, the forces of bourgeois society had to carry out the following tasks. First, they had to create a free market. The rich bourgeoisie pursued their basic economic objectives more vigorously than the political reforms desired by the more democratic forces. Bent on expanding the internal market as the nursery of capital and the springboard for the capture of world trade, their political operations were guided by such material ends.

The free exchange of goods was the prime economic basis of the struggles for freedom of religion, democratic rights, civil liberties and parliamentary representation. Nowadays the existence of a nationwide and world market is taken for granted. However, the free market was not a gift of nature but a historical achievement. It was conquered and consolidated at this particular turning point in European and world progress through intense class battles and far-flung interimperial wars.

The free market is the outcome of the growth of capitalist relations ensured by a triumphant bourgeois revolution. The fight for the unrestricted exchange of commodities was the supreme aim of the early bourgeois revolutionists, whether or not the participants were fully aware of the fact. Certain of their more clear-sighted heads, like Alexander Hamilton, the first secretary of the U. S. treasury, were highly conscious of this economic desideratum and worked systematically to realize it.

This is the purely *bourgeois kernel* of the antifeudal move-

ment. The economic core of bourgeois freedom, equality and
fraternity is freedom of buying and selling without interference
from arbitrary powers ("free enterprise"). In addition to religious, political and legal liberties, even the Levellers demanded
such economic rights as freedom to buy, sell, produce and
trade, without license, monopoly, arbitrary regulation or arbitrary taxation.

So far as the wealthy bourgeoisie was concerned, these economic aims, not political democracy and liberties for the masses,
were the mainspring of their oppositional activities. As a rule,
the moneyed magnates were content if they could get the kind
of market and tolerant government they wanted without the
disturbances attendant upon a frontal challenge to the old
regime. In some situations, however, the rich businessmen were
hammered so hard by their plebeian allies and armies that
they took more radical steps than they intended. If they had
to accept some democratization in order to get the economic
measures and political predominance they sought, they would
under certain circumstances accommodate themselves to the
package deal.

The second task of the bourgeois-democratic revolution was
the transformation of agrarian relations. Before the industrial
revolution, agrarian reform was the most vital of all problems,
even in the most advanced countries. In order to liberate the
productive forces of bourgeois society from feudal fetters and
constitute a substantial and growing capitalist market, the
manorial lords had to be liquidated and their properties redis-
tributed to the cultivators.

The land taken from its previous possessors was then converted into a commodity that could be bought and sold without
restraint. That meant handing it over, either directly or through
the government, to private landowners, peasants, freehold farmers or large-scale capitalist proprietors.

In the colonies, the aboriginal population had to be swept
off their native ground. North America was held by the Indian
tribes who enjoyed the land in common. Since land was not
individually owned under their collectivist organization, it was
neither alienable nor marketable. The bourgeois forces and their
regimes had to clear the Indians from their ancestral hunting
grounds before parceling these out to private owners and placing them on the market. Later the colonial rebels took title
to the crown territories and expropriated Loyalist proprietors
for the same purpose.

In the process of uprooting feudal domination, the lands

held in perpetuity by the Catholic Church, the baronies of large-estate owners and the communal property of the people were all converted one way or another into private property. For the first time on a large scale, landed property was turned into an article of sale that could be priced and purchased like any other commodity and become capitalized.

In feudal Europe the Church, kings, nobles and landlords not only held title to the best lands but also kept their cultivators in servitude. The recurrent peasant wars under feudalism persisted as one of the main propellants of the bourgeois revolutions. Their uprisings were fueled by the determination of the laborers tied to the soil to mitigate or abolish the oppressive and crushing burdens of feudal dues, tithes and obligations and gain possession of the plots they worked upon.

Under feudalism the laborer was tied to the lord and his labor was not available for capitalist enterprises. The conversion of labor power into a commodity was as indispensable for capitalist production as the change in the conditions of land ownership was for capitalist exchange. The formation of a class of propertyless workers was the third major prerequisite for capitalist development and it had to be promoted by various means to provide an ample supply of free labor which could be drawn upon for exploitation by the capitalist entrepreneurs in Western Europe.

The fourth task was to do away with particularism and unite the people in an autonomous sovereign state. To constitute a national market, provincialism had to be broken down, the small states and petty kingdoms amalgamated or abolished, and uniform coinage, weights and measures, and customs duties established. Restrictive tariffs and tolls levied by governments and privileged landowners had to be lifted for the uninhibited passage of people and goods. (In the colonial period, taxes and tolls were levied on travelers and on trade between one Atlantic colony and another) The power of taxation had to be centralized and the economic activity of the country stabilized by means of a secure currency and uniform fiscal regulations.

The struggle against particularism logically led to the unification of the separated or dismembered parts of the nation, as with the United States in the eighteenth and Germany and Italy in the nineteenth century. This demand for national integrity went hand in hand with the struggle for independence from foreign oppressors who, even if they had once been a stimulant of progress as a mother country, had become intolerably exploitative and tyrannical. Thus Holland threw off the despotism of Spain, the United States broke loose from England and Italy cast off the Austrian yoke.

The fifth task was to shatter the grip of the Roman Catholic Church. Just as every revolutionary movement of the twentieth century, no matter where or on what issues it originates, runs up against resistance from imperialism, so in Western Europe any sizable expression of unrest or revolt during the transition from feudalism to capitalism met fierce retaliation from the Catholic hierarchy. The papacy, which claimed to be built upon the rock of St. Peter, actually clung to the rock of counterrevolution.

The Catholic Church dominated the minds of men on earth and held the keys to Heaven and eternal life. But it did more than defend its monopoly over the spiritual and intellectual realms; it was also a mighty temporal potentate and property owner. It possessed much of the best land in Europe; it held immense treasures in precious metals. It protected obsolete trade and monetary relations, frowning on usury. It drained the wealth derived from the productive enterprises of the bourgeois classes into wasteful expenditures which enfeebled capitalist economic development. It was in league with the most tyrannical imperial regimes.

Thus every rebellion against the status quo promptly acquired a heretical, anti-Rome, Protestant-reformist edge. Protestantism was the religious credo par excellence of the bourgeois-democratic revolution in its pristine state. As John Strachey so well and wittily observed: "Protestantism is the free market in God." The dissenting creeds and sects introduced competition and free enterprise into theology and religious life against the monopoly maintained under the papacy, just as up-and-coming businessmen championed competition in place of the medieval and royal monopolies.

This explains why the class struggles against the feudal powers in Western Europe took the form of religious crusades and national liberation movements. The cause of religious freedom became fused with the fight for national identity, independence and unification.

The most dramatic instance of this synthesis was the first-born of the bourgeois revolutions, the uprising conducted by the Low Countries at the end of the sixteenth century. Headed by William of Orange, the Dutch dissidents went over to Protestantism of one denomination or another as they took up arms against the Catholic state of Spain which held them in subjugation. (The Church Inquisition as wielded by Philip II of Spain was the most terrible instrument of oppression.)

The sixth task consisted in bringing about political reforms along democratic lines. As Harrington, the chronicler of the Civil War in England, first pointed out, every upheaval in property relations brings with it a drastic rearrangement of the previous power structure. The bourgeois revolutions resulted in the large-scale dispersion and transfer of property in both the urban and rural areas. After the papal, monarchical and noble powers were weakened or overthrown, new claimants of political rights came forward to collect what was due to them. First in line were the grasping upper bourgeoisie, the merchants, bankers, manufacturers and large capitalist farmers. Next in order were the lesser classes of the cities and towns, the artisans and tradesmen. Behind them came the country folk, small farmers, yeomen and peasants. Below them were the propertyless laborers, the embryonic proletariat. Bringing up the rear were the vagabonds, the marginal workers, the black slaves and the female sex.

At one point or another in the progress of bourgeois society, spokesmen for each of these elements drawn into the democratic movements presented their own bill of rights to the ruling classes. Some received far more satisfaction than others; still others were completely denied. In every case it turned out that those who owned the most property and wealth ended up with the most political influence. In class society, governmental power inevitably gravitates to the strongest section of the property holders.

Religious reform rather than a share in government was the most elementary manifestation of the democratic demands of the rebellious masses. This priority was already evident in the last great peasant revolt of the feudal era which preceded the advent of the strictly bourgeois insurrections. The first of the twelve articles of the petition of the German peasants presented in 1525 called for democratic control over their church officials at the lowest level. It read as follows: "It is our humble petition and desire and also our will and resolution that in the future we should have power and authority so that each community should choose and appoint a pastor and that we should have the right to depose him should he conduct himself improperly." Other articles asked for the abolition of tithes, of serfdom, of excessive bonds and rents, the restitution of communal lands and rights, and better administration of the law courts.

A comparison of this request for minimal religious rights with the Bill of Rights appended to the Constitution of the United States gives a measure of the immense distance separating the last great peasant revolt against feudal bondage from the first successful colonial revolt of capitalist times. Article I of the U. S. Constitution states that "Congress shall make no law respecting an establishment of religion, or prohibiting the free exercise thereof. . . ." This guarantee of religious freedom is a long way from the timid request of the sixteenth-century German country folk for a say in selecting the shepherd of their flock. Moreover, most of the provisions in the American Bill of Rights concern political, civil and legal rather than religious liberties. That had become a settled question.

The establishment of a new political regime which could be counted on to promote and protect bourgeois interests was the paramount objective of a bourgeois revolution. The form of government most conducive to the stability of bourgeois society was a parliamentary republic. But in order to secure and maintain such a democratic system there had to be a powerful revolutionary thrust to bring it into being and a vigorous and prosperous capitalism to keep it going.

These conditions were not present in many of those countries that were drawn into the network of world capitalism. In fact, the one major power in the Western world to achieve a durable democratic republic on bourgeois foundations for two centuries was the United States.

5

ACHIEVEMENTS AND
LIMITATIONS OF
THE BOURGEOIS REVOLUTIONS

The mass of participants in the revolutionary events who shouldered these historical tasks and carried them through were not endowed with exceptional individual abilities. They were indeed less literate, well-informed and historical-minded than the average citizen of today. But peoples who get caught up in and swept along by a mighty and irresistible tide of social change are capable of hitherto unimaginable accomplishments.

The creative capacities of the insurgent masses were shown in the successive revolutionary combats which toppled the old regimes in the West and ushered in the new bourgeois order. During the formative stages of capitalism, six great upheavals marked the decisive steps in the forward march of the bourgeois-democratic revolution.

The first was the Dutch revolution of the late sixteenth century by which the Netherlands won its independence and set up its republic. The second was the English revolutions of the seventeenth century, which secured the supremacy of the British bourgeoisie and their parliament. The third was the revolt of the American colonists, which created the United States. The fourth was the French Revolution, which was decisive in demolishing the old order in Western Europe. The fifth was the less successful Revolutions of 1848 on that continent. The American Civil War was the concluding act in this series of struggles by which the world bourgeoisie attained sovereignty and the democratic revolution fulfilled its mission. Let us review their achievements and failures.

The Revolt of the Netherlands

The bourgeois-democratic era opens with a thundering drama — the eighty years' war from 1568 to 1648 between the inhabitants of the Low Countries, Holland and Belgium, and the Spanish tyranny. Moralizers who shake their heads over the agonizing difficulties of the first fifty years of the Soviet Union and the world socialist revolution disregard the still more prolonged birth pangs of the first bourgeois republic — which was still far removed from a popular democracy even after it had been won.

The mighty movement of the masses for national self-determination in the Low Countries began in the middle of the sixteenth century as a drive for religious self-determination under the leadership of dissenting nobles and landowners. The reformers, who were sentenced and executed by the thousands under the Inquisition, engaged in furious attacks upon the Catholic churches and convents long before they dared directly defy the sovereignty of the Spanish crown. Calvinists and Lutherans went forth in armed bodies thousands strong to worship in the open fields before they took the field in warfare against the oppression of the Spanish masters.

In 1566 the opposition nobles banded together to resist the "barbarous" Inquisition while still swearing "to maintain the monarch in his estate, and to suppress all seditions, tumults, monopolies and factions." On August 23 of that year they concluded a compromise with the Spanish monarch which permitted preaching wherever it was already practiced, provided the people laid down their arms and did not interfere with the old religion. This truce did not last long.

It took another fourteen years after this conquest of religious tolerance before the Estates General proclaimed a republic with a constitution that gave representatives of the people not only legislative but executive powers, including the direction of foreign affairs. It was a breathtaking — and exceedingly painful — departure to forsake the monarchy. The Estates General found it easier to make the break in practice than to recognize the result in principle and openly proclaim a new kind of government.

None of the nobles broached the idea of a republic or repudiated hereditary sovereignty. When the liberators decided to cut loose from the Spanish king, they thought of replacing him with some other permanent head of state, either a hereditary chief magistrate or a more compliant prince, as the British bourgeoisie did a century later. Their commander-in-chief, William of Nassau, could have grasped the scepter but declined to become a sovereign. In any case, he did not envisage a democratic republic after his country's liberation.

When the United Provinces declared their independence on July 26, 1581, they did not announce a new form of government, although the de facto republic they set up was destined to flourish for two centuries before it was replaced by the present constitutional monarchy. As Motley, the American chronicler of the *Rise of the Dutch Republic,* aptly commented: "The fathers of the commonwealth did not baptize it by the name of Republic. They did not contemplate a change in their form of government. They had neither an aristocracy nor a democracy in their thoughts." [1] As they dethroned the Spanish king, they even spoke of upholding the divine rights of kings.

The republic came in by stealth and remained by default. Nevertheless, the wavering between the old regime and the new, manifested in the contradiction between their intentions and their actions, did not nullify the epoch-making significance of the act of abjuration nor detract from its immense consequences. The upper-class leaders of the Calvinist revolt stumbled blindfolded into republicanism and stayed there *faute de mieux.* Although they refrained from giving equal rights to the masses of the people, they did much to legitimize republican sentiments and popularize antimonarchical ideas by maintaining the sovereignty of the representative assembly. They turned traditional relations upside down by asserting that princes were made for the sake of their subjects and not vice versa.

Whereas in their original stronghold in Geneva, the Calvinists imposed a theological monopoly as stringent as the Roman Catholic, the extraordinary popular upheaval, the multiplicity of rival Protestant sects in the national camp and the extensive trading relations of the bourgeois republic made ecclesiastical exclusivism out of place in revolutionized Holland. The Dutch ratified religious toleration, freedom of conscience and expression of opinion. William of Nassau forbade interference with the conscience of the citizen in religious matters.

The sturdy bourgeois republic established by the Dutch pioneers was far more oligarchic than democratic. In 1640 the Dutch statesman Francois Van Aersens declared that the government of the Low Countries was really an aristocracy "where the people have no say and indiscretion no place." Yet under the governance of its landed and mercantile classes, Holland became the foremost maritime, monetary and commercial power in the world during the seventeenth century. Its citizens were not only the wealthiest and most cultured but enjoyed greater freedom than any other country on the European continent. Costly and bloody as it was and despite the extremely restricted scope of the peoples' rights, the first bourgeois revolution was fully justified by its fruits.

The English Civil War

The English revolution of the following century took off from a more advanced point than its Dutch predecessor, since a centralized national state had been set up and all ties with Rome severed several generations before it broke out. The revolutionary decade of the 1640s began with attacks by the parliamentary representatives of the bourgeoisie upon the prerogatives of the monarchy and the Established Church, the twin buttresses of the obsolete medieval economic and social relations which thwarted industrial and commercial development.

In England, as in Holland, the struggle to democratize religious life went hand in hand with demands for reforming the regime and even dominated the first stage of the battle with the monarchy for power. The question of the Established Church involved much more than religious considerations. The Church of England was a great landowner; it directed education and molded public opinion; it was the main support and servitor of royal authority. The parish was the unit of local government; everyone had to attend services on Sunday, pay tithes and be subject to the jurisdiction of the ecclesiastical courts. Control of the Church was fundamental to the control of society, as James I recognized when he proclaimed: "No Bishop, no King."

When Puritans and Presbyterians assailed the hierarchy of the Church and tried to change its administration or set up congregations outside of it, they were striking at the breastworks of royal power and threatening to disrupt the feudal structure of the country. The Civil War was precipitated by the refusal of Charles I to surrender his authority over the army to Parliament and abandon the Church of England to Puritan rule.

The "root-and-branch" men like Cromwell, who were the most robust leaders of the bourgeois opposition, did not start out intending to overthrow the crown, although they were determined to break the monopoly of the Church. They sought to curb the exactions and excesses of Charles's personal regime, limit its absolute powers and teach the king a lesson. But once the monarch referred the issue of power to the test of arms in 1642, they had to reconsider their political attitudes. The moderate Presbyterians, on the right wing of the Long Parliament which sat for the rest of that decade, vacillated between the peerage and the people and continued to stand for a limited monarchy. The Independents, who directly represented the more radical country gentlemen and city merchants, placed their class objectives above the maintenance of the crown as well as the Church.

The defeat of the king's armies sealed the fate of the Established Church. Archbishop Laud, the henchman of absolutism, was executed in January 1645, the episcopacy was abolished, and the bishop's lands offered for sale in October 1646. At that point the revolutionary forces left the status of the monarchy in abeyance. The Presbyterians, Independents and some Leveller leaders were all still willing to work out a compromise with the king.

But when Charles decided to take up arms again in the hope of regaining absolute power, the Cromwellians were finally convinced that the monarch was too great a counterrevolutionary menace to be permitted to survive. Overcoming their reservations, Cromwell and his generals condemned the king as a traitor, led him to the scaffold and abolished the monarchy and the House of Lords. After nine years of parliamentary and military conflict, the revolution had succeeded in destroying the principal defenses of feudalism.

In addition to demonstrating how a revolutionary dictatorship can shatter the props of the old order, seventeenth-century England provided a clear-cut case of the divergences which generated irrepressible conflict between the big and the little bourgeoisie, the patricians and the plebeians in the revolutionary camp. As the country was shaken up by intensified civil strife during the early 1640s, the common people, who had hitherto been excluded from politics, moved onto the stage as a distinct force. They were brought together in a revolutionary democratic formation called the Levellers, the most resolute representatives of the plebeian masses and the stubbornest fighters for the program of radical democracy. Their religious, political and economic ideas expressed the interests and outlook of the artisans, apprentices, shopkeepers and other small property holders in the cities and the yeomen in the country districts.

The Leveller party had a short life. It began to take shape in 1646, went through three years packed with upheavals and was crushed by Cromwell in 1649. During the critical turning point in the Civil War, its partisans were strong enough to propel the revolution forward through their mobilizations of the masses for struggle and through the pressures their followers in the army exerted from the left upon the bourgeois Grandees led by Cromwell.

The Levellers started as a propaganda group which was transformed into a party as their mass influence extended and the revolutionary tide mounted. They were the first popular revolutionary party in English history.

The party was centered in London but spread throughout England. The Levellers were primarily an extraparliamentary organization of mass action; they remained unrepresented in the House of Commons whose seats were reserved for the nobility and wealthy. Their leaders addressed themselves first and foremost to the common people, educating, guiding and organizing them for direct intervention on the key questions of the day. The mass petition was the principal means they used to inform and arouse the people. These petitions, citing the grievances and demands of the populace, were widely circulated for signatures, submitted to Parliament and backed up by meetings and demonstrations.

Most of the Agitators in the New Model Army either belonged to the Levellers or were inspired by their ideas. The Levellers advocated elections of soldiers' delegates and promoted the formation of the regimental committees which were comparable to the soldiers' soviets that sprang up in the Russian army of 1917. The committees of Agitators took up the grievances of the ranks and favored a democratically controlled popular militia.

The conflict between the patrician leadership and the lower ranks of the antimonarchical movement grew extremely tense soon after victory over the king brought to the fore the problem of the new revolutionary rulership. This would have to be decided by the New Model Army itself, which through the march of events had become an armed party, the political hotbed of the revolution, the master of the land.

The Cromwellians wanted a regime — with or without the king — in which political hegemony firmly reposed in the hands of the large property owners. The Levellers demanded a government based upon the power of the people and responsive to their needs.

The mutinous rank-and-file soldiers were not only hostile to the king and the parliamentary majority but fearful that Cromwell and his officers would sell them out. They were alarmed by the tenor of a "written constitution," drafted by the council of officers, known as the "Heads of the Proposals," which presented a cautious and conservative program of political changes. The Levellers put forward their own democratic and republican counterproposals in the first "Agreement of the People," published in October 1647.

Both sides agreed that the freedom of Parliament must be secured, that frequent sessions should be held, that there should be a more equitable and representative distribution of seats, and that Parliament must control all executive and military officers. Both agreed upon religious toleration for all Christians but Roman Catholics, who were regarded as potentially subversive agents of foreign powers. If these reforms were accepted, the officers were inclined to restore the prerogatives and liberty of the king, who was their captive.

The Levellers took a different attitude toward both the king and Parliament. Their leaders were definitely republican (one of their principal spokesmen, Overton, stated that monarchy was "the original of all oppression") and their manifesto ignored and virtually abolished the monarchy and House of Lords. The officers envisaged a Parliament which would be independent of the king on the one hand and the people on the other and thus function as the instrument of the big bourgeoisie. The Levellers maintained that Parliament should be subordinate to the people, who would hold the supreme power and temporarily delegate it to elected representatives. The Levellers accordingly favored a broad franchise, while the officers insisted on restricting suffrage to merchants and landowners.

In an effort to reconcile their differences, or at least discuss them, the Council of the Army held an important meeting at Putney, near London, at the end of October 1647, with Cromwell himself as chairman. The clash of opinions during these debates between the spokesmen for the officers and the regimental ranks was the most dramatic direct confrontation of the democratic and oligarchic tendencies in the English revolution.

Cromwell's son-in-law, General Ireton, objected to the first article of the Agreement which he interpreted as meaning that "every man that is an inhabitant is to be equally considered, and to have an equal voice in the election of those representees, the persons that are for the general Representatives. . . ."

That is precisely the point, rejoined the delegates of the soldiers. Said Petty: "We judge that all inhabitants that have not lost their birthright should have an equal voice in elections." Colonel Rainborough backed him up with these famous words:

"For really I think that the poorest he that is in England hath a life to live, as the greatest he; and therefore truly, sir, I think it's clear, that every man that is to live under a government ought first by his own consent to put himself under that government."

This democratic assertion was too much for Ireton, who replied: "No person hath a right to an interest or share in the disposing of the affairs of the kingdom, and in determining or choosing those that shall determine what laws we shall be ruled by here . . . that hath not a permanent fixed interest in this kingdom. . . ." Otherwise, the poor can despoil the property of the rich. "All the main thing that I speak for," he went on, "is because I would have an eye to property. I hope that we do not come to contend for victory — but let every man consider with himself that he does not go that way to take away all property. For here is the case of the most fundamental part of the constitution of the kingdom, which if you take away, you take away all by that." [2]

This plain-speaking dialogue drew a sharp line between the bourgeois parliamentarians and the radical democrats. Were property rights to be paramount to individual rights? Were property qualifications to be set so high as to reserve parliamentary representation to the rich, or made low enough to include a large part of the citizen body? More immediately, were the economic and political interests of the new masters to prevail over the democratic liberties of "the poorest he" and were the common people to remain under the domination of the landed and commercial oligarchy? We did not fight for that, proclaimed the Levellers.

The disputed issues were not adjudicated according to the merits of the arguments weighed on democratic scales. They were settled by the further developments of the Civil War over the next two years. After some hesitation, Cromwell aligned himself with the Leveller ranks, ceased negotiations with Charles and broke with the Presbyterians. To crush the counterrevolution and concentrate power in the hands of the Independents, his forces beheaded the king and proclaimed a republic in 1649.

Having disposed of the royalist danger to the right, he then proceeded to settle accounts with the Levellers on his left. When discontent in the army erupted into mutiny, Cromwell was overheard to say: "There was no other way to deal with these men, but to break them to pieces. . . . If you do not break them, they will break you." This he proceeded to do. While Parliament tried the Leveller leaders for sedition, Cromwell

crushed the Agitators in his regiments in April 1649. Upon
the consolidation of his personal dictatorship, the Levellers
declined, disintegrated and disappeared as an organized force.

The significance of the Leveller movement in the struggle
for petty-bourgeois democracy cannot be measured by the
brevity of its political existence. Although it was active for only
a few years on the stage of English history, it left a durable
imprint on the development of democratic thought.

The Levellers were the first to formulate many demands which
became part of the permanent heritage of bourgeois-democratic
ideology. They called for a sweeping democratization of both
the church and the state and the suppression of tithes. They
proposed a constitutional republic, annual election of a Parliament responsible to the people and to them alone and a wide
manhood suffrage. They also tried to democratize the government of the city of London and the companies that restricted
the crafts and trades. In the sphere of legal reform, they demanded the right to trial by jury, no Star Chamber hearings,
an end to capital punishment and to imprisonment for debt.
They called for freedom of the press and no license on printing.

Most of these proposals and the doctrinal justifications for
them have since become commonplaces in the lexicon of every
garden-variety liberal. But at this birth-time they were audacious innovations that horrified their conservative contemporaries and cost their more prominent champions, such as John
Lilburne, Richard Overton and William Walwyn, tortures, fines,
persecution and prison terms.

The Levellers were the most full-blooded exponents of the
militant democracy which characterized the climactic points in
the struggles for human rights and liberties against despotism
during the rise of capitalism to world power. The Sons and
Daughters of Liberty, the Jacobins of the left and the Enragés,
the black and white Abolitionists were their lineal descendants
in the bourgeois-democratic revolutions to come.

They did not hold the most extreme positions in the social
conflicts of that period; the farthest left was occupied by the
dispossessed peasants who formed the agrarian communist sect
of the Diggers. The Diggers, who described themselves as "True
Levellers," went beyond the demands for political equality and
attacked the principle of private property in theory and practice.
They aspired to eliminate social ills by common ownership
of the land and collective cultivation of it.

The Levellers were not communistic but held the views of
small property owners who belonged to the less prosperous

part of the middle classes. As exponents of a petty-bourgeois democracy, they worked for equal political and legal rights against the discriminations imposed by the landed gentry and well-to-do. They wanted to spread and equalize property owner-ship rather than to abolish private property as the source of social and economic inequalities. Their petty-bourgeois status and standards were shown by the limitations they put on the exercise of the franchise. They specifically proposed to exclude wage workers and recipients of poor relief from the voting roster.

The radical democracy upheld by the Levellers was egali-tarian in spirit and plebeian rather than proletarian in its social support and popular appeal. Its agitators in the army and among the civilian population trusted in the self-action and self-organization of the masses. The Levellers opposed the arbitrary authority of any minority or aristocracy, whether under the patronage of the king, the bishops, the Presbyterians or the squirearchy.

They were not pettifogging legalists. They appealed away from established precedent to some higher law, justified by a natural or divine right, that promoted the safety and welfare of the people. Their conduct was guided by the maxim of every great struggle for human rights: the necessities of revolutionary progress constitute the supreme law. They stood for popular sovereignty — all power emanated from the citizen body and reverted to it, while the government remained at all times re-sponsible to the people for its conduct of public affairs.

The Levellers were individualistic in both a personal and propertied sense. They believed that everyone should have the right to work, worship, practice freedom of conscience, choose the government, speak freely, publish and petition. Nor should there be any infringement on the right to own and dispose of private property. Although they did not accord equal legal or voting rights to women, they did believe that women should have some voice in public affairs and encour-aged their participation in mass actions.

The expressions of extensive democracy from below were strongest when the popular revolt was rising and at the peak of its powers. They subsided and went underground as the revolution ebbed and the bourgeoisie stabilized its domination.

The popular democracy to which the Levellers aspired was cut down by the sword of Cromwell's dictatorship. His stern military regime purged and dispersed one Parliament after another. Although Cromwell and his generals carried out that part of the Leveller program which aimed at the abolition of the monarchy and House of Lords, they did not adopt its democratic reforms. From his accession to personal power in 1649 to his death in 1658, the Puritan general was the Lord Protector of the new bourgeois order "by any means necessary."

Cromwell's one-man rule consolidated the social conquests and furthered the economic and foreign policies of the bourgeoisie. Cromwell did not take the crown and inaugurate a new dynasty; he was deterred by resistance from the veterans of the New Model Army and the Independent preachers and congregations which had trusted him. He acted like William the Silent before him and George Washington after him, rather than like Napoleon. When the Cromwellian Protectorate was succeeded by the Restoration government in 1660, it was unable or unwilling to undo his work. The social and economic supremacy of the bourgeoisie had been secured beyond revision; the revolution of 1688 was to clinch the political ascendancy of the bourgeoisie.

Unlike the radical democracy advocated by the Levellers, the parliamentary form of government instituted after 1688 was conservative and moderate in temper. It relied upon indirect rather than direct representation. It was not plebeian but aristocratic, plutocratic and oligarchic in its social basis. It leaned upon precedent and tradition, in preference to higher law. It frowned upon independent and self-reliant activity by the masses and viewed electoral action hedged about by restrictions as the sole legitimate means of registering the popular will. It was hierarchical rather than equalitarian in orientation. It was not republican in principle but monarchical so long as the court was obeisant to the bourgeois Parliament.

The two English revolutions, the Great Rebellion of the 1640s and the Glorious Revolution of the 1680s, benefited the mercantile interests and landed gentry more than any other sectors of British society. Although the state church and the monarchy were retained, these relics of feudalism never again dared to assert absolute power or defy the will of the bourgeoisie.

The disregard of the upper classes for genuine democracy, even on bourgeois terms, was evidenced in their shifting attitudes toward the monarchy as an institution. Before the midseventeenth century, the London merchants and moneylenders had gotten along well enough with the royal house and were content to bid for and enjoy its patronage and protection. However, when the Stuart king stood immovably in their way, the insurgent Puritan army of the city and country bourgeoisie cut off Charles's head. Once they had achieved their major objectives and assured the supremacy of Parliament, the triumphant merchants and landowners brought back the monarchy of another lineage. To this day the English capitalists have found it a useful appendage of their domination. A similar choice in favor of a bourgeois monarchy over a democratic republic was made by the conservatized Dutch bourgeoisie after the vicissitudes of the French Revolution, as well as by other capitalist governments on the European continent.

In seventeenth-century England, the bourgeois side of the revolution succeeded; its republican and democratic movements failed. Nevertheless, the acts and achievements of the bourgeois revolution rid the country of much rubble from the feudal past and erected a framework in which democracy could reassert itself, with the rise of the working class after the Industrial Revolution.

The First American Revolution

The bourgeois revolution was relatively quiescent for almost a century after its consolidation in England. Then the struggle for democracy rose to flood tide and registered its greatest successes on both sides of the Atlantic.

Professor R. R. Palmer has characterized the four decades from 1760 to 1800 as "the age of the democratic revolution." In two detailed volumes he has described the challenge of the democratic forces to the aristocracies, patriciates, oligarchies and privileged orders in a series of places — Switzerland, America, Ireland, Britain, Holland, Belgium, Poland and Hungary — during the latter part of the eighteenth century. When these protest movements had died down or been extinguished by 1800, the revolution had won out only in America and France. But the magnitude of the accomplishments in these countries on two continents warrants such a designation for this period.

The resurgence of the democratic movement began in England's possessions on the Atlantic seaboard. The colonists of the thirteen states were the first people in the Western hemisphere to throw off subjection to the European powers and embark on their own national career. Theirs was the first victorious colonial revolt of the capitalist epoch — a feat all the more unprecedented since, from Roman times on, no colonial people had successfully thrown off the rule of a mother country.

The coalition of classes that made the first American revolution was held together by one overriding aim: to achieve self-determination as a nation through liberation from English tyranny. After winning independence from British crown rule through seven years of war, the founding fathers of the United States went on to unify the people in a federated democratic republic, the most favorable type of regime for the promotion of economic, political and cultural life under bourgeois auspices.

The American rebels, who acted at a more advanced stage of bourgeois development than their Dutch and English forerunners, had to expend much less energy to combat and reform the church. Religious toleration had long flourished in the colonies. Roger Williams had founded in Providence the first settlement which completely separated the state from religion, a principle legalized in the charter granted by Charles II in 1663 to Rhode Island. The official Church of England was neither powerful nor popular and was easily disestablished once the crown and its agents were overthrown. The tithes extracted to support its ministry were abolished and total separation of church from state was enacted, both on a state and federal level. The patriots used the prosaic and legalistic formulas of constitutional democracy more than Biblical citations to justify the cause and the course of their fight for freedom.

The War of Independence made important changes in economic relations. Until the revolution, Yankee merchants and shipowners had been heavily handicapped by the insistence of the British overlords that colonial trade go through British ports and operate under the restrictive regulations of the London-based Board of Trade. Thanks to independence, United States commerce enlarged its home market by removing the curbs on trade between the colonies; above all, it gained free access to the world market.

One of the key questions in all the bourgeois-democratic upheavals has been: who shall hold the land? All segments of the patriot camp — merchants, planters, financiers, landlords, speculators, farmers, mechanics and frontiersmen — had a stake in the contest over land ownership. They entered the fight against the royal, feudal and loyalist proprietors not simply for political power but also for title to the territories they eyed.

During the revolution, feudal encumbrances were cleared away and replaced by bourgeois economic and legal relations. Royal limitations on occupation of vacant lands were removed and the vast domains of the crown handed over to state and federal legislatures for disposal. Such feudal obligations as quitrents owed to the king and proprietary families were wiped out. Tory estates of considerable value were confiscated. The right of entail and primogeniture, by which great estates were kept intact from generation to generation, was ended and the feudal baronies divided.

In both American revolutions, the lands taken over by the federal and state governments were distributed according to bourgeois standards: immense tracts were sold cheaply to big speculators and well-placed moneyed interests, while smaller plots were parceled out to pioneer homesteaders, small farmers and army veterans.

To be sure, the agrarian reforms were by no means complete. Although slavery withered away in the North when it was no longer profitable and was legally prohibited in the Northwest Territory, it remained rooted in the South. Within the United States, the agrarian revolution along bourgeois lines had to be carried through in two separate stages, one in the eighteenth, the other in the nineteenth century.

In addition to breaking away from the most powerful empire in existence and sweeping away the institutions of colonialism, the royal government, the Established Church and the crown ownership of lands, the American revolutionaries created the first of the great constitutional conventions (constituent assemblies) which replaced an outworn system with a new government. They drew up a written constitution which spelled out the powers the government might and might not exercise, and to which subsequent amendment attached a specific Bill of Rights. They explicitly made the civil authority superior to the military. They also devised an effective federal system of states operating within a united democratic republic. These political innovations were unprecedented achievements.

Although still limited in many respects, the rights of the people were considerably extended in several areas. The franchise was widened under many state constitutions and representative governments set up. The terribly harsh criminal codes directed against the poor were softened.

Despite its shortcomings, the Yankee republic was the most progressive democratic government in the world at that point in the expansion of world capitalism. Its existence encouraged democratic forces in the Old World in their often disheartening struggles against the ancient and oligarchic regimes. Its example of successful resistance to the greatest empire in the world gave a strong stimulus to the wars of independence waged by the Latin American peoples against the weaker Spanish domination in the next century. The United States then provided a working model of democratic and republican gov-

ernment, born through revolutionary mass action, which served
as a source of hope and inspiration in the first half of the
nineteenth century, much as the early Soviet republic under
Lenin and Trotsky did in the first half of the twentieth century.

The French Revolution

The central revolutionary event of the bourgeois epoch was
the upheaval in France at the end of the eighteenth century.
The French Revolution did more than overthrow all three of
the main bulwarks of the old order in that country. It broke
the back of European feudalism and in Haiti helped bring on
a successful slave revolt.

The cycle of revolution stretched out for a quarter of a century from 1789 to 1814. Upon its completion, the most palpable result was the triumph of the bourgeois principle of
private property and its mode of exploitation. However, the
bourgeoisie had not attained political sovereignty along with
its social domination. The Bourbon dynasty, against which
the nation had contended for so long, had been put back on
the throne by the Great Powers. It would take more than another half century before the French bourgeoisie could dispense with the kings and Bonapartes and rule in its own right
through a democratic republic.

The anomalous fact that the bourgeois revolution failed to
vest political hegemony securely in bourgeois hands is to be
explained by the complicated class dynamics of the entire revolutionary process. The first moves against the crown did not
come from the commoners of the Third Estate, as in England,
but from dissenting nobles. Their initiative aroused the oppositional bourgeoisie, who promptly made common cause with
the liberal aristocracy. Together they took the decisive step of
converting the Estates General into the National Assembly,
which proceeded to govern in place of the king.

The dialectics of this sequence was noted by Robespierre
while the events took place. "In states constituted as are nearly
all the countries of Europe," he said, "there are three powers:
the monarchy, the aristocracy and the people, and the people
is powerless. Under such circumstances a revolution can break
out only as the result of a gradual process. It begins with the
nobles, the clergy, the wealthy, whom the people supports when
its interests coincide with theirs in resistance to the dominant
power, that of the monarchy. Thus it was that in France the
judiciary, the nobles, the clergy, the rich gave the original

impulse to the revolution. The people appeared on the scene only later. Those who gave the first impulse have long since repented, or at least wished to stop the revolution when they saw that the people might recover its sovereignty. But it was they who started it. Without their resistance, and their mistaken calculations, the nation would still be under the yoke of despotism."

The upper bourgeoisie regarded itself as the natural inheritor of the royal power and the appointed custodian of the sovereignty of the people. Its representatives did exercise state power from 1789 to the ousting of the Girondins on May 31, 1793, when they had to yield it for a time to the Jacobin dictatorship. They again assumed supreme authority after the Thermidoreans got rid of Robespierre, only to surrender the last shreds of it in 1799 to Napoleon's military coup. That ended their direct rule during the course of the revolution.

The bourgeoisie was mortally afraid of the disorders arising from popular tumult. One of their deputies to the National Assembly wrote that "one must work for the good of the people, but the people must do nothing for themselves." Actually, the masses not only had to do everything for themselves but a lion's share of revolutionary reconstruction for the bourgeoisie as well.

If the big bourgeoisie did not set the revolution going, neither did it carry the struggle against Bourbon absolutism through to the end on its own. At critical junctures in the contest with the counterrevolution, its representatives wavered, faltered and held back. Left to their own devices, the men of wealth would have accomplished far less than the necessities of the struggle demanded and the situation permitted.

If the upper classes challenged and upset the old regime, the plebeians in the city together with the peasants in the country overwhelmed and demolished it. The revolutionary offensive made its big strides forward through the interventions of the lower middle classes and laboring poor who, animated by their own grievances and aspirations, shouldered the heavy and bloody tasks of giving battle to the watchdogs of the feudal system and safeguarding the welfare of the revolution. As George Rudé has demonstrated, the interventions of ordinary men and women in the streets and markets were, except for the year 1790, "an almost continuous feature of the life of the capital during the first six years of the Revolution and for nearly two years before its outbreak."[3]

The revolution kept ascending from 1789 to the end of 1793,

as the plebeians shifted farther and farther to the left and the
more radical parties superseded the more moderate. The agita-
tion of the masses reached its crest with the bid for power of
the Enragés in August 1793 and the dechristianization campaign that autumn; it did not completely die down until the
insurrection of the Paris poor was subdued in May 1795.

The popular revolution started on its downward path after
Robespierre crushed the forces to his left in 1793. Thereafter
the autonomous actions of the masses played a constantly
diminishing role in the shaping of events. The reaction based
on the passivity of the masses was accelerated by the downfall
of the revolutionary republicans and continued to deepen under
the Directorate until the last embers of the revolution were
snuffed out by Napoleon.

Throughout the first period the spontaneous interventions of
the masses spurred on the revolution, by exerting radicalizing
pressures upon the hesitating bourgeoisie and forcing its hand
in proceeding against the old regime. This direct action began
with the storming of the Bastille, which also gave the signal
for the takeover of the provincial cities and towns and incited
the revolt of the peasants, who numbered twenty out of twenty-
six million Frenchmen. The peasant insurrection attacked the
throne from the rear while the risings in Paris engaged it in
frontal assault. The combination of these two movements made
the revolution irresistible.

The first response of the National Assembly was to call on
the troops to suppress the insurgents. Upon consideration of
their weakness in face of the people on the march, the delegates took the opposite tack. In August 1789 they issued the
Declaration of Rights, decreed that the feudal regime was entirely destroyed and withdrew the king's veto over legislation.
These were the first major concessions torn from the bourgeoisie by the masses.

Paris was the head and front of the revolution and the populace of the capital was its main motive force. They proved this
for the second time in the October 1789 days when twenty
thousand demonstrators, including the National Guards of the
Paris districts, led by a band of housewives and market women
demanding bread, invaded Versailles and slaughtered part of
the royal bodyguard. They forced Louis XVI to sign a decree
providing food for the city, to approve the Declaration of
Rights along with the nineteen articles of the constitution presented by the National Assembly and to take up residence in

the capital under the surveillance of its citizens. For the next five years, the moods and moves of the inhabitants of Paris were to be the most decisive factor in the development of the revolution.

". . . The essential work of the Revolution of 1789 may be found registered in the resolutions of August 4 and in the Declaration of the Rights of Man and the Citizen," wrote Georges Lefebvre. "But it would be childish to emphasize only these legislative enactments, throwing into the background the events that gave them birth. . . . The Old Regime did not bend before the judicial revolution. Having taken to force, it was destroyed by force, which the people, descending into the street, put at the service of what they regarded as right, though even their own representatives had not dared to ask such assistance from them."[4]

The constitution finally brought forth by the National Assembly in the spring of 1791 made plain how much the bourgeoisie who dominated it dreaded the extension of democracy. It divided Frenchmen into active and passive citizens and only the former were given the right to vote for the legislature. These qualified as active by the payment of a small direct tax certifying the ownership of a considerable amount of real estate. The limitation of the franchise to a small minority of property holders was deliberately designed to exclude the common people from participation or representation in the national government. For the bourgeoisie, the Rights of Man did not include equal electoral rights.

They wanted a monopoly of power for the notables headed by the men of wealth. Dupont de Nemours, who was to be one of the Thermidoreans and the founder of the Dupont dynasty in the United States, justified the property qualifications for suffrage imposed by the upper bourgeoisie in the most class-conscious spirit. "It is obvious that the property owners, without whose consent nobody in the country would have either food or lodging, are that country's leading citizens. They are sovereigns by the grace of God, of Nature, of their work, of their progress, and of the work and progress of their ancestors." Though his contemporary American descendants are not that candid, they behave in the family tradition.

The ideal system for the bankers, merchants and manufacturers composing the upper ranks of the bourgeoisie was a constitutional monarchy. They ultimately obtained this through the July 1830 overturn in the bourgeois monarchy of Louis

Philippe. But so restricted and undemocratic a regime could not be maintained in the raging torrent of the revolution at full flood.

The Legislative Assembly elected on the basis of the bourgeois constitution was swept away by the uprising of the working-class quarters of Paris on August 9-10, 1792. At that turning point, the "passive citizens" again showed themselves to be the most energetic of revolutionary forces. Rightly suspicious of the treasonable complicity of the royal family with the counterrevolutionary interventionists and émigré aristocrats who had invaded the country, they rose up in defense of the revolution. The insurgents stormed the Tuileries, overpowered and killed the Swiss Guards, seized the king and the royal family and, in effect, overturned the throne.

This "second revolution" destroyed the authority of the Legislative Assembly, doomed the monarchy and delivered de facto power to the insurrectional Paris Commune. This body, dominated by Danton, Robespierre and Marat, had overthrown the municipal government, taken over the city hall and set up its revolutionary rule. Feeling the hot breath of the masses on its neck, the dying Legislative Assembly suspended the king from office and ordered elections for a National Convention to draft a more democratic constitution.

The Convention became the arena of a struggle for supremacy between its right and left wings headed by the rival factions of Gironde and Mountain. The leaderships of the moderate Girondins and the radical Jacobins represented different sectors of the possessing classes. They had come into violent collision with each other under the conditions of foreign war and civil commotion which sharpened all antagonisms and strained social relations to the breaking point.

Although both contending factions were staunch defenders of private property, they were actuated by divergent interests and had different relations with the plebeians. The more conservative Girondins, who controlled the majority in the Legislative Assembly and the Convention that succeeded it, were intent on protecting the bourgeoisie involved in the export trade and the textile manufactures. They were anxious to shield the king and keep the masses immobilized.

The Montagnards were headed by those elements of the bourgeoisie newly enriched by inflation, the acquisition of national properties and profiteering on military supplies and war contracts. More republican than monarchical in sentiment, they had been thrown to the fore by the revolutionary events as the most radical and aggressive force among the propertied classes. The Jacobin leaders had close ties with the lower orders of shopkeepers, artisans, laborers — the sansculottes who were the principal sufferers from the economic and social effects of the war and the most resolute adherents of the revolution, which they were determined to democratize and drive forward.

The Montagnards opposed the Girondins not only over the fate of the monarchy but over the conduct of the war against Austria, Prussia and the monarchical powers. The war had the dual character of defending the revolution and promoting commercial and territorial conquest. Both of these aims required total mobilization of the nation and its resources. In order to assure their primary objective, the Montagnards, who were committed to win commercial superiority over Great Britain and to territorial and military aggrandizement, joined with the sansculottes to sweep the concilatory Girondins out of the way.

The external threat immensely accelerated the pace of revolutionary action. As the armies of the enemy came close to the gates of Paris, the revolutionaries of the Commune called upon the people to defend "the land of liberty" to the death — and they responded. Although the Convention had to proclaim the Republic, the Girondins lost the bases of their support by their futile efforts to save the monarchy, their equivocal attitude toward the trial and execution of the king, their narrow class policies and the military reverses of the French armies under their command.

The exasperated sansculottes of Paris who had toppled the monarchy rose up against the Girondins at the end of May 1793 and installed the left Jacobins in power. The revolutionary regime of Robespierre was led by the most intransigent of the middle-class revolutionists, who were most conscious of the necessities of the struggle and most responsive to the demands of the masses. The Jacobin dictatorship rested upon an alignment of forces, in which the weight of the conservative elements had been reduced to a minimum, while the power of the people rose to its height. Its rule signified the greatest victory of the democratic forces of the revolution over its bourgeois-bureaucratic tendencies.

This most advanced stage of the revolutionary decade from 1789 to 1799 demonstrates how shallow the liberal view of the absolute counterposition of democracy to dictatorship is. The revolutionary government did not have any constitutional legitimacy and its Committee of Public Safety exercised its executive functions without legal restraints. Yet this agency of

the revolution provided the fullest measure of democracy the
French people had ever enjoyed. It was a democratic dictatorship.

The Jacobin regime was the outgrowth of all the power that
the insurgent masses had managed to accumulate since 1789.
It formed the apex of an extensive structure of democratic institutions, chief among them the sections and the Commune of
Paris, the popular societies, the revolutionary committees and
the revolutionary army.

The source and seat of the power of the people were the
forty-eight sections of the capital which, ironically, the Legislative Assembly had set up in 1790 after the taking of the
Bastille and the October Days to forestall any further interference of the plebeians in political affairs. As the revolution
intensified, these electoral subdivisions became converted into
autonomous political assemblies where the people could voice
their sentiments for or against the existing regime and organize
themselves for action. Thus the August 10, 1792, insurrection
was politically prepared by a petition passed by all but one
of the Parisian sections calling for the dethronement of the king
and summoning a National Convention. Representatives from
twenty-eight of the sections constituted the body that carried
out the insurrection.

The insurrectional Commune based itself upon the sections.
This organ of municipal self-government not only ruled Paris
after the August action but acted as a counterpower to the
Assembly and Convention. The revolutionary Commune held
Louis XVI prisoner, took control of the National Guard, abolished passive citizenship and introduced manhood suffrage,
suppressed the remaining feudal charges without compensation
and put up confiscated émigré property for sale in small lots.

The political leadership of the radical forces in the sections,
Commune, Convention, Committee of Public Safety and the
army, was drawn from the popular societies. There was a multiplicity of these, ranging from the right-wing Club des Valois
to the left-wing club of the Cordeliers, to which Danton and
other prominent agitators belonged. The most important were
the Jacobins, who developed through a series of secessions
and splits into the principal revolutionary party of the country.

These voluntary associations which sprung up on all sides
from 1789 to 1791 federated on a provincial and national
scale. On July 14, 1790, the first anniversary of the fall of
the Bastille, the Féderés marched into Paris from all parts of
France to celebrate their liberation from feudalism and despo-

tism; the Fete of the Féderés became an annual muster of active partisans of the revolution.

By 1793 France was covered by a network of between five to eight thousand such clubs with a membership of around half a million. Many of these local clubs were in correspondence with the Paris Jacobins, which provided a national organizational mechanism capable of mobilizing the most militant and devoted individuals for the execution of revolutionary assignments.

The Jacobin membership was largely of middle-class composition and its principal figures formed the backbone of the left wing in the Convention and the nucleus of the Committee of Public Safety. Through their close connections with the masses, the Jacobin leaders could summon them into action — or hold them back. They organized their armed interventions through the sectional meetings and popular societies.

The Jacobins and their press exercised critical pressures upon the Constituent Assembly and other government bodies until they took over power in the capital and the country. The popular societies were the sword and the shield of the Jacobin dictatorship in the communes of the towns and villages. Thus in Metz, 61 Jacobins out of 148 held government office and at Toulouse, 103 out of 731. In November 1793 the Committee of Public Safety hailed their vanguard role as follows: "Vigilant sentinels holding the most advanced posts of public opinion, they sound the alarm in every danger, and against every traitor. It is in the sanctuary they provide that Patriots sharpen the weapon of victory." [5]

Robespierre's authority among the Jacobins lifted him to the helm of the dictatorship, and his loss of authority over the clubs in the summer of 1794 enabled the Thermidoreans to unseat him and bring him and his associates to the scaffold.

The popular societies bloomed and faded with the vicissitudes of the revolutionary cause. Their numbers and power crested at the flood tide of the revolutionary upsurge and sank with its ebb as the political role of the people drew to an end. They were among the first casualties of the Thermidorean reaction and repression and had virtually disappeared by 1796.

The host of revolutionary committees which took over a wide range of governmental functions was another instrumentality of the popular democracy under the Jacobin dictatorship. Each section formed its own revolutionary committee. The Central Revolutionary Committee of the Paris Commune organized and led the uprising of May-June 1793. The vigilance committees

of the communes exposed corruption, ferreted out counterrevolutionary conspirators and meted out revolutionary justice to
the culprits.

Every great revolution breaks up the old army and creates
a new one in its own image. Democratic France did this. Upon
the initiative of the Féderés a compulsory universal enlistment
of all able-bodied males was decreed on August 1792 and eight
thousand of the Féderés engaged in its enforcement throughout
the country. This was the first egalitarian mobilization of an
entire people in a national war of liberation in modern history.
The citizen army of the revolutionary republic was the antithesis
of the monarchical military forces directed by an aristocratic
officer caste and manned by mercenaries.

The revitalized and democratized French army was the most
formidable and enduring creation of the Jacobin republic. Its
mass levies conducted a popular war which brought great
triumphs to the revolutionary armies.

The aureole that surrounds the Jacobins in French radical
tradition derives in large measure from their energetic defense
of the revolution and its democracy. However, this progressive
bourgeois dictatorship sowed the seeds of the military dictatorship of a later stage just as the Cromwellians did. Not only
Robespierre and St. Just but Napoleon were Jacobins. Bonaparte upheld the republican principles of the Jacobins against
the Girondins in the critical summer of 1793 and the young
officer owed his rapid promotion to the Jacobin leader. Neither
flinched from putting down the restless plebeians on their left
flank.

Ironically, as the revolution receded, this new military organization served as an instrument of oppression at home.
Napoleon, who owed his career and victories to the grand
army, took over its command and turned it against the people. This development drove home the point that revolutionaries must control the army or sooner or later the reactionaries among the officers will suppress the revolution — a lesson
which the Algerians led by Ben Bella learned to their sorrow
more than a century and a half later.

The revolutionary regime which lasted for almost a year under the Committee of Public Safety had tremendous achievements
to its credit. Brought into existence by the extreme danger to
the revolution in 1793, it repelled the invasion, putting down
the counterrevolution in the Vendée and reconquering Belgium.
It centralized the government and broke the remaining roy-

alist resistance by means of its revolutionary tribunals and terror.

As significant as the dictatorship's military successes were the social measures it enacted. The revolutionary government obtained control over the economy and halted inflation by means of requisitioning and the *maximum* which gave the poor bread at a reasonable price. It put the unemployed to work manufacturing arms and doing guard duty. It gave the peasants the national estates, which were partitioned into small lots and placed on sale. It established free medical services, old-age assistance, allowances to the relatives of soldiers and the right of compensation for war damages. It obtained the money for these measures by means of forced loans and taxes. The monopoly of public affairs was shattered and the doors of administration opened to the lower middle classes.

Politically and socially, the Jacobins went about as far as any revolutionary bourgeois regime in alliance with the insurgent masses has ever gone in ministering to the needs of the people, releasing their constructive capacities and permitting the free exercise of their powers. Even so, they could not and did not go far and fast enough to satisfy the clamorous demands of the sansculottes and rectify their grievances.

If the positions, tendencies and social components of the parties of the French Revolution are compared with those cast up during the English revolution, the Girondins were roughly analogous to the Presbyterians, the Robespierrists with the Cromwellians, the Enragés with the Levellers, and the followers of Babeuf with the Diggers.

The Jacobin dictatorship rested upon a coalition of the revolutionary bourgeoisie with the plebeians. The Jacobin leaders were ready to call the masses for political protests and even armed insurrection when that suited their purposes. But they feared to give free rein to the energy of the masses and hastened to curb any moves from below which menaced their positions and wealth.

The shopkeepers, craftsmen, journeymen and laborers who made up the ranks of the sansculottes readily accepted direction from the radical bourgeoisie in the struggle between the monarchy and the republic. But if their political objectives coincided, their economic interests and social welfare diverged widely. Though they were unhappy about restricting freedom of trade which kept profiteering down, the leading Jacobins agreed to regulate the prices of prime necessities. But they also wanted to freeze wages. The laboring poor insisted on price-fixing but opposed wage-freezing. The stresses arising from such issues led to a disruption of the partnership between the Jacobins and sansculottes.

The Enragés, led by the "red priest" Jacques Roux, Eugene Leclerc and Jean Varlet, most vigorously voiced the discontents and the egalitarian aspirations of the plebeians. They did not hesitate to assail all the agents of the upper classes who sought to shift the costs of the war and the burdens of the revolution onto the backs of the poor.

The Enragés agreed with the Jacobins on the necessity of waging war to the death against the foreign interventionists and their royalist accomplices within the borders. But they were as strongly opposed to the newly installed aristocracy of wealth as to the nobles and priests. They kept pressing the Robespierrists to take sterner measures to curb the profiteers, relieve the misery of the poor and fight for social equality. Robespierre, besieged on all sides, found the pressure from the left intolerable.

Jacques Roux wrote bitterly: "They always use men of high character to make revolutions. Then when they're no longer needed, they're smashed like a glass."[6] This was a prophecy of his own fate. After having disposed of the Girondins on the right, Robespierre proceeded to a showdown with the recalcitrant Enragé agitators, who were stirring up the poor and hungry. He broke these spokesmen for the common people by slandering them as hired agents of the enemy. Jacques Roux, the framed-up chief of the Enragés, escaped the guillotine only by committing suicide on February 10, 1794.

This did not end resistance on the extreme left. The Hébertistes, who had been in league with the Enragés in the forefront of the Parisian masses, undertook an offensive against the Christian religion. To combat their program of tighter popular control over the administration, on November 21, 1793, Robespierre also denounced the dechristianizers on false charges, tried and condemned them to death.

Ronsin of the Revolutionary Army, who was one of the victims, exclaimed: "Liberty cannot perish; and those who are now sending us to death will follow in their turn." So it happened. Robespierre was squeezed between two categories of enemies he could not help but create: those who felt he was going too far and too fast in his actions against the possessing classes and those who felt he was going too slow and growing callous to the plight of the poor.

By striking down the Dantonists on one side and the most uncompromising revolutionists in the Commune on the other, by suppressing the most combative elements of the *bras nus* and dislodging the masses from the positions of power they had won, Robespierre cut away the foundations of his previous support. The grave he had dug for others had room for himself. He was deposed on the ninth of Thermidor (July 27, 1794) by a mixed cabal of opponents whose assumption of power reversed the direction of the revolution.

The guillotine that beheaded the Robespierrists cut short the flowering of revolutionary democracy in the French Revolution. The Republic which continued under the Directory reverted to the narrow franchise of the original bourgeois constitution and pursued a course of social and political reaction.

The masses engaged in several desperate rearguard actions before their revolutionary ardor was completely crushed. In May of the next year, the Paris insurgents nearly dispersed the Convention by force and built barricades in the streets of the working-class quarters. Troops had to be called into the capital for the first time in six years to put down the uprising. The Convention arrested, imprisoned or deported ten thousand rebels and guillotined a few of their leaders.

The Conspiracy of the Equals was the final flare-up of the plebeian struggle for social equality. This abortive attempt to seize power in 1796 had a twofold significance. It brought to a logical culmination all the strivings for direct democracy which had been churned up by the hopes and idealism of the revolution. But Gracchus Babeuf thrust these onto a higher ground by advocating a communist solution for the problems of the poor.

Babeuf utilized the same methods of organization and action as his radical predecessors. He published an influential journal called the *Tribune of the People,* formed a society called the Pantheon Club which attracted about two thousand members and then, when this was disbanded, organized a secret group to prepare an uprising and win over the armed forces for the project. However, the conspiracy was betrayed by one of the inner circle around Babeuf and Buonarotti and broken up by the police on May 10, 1796, a few days before the date scheduled for the insurrection. Babeuf was tried and put to death while Buonarotti, who was sent to prison, lived to record the history and ideas of the movement.

The would-be insurrectionists represented a coalition of left Jacobins with a small core of communists. The neo-Jacobins viewed themselves as continuators and consummators of the unfinished work of the revolution cut short by the Thermidoreans. They had an immediate program to distribute the *milliard* that the Convention had promised from sales of the national properties among the defenders of the country and to award the property of the suspects to the poor. They wanted to restore the Constitution of 1793 and reinstitute the taxation, requisition and rationing policies of the revolutionary republic.

These aims were not very dissimilar from the program of militant Jacobinism. Babeuf also planned to set up a provisional dictatorial government, like that under the Committee of Safety, which would lean upon the most revolutionary forces, go forward to strengthen the democratic rule of the people and achieve genuine equality.

But if his short-range program was not new, Babeuf did introduce two memorable ideological innovations into the history of the bourgeois revolution. One was the concept of the uninterrupted revolution which was to carry the war between the patricians and plebeians, the rich and the poor, to its very end. This doctrine of consistent class struggle prefigured the dictatorship of the proletariat without the scientific grounding of historical materialism.

The idea was strikingly formulated by Sylvain Maréchal in his *Manifesto of the Equals:* "The French revolution is only the forerunner of another revolution, far greater, far more solemn, which will be the last of them all."[7] Herein can be discerned the germ of the theory of permanent revolution later taken up by Marx and Engels and most fully developed by Trotsky in the twentieth century.

Babeuf most of all transcended his precursors in the way he proposed to realize equality and secure democracy. The left Jacobins, Enragés and Hébertistes were no less vehement partisans of equality. The sansculottes they spoke for wanted social as well as legal equality and full political rights. But all these other forces and tendencies held different economic views than the Babouvists; they hoped to achieve these aims within the confines of private ownership.

The Robespierrists were as much champions of large holdings as the Girondins; the Enragés and their followers upheld the small-property ownership congenial to shopkeepers, artisans and peasant proprietors. None of them envisaged or welcomed the abolition of private property in industry or agriculture. They hoped to extend its possession to many more citizens through agrarian reform, the distribution of confiscated goods and the sale of lands at the disposal of the republic and the municipalities. All these layers of bourgeois society saw the multiplication of petty proprietors as the guarantee for the protection of individual freedom and national prosperity. They put strong emphasis on small private property, small private enterprise and small private workshops.

That was in fact the actual direction taken by the revolution which converted feudal France into a nation of petty proprietors. This dispersion of property holdings among small cultivators, shopkeepers and artisans was to retard its industrial development during the nineteenth century.

Babeuf, on the other hand, proposed to abolish private property. Here is how he expounded that cornerstone of his position in his defense at the trial, February-May 1797: "It is necessary *to bind together everyone's lot,* to render the lot of each member of the association independent of chance, and of happy or unfavorable circumstance; *to assure to every man and his posterity, no matter how numerous it may be, as much as they need, but no more than they need,* and to shut off from everybody all the possible paths by which they might obtain some part of the products of nature and of work that is more than their individual due.

"The sole means of arriving at this is to establish a *common administration;* to suppress private property; to place every man of talent in the line of work which he knows best; to oblige him to deposit the fruit of his work in the common store, to establish a simple *administration of needs,* which, keeping a record of all individuals and all the things that are available to them, will distribute these available goods with the most scrupulous equality, and will see to it that they make their way into the home of every citizen." [8]

Babeuf had in view a communism of the distribution and consumption of goods rather than of production. Since "stomachs are equal," everyone should draw a perfectly equal share of the available goods from the common store to which they would contribute.

His system was directed toward an equally radical democracy. "Our dogmas are pure democracy, equality without blemish and without reserve," he insisted. He realized that political democracy could only be assured and had to be complemented by a social democracy and that a consistent popular democracy leads through the abolition of private ownership to communism. He proposed to abolish inheritance to implement and maintain the thoroughgoing egalitarianism he envisaged.

Babeuf was incontestably a link between the bourgeois and the proletarian revolutions; despite their immaturity, his views marked a significant step in the development of communist thought. He gave the most advanced expression to the experience of the plebeian elements, who were the democratic mainspring of the bourgeois revolution. His ideas and proposals ran far ahead of his time. If France could not arrive at a stabilized bourgeois democracy toward the end of the eighteenth century, it was far less ready for socialism at that level of economic development. The productive forces of society had to be expanded under capitalist conditions before they were ripe for postcapitalist forms.

The pillars of small-scale private property were sunk deep into French soil by the exceptional thoroughness of the agrarian revolution. The transfer of land ownership from the feudal lords and the Church was not accomplished all at once but in several installments. In the glare of burning country houses, the delegates to the Versailles Assembly in 1789 bravely pledged that the feudal regime was totally finished. However, on August 4 they included a proviso that rents would continue to be collected until they could be redeemed. The ungrateful and cheated peasants resisted payment on these claims for the next three years.

After the fall of the Gironde in 1793, the Convention voted to wipe out the last feudal rents. Unlike the peasants in the rest of Europe, who either lost part of their land or were crushed under installment payments lasting many years, the French cultivators of the soil got rid of all feudal burdens and received the land without cost to themselves. This radical agrarian reform converted the peasantry into staunch supporters of that part of the revolution. Nowhere in Europe was the ownership of real property so widely dispersed as in France. But the material possessions of this mass of small proprietors made them into an equally solid prop of the bourgeois order and a conservatizing force within it throughout the next century.

The revolution found it easier to deal with the Church than the crown. The Constituent Assembly swept away its tithes and privileges and instituted religious tolerance. It confiscated ecclesiastical property, put up the Church lands for sale and issued paper money called *assignats* backed by the proceeds from the sale of the nationalized land. The first constitution dissolved the religious orders and turned the clergy into salaried servants of the state by forcing them to pledge loyalty to the Civil Constitution.

This requirement, taken over the resistance of Louis XVI,

split the clergy into those who complied with the constitution and those who refused to take the oath. The opposition between the constitutional and nonjuring priests persisted throughout the revolution. However, these measures effectively secularized the state and broke the power of the Church. Neither under Napoleon, who signed a concordat with the Vatican, nor under the Restoration did the Church regain its ancient privileges. Here material interest prevailed over religious conviction. Too many Frenchmen of various classes had too much to lose from any repossession of property rights by the Church.

In addition to the intensity of its class conflicts, the swiftness of its development and the clean sweep of its agrarian and ecclesiastical revisions, the French Revolution had by far the greatest international impact and influence of any social and political upheaval of the bourgeois epoch. There would be nothing like it until the Russian Revolution of 1917. Whereas the democratic revolution in the New World had had only marginal effects upon the Old, the revolution of 1789 unfolded in the richest, most populous and most cultured country of the continent. Its events, ideas and institutions, as well as its armies, flowed over the national boundaries, spreading throughout Europe and reaching as far as the Americas through the Haitian Revolution.

The spectacle of the crown, the Church and other venerable institutions being toppled by the uprisings of the people aroused enthusiasm and invited emulation among oppositional elements from one end of Europe to another. It kindled hopes of liberation among the lower orders and divided the politically alert sections of the population into pro-French and anti-French partisans.

Even without direct intervention, the advent and very existence of the antimonarchical and antifeudal regimes set up by revolutionary means were an incitement to discontent and an encouragement of radicalism and rebellion. The revolutionary wars conducted by the Girondins and Jacobins against the coalitions of monarchical powers heightened their incendiary role. The Convention of 1792 issued two decrees calling for an international people's revolution. One announced that the French Republic would assist "all peoples who might wish to regain their liberties" and the other ordered French generals to confiscate property and repress counterrevolutions in the territories they occupied.

The international repercussions of the revolution did not cease with the revolutionary republics. While Napoleon's personal regime extinguished the last flickers of revolutionism at home, as the champion of the new bourgeois order against the decadent forces of feudal and semifeudal reaction, the little Corsican carried embers of that revolution abroad.

Though Bonaparte did not accord self-government through elected legislative bodies to the peoples under his imperial jurisdiction, he did subject Italy and Germany to an internal reorganization which purged them of feudal hangovers. Ranks were abolished and the nobility deprived of its privileges of taxation, officeholding and military command. Equality before the law was instituted. The manorial system was liquidated, though the assault upon feudal property was less thorough-going than in France, since the old landed proprietors continued to receive dues. The landlord replaced the lord. The tithes and privileges of the Church were swept away and religious tolerance and a secular state brought into being. The guilds and other medieval restrictions upon labor and commerce were abolished. Thus the Napoleonic conquests not only set up and knocked down republics but reshaped the social structures of Western Europe.

All the achievements of popular democracy were packed into the four years of intense revolutionary actions by the plebeians and peasants and their bourgeois allies. After the Thermidorean reaction set in, democracy was eliminated from the social and political life of France for nearly a century. The recession of the revolution set in motion a tide of reaction that produced a succession of regimes, each more conservative than the last: the Directory, the Consulate and the empire. This counterrevolutionary swing culminated, after Napoleon's final military defeat, in the stabilization of a new balance of social forces crowned by the restored Bourbon monarchy.

However, Louis XVIII governed over a fundamentally different social order than his beheaded namesake. His charter did not recognize the principle of popular sovereignty that even Napoleon tipped his tricorne to through his plebiscites; it restricted participation in the government to a very few large landowners. Nonetheless the restoration left intact the essential social conquests of the revolution: the abolition of feudalism and its privileges, manorialism and its tithes, the principle of equality before the law and, above all, the redistribution of landed property effected by the revolution. The Bourbon king kept his hands off the rights of private ownership and did not interfere with the operations of capitalist enterprise. The regimes of both the revolution and the restoration held sacred and inviolate the public debt held by the men of money and private property. France had become definitively bourgeoisified; power and prestige went with wealth and no longer with birth.

The principal beneficiaries of the revolution turned out to be the big and little bourgeoisie, the well-to-do property owners and richer peasants. The laboring poor had little material benefits and improvements to show for all their sacrifices and sufferings. The bourgeois character of the revolution was shown, among other ways, in the harsh labor laws. When the Constituent Assembly abolished the guilds, it passed the Le Chapelier law which forbade strikes and any associations of labor. The left bourgeois republicans did not oppose this law which left the wage workers vulnerable to unrestrained exploitation by the employers. Still worse was the antilabor bias of the Napoleonic Code, which not only banned trade unions and forbade the workers to change their residence or employer but would not accept the word of an individual worker against his boss in court — an exceptional departure from strict equality before the law. The bourgeois revolution took care of its own — and let the devil look after the rest.

Every bourgeois revolution — and not them alone! — has suffered from an insuperable contradiction between the aspirations of the masses and the impassable limits on their fulfillment. As the French Revolution gathered momentum and progressed from one stage to the next, it flattened obstacles in its path as does a steamroller. Then its most dynamic forces ran up against insurmountable barriers set up by the objective historical conditions, were stopped short and flung back.

The level of the productive forces dictated that the historical mission of the revolution was to affirm the most highly developed type of private property rather than to overstep its boundaries. This fundamental economic factor prevented the unpropertied forces from becoming the ruling class or their spokesmen from acting as the heads of state. These functions were to be reserved for the agents of one or another fraction of the possessing and exploiting classes.

The small-property owners and wage workers suffered from the same political disability and organizational weaknesses as the plebeians of Athens, Rome and the medieval communes. Their leaders did not usually come from their own ranks. With very few exceptions, they received political direction from members of the commercial bourgeoisie, the professions or liberal aristocrats. They did not have much expertise in the art of politics or managing the affairs of state — or much time to spare for these occupations. However quick they were to defend their rights and welfare, they were often confused and uncertain on the course they should take, liable to be tricked by unreliable leaders or let down by those they trusted. In the end they were isolated and subdued by force.

The historical necessity for their subordinate status was certified by the final outcome of the class struggles. However, the end result of a revolutionary process is one thing and its inner mechanism and specific course of development is another.

When insurgent peoples enter upon the revolutionary arena, they are neither concerned with nor aware of the objective restrictions placed upon the scope of their achievements. They seek immediate relief for their urgent problems and use whatever ways and means are at hand to serve their aims.

A revolution on the French scale is a gigantic experiment in social reconstruction carried on in the laboratory of history. It was conducted by its participants in an empirical manner, whatever they recalled of like events in history. No one could tell in advance what its outermost terminals would be. These had to be discovered and determined by its contending forces in the course of prolonged encounters.

The state of economic development constituted the material framework of the revolution. But within these given conditions, the revolution contained a wide margin of elasticity, of open possibilities, of uncertainty. How far the revolutionary movement could advance and how many of its latent possibilities could be realized depended upon many things: the amount of energy displayed by the major revolutionary forces, the quality of their leadership, the internal and external resistances they met and other secondary and accidental circumstances.

The masses in motion had to exert tremendous efforts to overcome all handicaps, beat back their enemies and approach their objectives. They tried to push the revolution as far as it could go — and even beyond. Such "excesses" are inherent in every genuine popular upheaval. If the reach for a better world does not exceed their grasp, what's a revolution for!

These outbursts were absolutely indispensable for breaking the resistance of reaction, liquidating the old order and making possible the acquisition of economic, social and political mastery by the bourgeoisie. In politics, as in economics, it is not uncommon for one class to do work for another. In this case, the plebeians performed the immense service for the wealthy bourgeoisie of completing the settlement of accounts with the feudalists. Without their independent combativity, the revolution would have marked time at various points, slipped back and accomplished far less than it did.

But the militant masses were not simply subalterns of a crafty bourgeoisie. They did a great deal for their own cause. Although a few republics had existed in monarchical Europe prior to 1789, these were dominated, as in Holland and Switzerland, by noble families and merchant patriciates. There were no genuine democracies where the citizen body had a say in government.

The French Revolution did more than any other up to its time to propagate and popularize the idea of the sovereignty of the people and show how much could be realized through their own action. The interventions of the masses during the great "days" of 1789, 1792 and 1793 imprinted on the minds of the late eighteenth and nineteenth centuries the decisive part played by popular revolution in bringing democracy to birth.

Even though the democratic phase of the revolution was short-lived, and the plebeians had to relinquish the political positions they had won, they exercised control over their affairs and destinies long enough to give examples of democratic rule in both its direct and representative forms. The first was manifested through the local initiatives of the clubs, sections, committees, volunteer armed forces and ad hoc actions undertaken by the assemblies of the populace; the second through the revolutionary Commune and the Convention.

The subsequent reversals of the revolution did not obliterate these traditions either in France or the rest of Europe. The common people of France, and especially the plebeians of Paris, acquired a sense of their latent power and just rights and a remembrance of their heroic deeds during the revolutionary years which have never left them. To be sure, these democratic revolutionary traditions were to be much abused by demagogues and misleaders of diverse stripes. But they have continued to reassert themselves as a living force in critical clashes between the rulers and the ruled in that country ever since.

The Revolutions of 1848

The defenders of the status quo had far greater grounds for satisfaction in the first half of the nineteenth century than the partisans of democracy. "As for democracy, by 1815 aristocracy or monarchy had won the struggle everywhere, except to a limited extent in the newly independent United States, and democracy seemed farther off than ever." [9]

Europe witnessed few revolutionary upheavals between the close of the Napoleonic wars and 1848. Then the extremely rapid expansion of industrial capitalism precipitated a round of wars and revolutions which lasted for almost twenty-five years until the crushing of the Paris Commune in 1871. The revolutions of 1848 and 1871 in France were the principal events in the first and final chapter of that turbulent bourgeois-democratic movement of the mid-nineteenth century; the Civil War in the United States was the central event in its second chapter.

The development of the democratic movements of that era proceeded at different tempos, assumed different forms and had different results in the various countries. From Ireland to Austria the uprisings of 1848 in Europe uniformly ended in disaster and the restoration of the old order — with superficial changes at the top. At the same time these frustrated assaults made possible numerous reforms in the ensuing decades and prepared the way for further advances by the progressive forces.

The struggles of the second and third waves were more successful in attaining their objectives. The triumph of the Union in the United States was of far greater historical import than the failure of the Polish insurrection in 1863. The national unification of the German and Italian peoples was more significant than the fact that it was achieved under monarchical auspices.

Even where the revolutionary movements failed to reach fruition, they engendered valuable reforms (extension of the franchise in England, national autonomy for the Swiss cantons, limited constitutional liberties in Hungary, etc.). By 1871 the bourgeoisie had secured liberal constitutional governments in most of the leading countries of Western Europe with the exception of Germany, Russia and Austria-Hungary.

Except for the United States, social reforms were largely restricted to the removal of the vestiges of feudalism which hampered capitalist development. Thus the Revolution of 1848 led to the abolition of serfdom in Hungary; in 1863 Alexander II decreed the emancipation of the serfs within Russia's dominions. In southern United States alone did a really revolutionary transformation of social relations take place.

The upheavals which convulsed France, Germany, Austria,

Italy and Hungary in 1848 were especially noteworthy in the
procession of bourgeois revolutions for three reasons. The
course of these events everywhere exposed the incapacity of
the liberal bourgeoisie to lead the people in liquidating the
old order and realizing the democratic demands and aspirations of the nation.

They further demonstrated that all segments of the petty
bourgeoisie from the students and shopkeepers in the cities
to the peasants in the villages lacked the political initiative,
independence and strength to smash the feudalists completely
and consolidate a democratic state. In the third place, they
showed that the industrial proletariat, despite the bravery and
energy it exhibited, was still far from having acquired the political consciousness, party organization, knowledge and experience required to rally all the oppressed around its banner
and secure victory for the revolutionary upsurge. This immaturity of the class was confirmed by the experience of the Paris
Commune of 1871.

As a result of these factors, every one of the insurrections
of 1848 went down to defeat. The industrial bourgeoisie did not
attain its political domination but surrendered its right to rule
for the right to make money. The Hungarians, Poles and Ital-
ians failed to win their national independence. The counterrevolution triumphed all along the line and the Continental countries wound up under a military despotism in France and
a restored monarchy in Germany, Austria, Hungary and Poland.

The abortive Revolutions of 1848 stood midway between
the brilliantly successful revolutions of the bourgeois past and
the proletarian victories to come. The fiasco of the antimonarchical bourgeoisie, along with the vacillations and impotence
of the intermediate layers of bourgeois society in defending
and maintaining a democratic state, had grave political consequences for European politics in the last half of the nineteenth
century.

But these features of the 1848 revolutions held less significance for the future than the emergence of the proletariat as a
decisive political force. The rigidly reactionary political regimes
which ruled absolutist Europe after 1815 had been overthrown
by the uprisings of the laboring poor in the capital cities of
Western and Central Europe.

The manifest power displayed by the proletariat in these
onslaughts sowed fear and panic among all elements of the
propertied classes. For the first time, "the specter of commu-

nism" began to haunt the Old World. The principles, program and outlook of scientific socialism received its classical formulation in *The Communist Manifesto,* which Marx and Engels finished a few weeks before the outbreak of the February Revolution.

Paris was again the center of the revolution, and there the confrontations between the contending class forces unfolded most clearly and sharply and were fought to a finish. The bourgeois republicans, who had overturned the monarchy of Louis Philippe with the workers in February, could not tolerate the coexistence of the armed Paris proletariat demanding substantial concessions for itself. On June 22 they hurled the army, the Mobile Guard, the Parisian National Guard and the National Guard against the insurgent workers and slaughtered several thousand of them.

This brutal civil war of capital against labor crushed the working class, thereby shattering the principal social support for the democratic republic and ruining its prospects. The bourgeoisie, in France as well as in Germany and elsewhere, permitted all the major institutions of the old state apparatus to remain intact, counting on establishing and preserving its supremacy with their help. The nobility, army and bureaucracy bided their time, allowing the bourgeois republicans to hold the center of the stage and shelter them so long as the insurgent populace threatened to overwhelm them.

Then, as soon as the mass movements had subsided or were repressed and the danger to their positions had passed, the feudalists, monarchists and reactionaries dispensed with the services of the liberal bourgeoisie and regained their dominion. Thus the constitutional republic of the Legislative National Assembly tottered along for three years after the revolutionary masses were quelled, until it was tossed aside by the coup d'etat of the second Bonaparte, which put the finishing touch to the counterrevolution.

The American Civil War

The American Civil War, which erupted thirteen years after 1848, has a twofold importance in the annals of the bourgeois revolution. It was the second and closing act of the democratic revolution in the United States. And it was the greatest revolution of the nineteenth century, the last thoroughgoing mass struggle carried through by the radical bourgeoisie in the Western world.

The second American revolution had both national and international roots. It was necessitated by the incompleteness of the first and by the vast economic and social changes brought about by the Industrial Revolution and the expansion of commercial agriculture on a domestic and world scale.

The first American revolution had liberated the thirteen colonies from British rule, created the federal union and set up a democratic republic. But it had failed to deliver state power firmly into the hands of the northern bourgeoisie or to extirpate slavery. The economic and political ascendancy of the cotton nobility during the first half of the nineteenth century held back the reconstruction of American society along purely capitalist lines and threatened to make the capitalist class along with the rest of the nation subordinate to the slave power. The Civil War was the showdown between these two chief contenders for supremacy in North America.

The victory of the Union shattered the last of the precapitalist social formations and ruling classes that blocked the expansion and challenged the hegemony of the native American capitalists. The defeat of the southern slaveholding oligarchy prevented the United States from becoming Balkanized and preserved the unity of the nation. The illegalization of chattel slavery formally liberated the black men from bondage and warded off the dangers to the democratic rights of the people posed by the aggressions of the ultrareactionary slave power.

The United States was the country of the nineteenth century where the bourgeois-democratic revolution solved its problems with maximum success. Here the magnates of industrial capital became the sole rulers of the Republic by destroying the slavocracy. Elsewhere, as in Germany and Italy, the bourgeoisie faltered for lack of revolutionary energy, fell short of its goals, and representatives of the landed classes retained the reins of government in their hands.

The American bourgeoisie was more brilliantly able to fulfill its historical mission because of the exceptional character of America's social development. Their drive for power was based upon the achievements of the first revolution. The American people had already attained national independence, gotten rid of the altar and the throne and enjoyed the blessings of republican democracy. These advantages gave the American bourgeoisie a head start that made it easier to outdistance the Europeans.

The economic power, political independence and social weight of the capitalists in the United States considerably surpassed that of their German and Italian compeers. The American masters of capital were no political tyros. They had taken almost a century to prepare themselves for this final showdown; they had once held supreme power and felt it was theirs by right. They had already created their own parliamentary institutions and taken legal possession of the state apparatus before the battle was joined. They entered the arena with their own party and program.

The role of the bourgeois Republicans as the defenders of the Union and its democratic institutions enabled them to rally around their banner the progressive forces within the nation and throughout the civilized world. The Republicans succeeded in winning over the bulk of small farmers in the North and West to their side while the slaveholders failed to draw their sympathizers among the governments of Western Europe into the conflict. The North could count on support from the blacks in the South; their unrest weakened the Confederacy, even where the Union leaders feared to encourage their self-action.

The economic strength and manpower of the northern bourgeoisie was much superior to that of their adversary. Finally, the clear-cut antagonism between the slavocracy and industrialists, on the one hand, and the immaturity of the proletariat, on the other, enabled the radical bourgeoisie to carry through the struggle against their southern rival to the end. The German bourgeoisie had to reckon at every point with the princes and Junkers to its right and with a distrustful working class on its left. Except for a brief explosion in the middle of 1863, the industrial workers in the United States did not assert themselves as a powerful independent factor during the Civil War.

The revolution was led to its conclusion by the radical Republicans. They were the last of the great line of bourgeois revolutionists. Thrusting aside the conciliators of every stripe and crushing all opposition to their course, they annihilated their class enemy, stripped the slaveholders of all economic and political power and proceeded to transform the United States into the colossus of capitalism, purged of the last vestiges of precapitalist relations.

The American people did not fight the Civil War to create a democratic form of government but rather to safeguard its existence and assure its perpetuation. For seventy years the tobacco and cotton nobility had been able to live and rule under the Constitution of the Republic. Some of its ideologists boasted that the southern states had revived the glories of

"Athenian democracy," which likewise rested on the pedestal of slavery. They conveniently disregarded the fact that the original type of political democracy, which had been epoch-making twenty-five hundred years before, was totally anachronistic in the nineteenth century.

The slaveholders found even the most restricted formal democracy too much to bear. They refused to accept the outcome of the electoral process when Lincoln won the presidency in 1860, because the Republican victory shifted the balance of national political power to their disadvantage at a time when they could ill-afford to forfeit continued control over the policies and resources of the federal government. That event detonated their decision to quit the Union and form the Confederacy.

The second big problem of democracy raised by the Civil War concerned the rights and status of the four million blacks who had been legally emancipated from chattel slavery. For a few years during the postwar Reconstruction of the South, the ex-slaves helped set up and participated in highly progressive state governments which replaced the despotism of the planters with an extension of the power of the people. The radical Reconstruction regimes improved educational facilities, equalized taxes, cut down illiteracy, abolished imprisonment for debt, did away with property qualifications for voting and holding office and instituted other reforms in city, county and state government. For the first time, black men were elected to state legislatures and Congress.

These governments rested on a coalition of freedmen and their allies among the small farmers and poor whites. But the decisive power was held by the federal government and its armed forces, which occupied the South and supervised its affairs.

The radical Republicans in Washington pursued a contradictory agrarian policy. In the unorganized western territories, they gave free homesteads to white settlers and immense tracts of land to railroad companies, real-estate speculators, lumber and mining interests. Their land policy in the South was very different. There they feared to carry through an agrarian revolution which would have involved the expropriation of the land owned by the secessionist planters and distribution of it among the landless laborers.

Although they nullified three billion dollars worth of property in slaves, the triumphant capitalists were unwilling to confiscate landed property for the benefit of the freedmen. To the contrary, in some places the blacks were deprived of the lands they had taken over and were cultivating on their own account.

This refusal to give Afro-Americans the "forty acres and a mule" and other material prerequisites for economic independence forced the landless, helpless freedmen into new forms of servitude to the merchants, moneylenders and landowners. Within a few years, their conditions of economic dependence led to the loss of their civil rights and political power under the terror of the white supremacists.

This period in American history is another example of how superficial it is to counterpose the bare abstractions of democracy to dictatorship, as though these two forms of rule were everywhere and under all conditions irreconcilable opposites which had no elements of identity with each other. The succession of regimes in the South from 1860 to 1880 indicates that the reality is much more complex.

Although it draped itself in pseudodemocratic forms, the slaveholders' dictatorship, smashed by the Civil War, was utterly reactionary. So was the Bourbon-bourgeois autocracy which has dominated the South ever since white supremacy was reconstituted on the bones of the subjugated freedmen.

On the other hand, the bourgeois military dictatorship backed by the black masses and poorer whites which held sway in the South following the defeat of the Confederacy was the shield and support of popular rule. It is an indisputable historical fact that the one time Afro-Americans have enjoyed any measure of democracy in the South and effectively participated in its political and social life was under the bayonets of the federal armies and under the protection of their own armed forces. This, too, was a democratic dictatorship.

The experience of Reconstruction and its aftermath also exemplified the incapacity of the capitalist class, even in its most radical days, to realize bourgeois democracy to the full or extend full and enduring equality to national minorities. So long as the northern bourgeoisie needed the black masses as a pawn in their combat against the cotton nobility, they granted a certain increment of freedom to them. But once they had cinched total mastery in the nation and over the South, the managers of the Republican Party turned against the southern masses. To keep the presidency in 1876, they made a deal with the new bourgeoisie and planters of the South at the expense of the plebeians and delivered the freedmen back into peonage.

The task of winning democracy and self-determination for Afro-Americans was thereby transmitted to the twentieth century for solution and has become a basis of the black liberation movement in our own time.

The Conservative-Bourgeois Transformations from Above

The nineteenth century became the golden age of capitalist supremacy, thanks to the conquests of all these revolutions crowned by its own industrial revolution. It witnessed the flourishing of international free trade, the unexampled spread of capitalist relations, the triumph of bourgeois culture and its values and the preeminence of parliamentarism and liberalism.

These historical circumstances fostered the conviction in the Western world that bourgeois society was the most conducive to political freedom and that private property, competition and free enterprise irresistibly carry democracy in their train. This proposition was to become less and less tenable as the next century grew older. But it had a limited validity even during the most exuberant era of capitalist expansion and most full-blooded manifestations of bourgeois revolutionism.

Every national capitalist class did not become the banner-bearer and promoter of a democratic state. Far from it. Only in those countries where the struggle of the contending classes exploded in civil war was the radical bourgeoisie compelled in its own vital interests to ally itself with the plebeian insurgents in the towns and countryside in overcoming the resistance of the old regime.

Most of these thoroughgoing bourgeois onslaughts took place during the age of commercial capitalism, when that system carried with it the hopes of all the virile forces of the nation. The American Civil War was the sole outstanding victory of the radical bourgeoisie during the rise of industrial capitalism.

Throughout this international consolidation of capitalist production and power, bourgeois democracy experienced an extremely uneven development. It did not have to conquer for a feudal country to change over into a capitalist one. The shift from one set of economic and social relations to the other could proceed along two different roads: either through a popular revolution resulting in a more or less democratic regime, as in the United States, or through a relatively orderly transformation from above which ended up with bourgeoisified imperial governments, as in nineteenth-century Germany and Japan.

The second course of political development became more likely as the world market and the capitalist forces of production reached a more advanced stage. The pioneers of bourgeois society had to fight tooth and nail to gain political supremacy and rouse the entire populace to dispose of the resistance put up by the defenders of the old order. The retarded German and Japanese bourgeoisie, which came to the fore at a later date, were able to effect the transition by making a deal with a section of the landed aristocracy on a program which gave each bourgeoisie what it needed without crushing the landed proprietors.

The Imperial Meiji Restoration (1862-1912) struck off the shackles on the free movement of persons and goods and encouraged economic development along capitalist lines. In 1869 the government declared equality before the law of all social classes, abolished land barriers to trade and communication and allowed individuals to acquire property rights in land. The suddenly rising Japanese bourgeoisie thereby succeeded in establishing a strongly centralized state under its patronage which went on to create a conscript army, modern shipping, heavy industry and a banking system. They acquired by government legislation many of those rights and powers which such trailblazers of the bourgeois order as the English and French had to wage bloody battles to win.

However, the nations which avoided a revolutionary upheaval had to pay heavily for the easier passage to bourgeois conditions. In those cases where the bourgeoisie shared power with archaic forces, economic progress was combined with a repressive regime. Without being revolutionized, the government could not become democratized. Neither the German nor the Japanese capitalists became the carriers of democratic ideas or the creators and sustainers of democratic institutions. The bargain they struck with a part of the feudalists involved the retention of monarchical rule, landlordism and militarism. Germany's government after 1870-71 was not liberal bourgeois. The executive power remained vested in the Prussian landed nobility, even though the latter had to support itself more and more upon the bourgeoisie which held all economic power in its hands.

As Hajo Holborn indicated, "the German bourgeoisie had never fought for or aspired to democratic government,"[10] either in 1848 or during the constitutional struggle of the 1860s. Saddled against their will with a democratic regime after 1918, they regarded it as a threat to their social and economic position and threw their support in 1933 to the party and the man who destroyed it.

The commercial and industrial bourgeoisie in their prime

must be credited with considerable capacities for progressive political action and, when they were associated in struggle with the popular masses, for revolutionary accomplishments in the furtherance of democracy. But they were not invariably attracted to and certainly not constitutionally wedded to democracy.

Like any other propertied and privileged class, the capitalists, whether they held paramount or secondary status, placed the preservation and promotion of their economic interests above devotion to democratic liberties. When these two considerations diverged and collided, they invariably chose to defend their property regardless of the injury done to popular rights.

The bourgeoisie proved to be a powerful, though neither a persistent nor reliable, force for democracy only during the rise of world capitalism and then only in the richest countries of Western Europe and North America. The more capitalism attained maturity and exercised world supremacy, the more conservative and less democratically inclined the men of money became.

The American Civil War marked the Great Divide between the two periods in the evolution of bourgeois politics. That turned out to be the final burst of firm revolutionary will exhibited by the world bourgeoisie. Nowhere since that time has the big bourgeoisie placed itself at the head of the rebellious masses, led it to victory and carried through the democratic tasks of the revolution. It feared to arouse or lead the insurgent workers and peasants because it had far more to lose than to gain in social terms.

The experiences of nineteenth-century Germany and Japan expressed the real character and prefigured the further political path of the bourgeoisie far more than the example of the United States. Even the French bourgeoisie, which could act in a revolutionary manner in 1789, became more and more conservative and turned reactionary during the renewals of revolutionary ferment in 1830, 1848 and 1870.

As world capitalism entered the era of imperialism, its leading representatives could no longer afford the risks of embarking on revolutionary action on their home grounds. As Plekhanov pointed out regarding Russia and Asia: The bourgeoisie becomes all the more cowardly the farther East you go. In the colonial and semicolonial lands, the weak, craven and dependent native bourgeois elements which mediated between foreign finance and their own national economy were to prove even less capable than the bourgeois classes of the advanced countries of revolutionizing archaic regimes and establishing democracy.

6

BOURGEOIS DEMOCRATIC
IDEOLOGY

The liberal with faith in the absolute value of bourgeois democracy gives little thought to the origins of his political notions. He feels that his democratic principles are more solidly anchored in history than the ideas of socialism, which are constantly contraposed to them. It would astonish him to learn that, if the teachings of Marxism have been current for little more than a century, his democratic doctrines are not much older. They are by no means a venerable possession of mankind.

During the seventeenth and eighteenth centuries, few people advocated democratic and republican ideas in the Western world. These convictions were then daring novelties and it was dangerously subversive to espouse them openly. The first body of militant democrats, the Levellers, were active for less than a decade during the English Civil War. Their democratic outlook did not bear further fruit for almost a century and a half, when British radicalism revived, under the spur of the American and French revolutions, in protest against King George III's arbitrariness.

Most of the leading theoreticians of the early bourgeois revolutions were not champions of popular democracy. Locke, for example, was not concerned about establishing majority rule, which is regarded as the essence of democracy by his liberal descendants. The Fundamental Constitutions of the Carolina Colonies, which he drafted in 1670, had as its avowed purpose to set up serfdom and thus "avoid a numerous democracy." This charter sought to enforce an iron-clad servitude, based on a provision forbidding any serf or his offspring "to all generations" from quitting the land of his particular lord.

Before the American and French experiences, only the boldest political figures challenged the monarchy in favor of republicanism. It was even more rashly innovative to uphold the sovereignty of the common people. They were considered too stupid, illiterate, anarchical and inexpert to handle the affairs of state, which were better left in the hands of some aristocratic, plutocratic or bureaucratic elite.

Two qualified scholars, Howard Becker and Harry Elmer Barnes, tell us "it is most significant . . . that during this entire period there was no systematic analysis of the meaning and implications of democracy, nor with the doubtful exception of Mably in France, Paine in England, and Jefferson in America, was there any important defense of democracy as the ideal form of government. Most of the radicals regarded a constitutional monarchy or, at the most, an aristocratic republic as the ideal form of government. Montesquieu and Rousseau, for example, both held that a democracy would be tolerable in a very small state and could never be successful in an extensive country." [1] In *The Social Contract* Rousseau wrote, "If there were a nation of Gods, it would govern itself democratically. A government so perfect is not suited to men."

The democratic ideology evolved slowly in the wake of capitalist relations and at a considerable distance behind them. It did not gain extensive circulation and become a permanent acquisition of the progressive forces until the nineteenth century.

This is confirmed by Professor Palmer who has made a thorough study of the use of the term democracy in Europe and America before that time. "It is rare, even among the *philosophes* of France before the Revolution, to find anyone using the word 'democracy' in a favorable sense in any practical connection. . . . The two nouns, 'democrat' and 'aristocrat', were coinages of the period, unknown before the 1780's. . . . Neither word was current in English before 1789; in France, *aristocrate* crops up in the reign of Louis XVI, *démocrate* not until 1789." [2] This political historian found that the constitution of the Helvetic Republic in Switzerland, which was proclaimed by the French in 1798, was apparently the only written constitution in the last quarter of the eighteenth century to explicitly characterize itself as "a representative democracy."

At the dawn of the bourgeois era, the demands put forward by the most democratic elements were extremely circumscribed. Their movement and political awareness advanced step by step from modifications of the institutions at the top of the social pyramid to its economic substructure. But this progression required several centuries for fulfillment.

The prebourgeois German peasants called for little more than a measure of democratic reform in the Catholic Church organization; the English Presbyterians and Puritans went further by demanding toleration for dissenting sects; finally, the American colonists took the decisive step of insisting on the separation of church from state. From the application of democracy to church-state relations, the most radical forces moved on to a rationalization of the political system. In its most advanced phases, the result was the installation of a republic on a more or less democratic basis.

While these accomplishments sufficed for the advent of parliamentarism, they left untouched the most important of all the factors determining the character and course of social and political life—the economy. This aspect of the problem of democratization was posed as early as Babeuf, who presented a communist solution to it. His line of criticism was more profoundly developed by Marxian socialism from the middle of the nineteenth century on. The anticapitalist thinkers exposed the limitations of a purely political democracy which could not represent the will and welfare of the majority so long as a small minority of capitalist property owners controlled the means of production and operated them for private profit.

Thereupon the aspirations for religious, legal and political democracy were extended and deepened to become what has been variously designated as industrial, economic, social or workers' democracy. This called for a social revolution of a proletarian nature to make democracy complete. Thus the inner logic of the democratic movement of the masses irresistibly carried it beyond the boundaries of bourgeois power and property, a dialectic which that class found highly distasteful.

The intermittent, protracted and hesitant character of the democratic movement trammeled by the bourgeoisie accounted for the slow growth of its pattern of thought. This was not perfected until well into the nineteenth century when its rival and successor was already knocking at the door. In this respect democracy was unlike scientific socialism, which set forth its fundamental principles and program in a comprehensive systematic way early in the advent of the working-class movement. Socialism has been from its birth a far more conscious and theoretically motivated movement than its predecessor.

All the same, bourgeois democracy was by its very nature

a far more articulate social and political movement than any before its time, since the popular masses as well as upper classes were drawn into active participation in its struggles. Revolution spurs critical thought on all levels, loosens tongues, brings like-minded people together. The sharp collisions of contending social forces and political tendencies on the open arena stimulate the give and take of argumentation for or against the courses they project or follow.

The printing press introduced greater cohesion and consciousness into the controversies that agitated the nation. The English, American and French revolutions were prepared, promoted and publicized by a popular press and a spate of pamphlets, broadsides and books whose contents were read by the literate and listened to by the illiterate parts of the population.

Thousands of pamphlets were issued during the English Civil War. In the first six months of 1776, Tom Paine's appeal for independence, *Common Sense*, sold 100,000 copies in a country of fewer than three million. Dr. Price's *Observations on Civil Liberty* (1776) had the remarkable sale of around 60,000 copies within a few months of the outbreak of the colonial revolt, which the English radical welcomed. Hundreds of political pamphlets appeared when the Estates General convened; its Declaration of the Rights of Man and the Citizen was distributed by the thousands. The inexpensive radical press became the indispensable medium for instructing, rousing and directing the popular movement.

Because of the importance of lively criticism and unrestricted discussion, freedom of the press and freedom of expression were placed high on the list of demands by radical spokesmen for the masses — and the exercise of these rights invariably became one of the first casualties of a triumphant reaction.

The most creative political theorists and publicists took advantage of their new-found freedom to bring forward arguments and formulate principles which legitimized the claims and defended the objectives of the social forces they spoke for. Out of their reasonings and polemics came a body of doctrine which crystallized into the basic ideology of the democratic movement. Its cardinal conceptions accorded with the requirements of political progress better than any other social philosophy of the era, even if several of the fundamental propositions concealed conflicting economic interests behind cloudy and unhistorical general formulas.

The credo of the bourgeois democrats (some of whom were more bourgeois than democratic) was a composite of elements derived from several stages in the development of Western civilization, extending from the Greeks and Romans to the plebeian-proletarian struggles of modern times. The threads woven into its fabric include a modification of some teachings of Christianity, the doctrine of natural rights which goes back to antiquity, the reflexive categories of commodity relations at the base of bourgeois society and a demand for thorough-going social equality emanating from the laboring poor. Two of these sources have a precapitalist character; the key component is unmistakably the influence of the highly developed market economy; and attached to these is an amendment on equality which has an anticapitalist potential for disruption of bourgeois rule.

The political philosophers of the democratic school discarded the obsolete theological underpinnings which justified the monopoly of power held by the monarchy and Church. The shift was first expressed in the replacement of divine right as the sanction for absolutism by a secular contractual basis for the constitutional monarchy. The social compact between the sovereign and the people was a conception appropriate to the predominance of market relations of exchange.

Yet, paradoxically, in the historical sequence of social philosophies in the Western world, the genealogy of democracy takes its place as a secularized offspring of the Christian teachings on the abstract equality of all men. Early in its career, Christianity displayed two opposing trends springing from the interests and orientations of different layers of society. On the one hand, its millenial expectations expressed the dreams and aspirations of the poor and the enslaved for the relief of their miseries, for social justice, emancipation and a better world. On the other hand, this religion, like others, postponed satisfaction of these desires to an afterlife. Faith in the divine justice of the heavenly kingdom tended to dull the revolutionary edge of the egalitarian hopes of the masses and deflect hatred from their immediate oppressors by reconciling them to the God-anointed and appointed kingdoms of this earth.

The conservative side of Christianity enabled its principalities and hierarchies to convert it into an instrument of the ruling and exploiting powers to reconcile its adherents with the successive forms of class servitude, from Roman slavery through medieval serfdom to capitalist wage labor and colonialist subjugation.

The Gospels taught that all men, regardless of social status, were the same in the sight of God. All members of the

Christian community were part of the body of Christ and partook of his eternal life, though in the existing social system a minority was rich and the majority poor, some were in bondage and others free. At the same time, the Catholic Church restricted its universality by reserving salvation to the elect. It therefore contained an exclusivist aspect which sharply divided believers from nonbelievers and the saved from the damned. Dissenters and heretics could always seize upon relevant passages from the Bible and egalitarian elements in the traditions of early Christianity to justify opposition to the dominant powers.

The radical bourgeois thinkers influenced by Protestantism likewise borrowed its teachings on the equality of all souls from the inventory of early Christianity. Their principles of political democracy brought Christian egalitarianism closer to earth by regarding all citizens as equal before the law and equally entitled to participation and representation in the political life of the country.

The attainment and exercise of these acquired rights were an immense step forward from the mystical and fictitious equality of Catholic theology and the rigid feudal hierarchy of obligations and rights. Their assertion brought its exponents into irreconcilable conflict with the upholders of feudal institutions.

At the same time, the new bourgeois ideology carried over in its own fashion the original Christian cleavage between a purely formal equality and the prevailing material conditions of inequality in life and labor. Bourgeois democracy was no more able than Christianity to disentangle itself from this chronic contradiction which plagued it from birth and grew more acute as it went along. It likewise perpetuated the division between the elect and the damned along secular lines by restricting representation to citizens with certain qualifications and to males of a certain age and by denying equal civil, political and legal rights to such categories of the population as women, resident foreigners, slaves and oppressed nationalities.

The early advocates of the democratic cause translated the mystical promise of equality in the hereafter into prosaic legal and political terms by means of the second strand in their system of ideas—the theory of natural law. All three of the epoch-making codifications of the democratic revolution—the English Bill of Rights (1689), the French Declaration of the Rights of Man and the Citizen (1789) and the Bill of Rights

appended as the first ten amendments to the U. S. Constitution (1791) — were inspired by the premises of the natural-
rights philosophy.

According to this doctrine, humans are born with certain
inherent and inalienable rights which no sovereign power can
deny, although they may be surrendered to a government
through a social compact. By the dictates of nature or the
decree of reason (theorists shifted with easy inconsistency from
one source of sanction to the other), all men were to be judged
equal before the law, as in Christendom they were equal before God. By logical extension this should entitle them to an
equal voice and vote in deciding the affairs of their community and the destiny of their fatherland.

This line of reasoning had had forerunners among the Greek
Sophists and the Roman Stoics and jurists, just as adumbra-
tions of the idea of equality can be heard among the Old Tes-
tament prophets and other opponents of oppression in antiquity.
But the confrontation of natural human rights with divine
right, vested in clerical monopoly and the absolute monarchy,
acquired its sharpest edge during the antifeudal struggles of
the seventeenth and eighteenth centuries.

Natural rights are a kind of legal Protestantism which go
hand in hand with the expansion of market relations. Just
as the Protestants tended to do away with all intermediaries
between the individual and God, so natural rights did not
require any external authorities or sanctions as a warrant
for their validity. They were lodged within the individual as
an autonomous entity, just as individual ownership was vested
in a commodity and the right of conscience in the private
person. In the Putney debates, for example, the Levellers asserted that "every man is naturally free" and therefore entitled
to a vote by the natural rights of every free-born Englishman.

This individualistic side of the natural-rights philosophy was
dialectically complemented by the notion of the social contract. According to the reasoning of Hobbes, Locke, Rousseau
and their ilk, men gave over their natural or God-given personal liberties and curbed their appetites and aggressions in
order to enjoy the safety and order of organized government.

The specific content of the natural rights affirmed by their
claimants varied considerably from one phase of the revolutionary process to the next, from country to country and
from one social layer to another throughout the bourgeois
era. They encompassed religious liberties, such as freedom
of worship according to the dictates of the individual conscience

or congregation, separation of church and state; political liberties such as freedom of speech and the press, unrestricted public assembly and association, the right to petition authorities for redress of grievances; and manifold legal rights. These were later extended, under pressure from the working class, to include the right of union organization and collective bargaining as well as the right to form political parties.

In the eyes of its foremost formulators, the natural rights of man in the field of economic activity were given equal and even higher rank than religious, political and legal liberties. These included full freedom to trade for the commodity owner and merchant; freedom of manufacture regardless of medieval patents, royal monopolies or guild restrictions; and, not least, freedom for the propertyless proletarian to sell his labor power on the market.

The twofold aspects of the natural-rights philosophy were trenchantly presented in the positions of John Locke, who was the most influential exponent of the natural-rights doctrines. In his *Two Treatises of Government* (1690) he asserted that all government rests upon the consent of the governed and that the people constitute a power anterior and superior to the regime. A government may therefore be overthrown and replaced by revolution if it persistently violated the lives, liberties and property rights of the body politic. As the founders of the United States interpreted this doctrine, their resort to revolt was justified by the flagrant and repeated violations of the rights agreed to in the social compact of the colonists with the crown.

This justification of popular insurrection when the sovereign state turns tyrannical and breaks its contract with the people is the democratic element in Locke's political theory. Interwoven with it was a narrow interpretation of who constituted the majority. While Locke favored representative government, he wanted to restrict representation to men of property and wealth.

Locke trimmed the democratic innovations of the Levellers to suit the requirements of bourgeois rule in partnership with the aristocracy. He was not a republican, like the Leveller leaders Lilburne, Overton and Walwyn, but a monarchist parliamentarian who accepted Charles II's restoration in 1660 and the accession of the House of Orange in 1689. He favored religious toleration for Protestants but not for Catholics, Jews or atheists. He had no objection to slavery in the colonies or servile relations in England.

In his eyes men had set up society and its political organization primarily "for the Regulating and Preserving of Propriety." He defended the inviolable right of private ownership as a keystone of the sacred rights guaranteed by the law of nature and reason. He considered the protection of individually owned property to be the chief end of government and was himself the possessor of a sizable estate.

The preservation and reinforcement of property rights, he argued, was at one and the same time the chief reason why men came out of the original state of nature, entered into a compact with the ruler and established a government. On this same account, men were justified in making a revolution against a government that threatened to abridge or annul property rights.

These opposing concerns for the protection of personal liberties and private property lent an incurably contradictory character to Locke's writings which is responsible for the influence they have exerted in different quarters and along divergent lines. The dual elements in his position made it possible for both radical reformers and social conservatives to lean upon his teachings and extract different aspects from them to support their stands. While moderates clung to his strongly argued case for "possessive individualism," his more radical disciples referred to the affirmation of popular sovereignty.

Locke's writings embodied in classical form the insoluble conflict between human rights and the claims of private property, which has persisted throughout the career of bourgeois democracy. By placing property rights on a par with the protection of civil liberties and even above them, Locke was destined to serve as the mentor of bourgeois liberalism as well as economic laissez-faire and free enterprise.

That made him the preeminent intellectual influence in the formative period of American democracy. Vernon Parrington wrote in *The Colonial Mind* that the *Two Treatises of Government* "became the textbook of the American Revolution." [3] The Declaration of Independence directly incorporates the following text of the conclusion of Locke's treatise: "The People have a right to act as Supreme, and continue the Legislative in themselves, or erect a new form, or under the old form place it in new hands, as they think good."

The fundamental factor in forming and sustaining antifeudal democratic ideology was not handed down from the past and refashioned to suit the political needs of the progressive bourgeoisie. The new democratic conceptions were most deeply rooted in the soil of capitalist commodity relations, sprouting and thriving where these were most powerfully operative.

The ultimate material source of the prevailing theoretical and practical forms of equalization at work in bourgeois society is the spontaneous equating, by the social process of commodity production and exchange, of nonuniform kinds of labor. Through the operation of the law of value, types of labor that differ in quality are equated in quantity according to the amount of socially necessary (abstract) labor incorporated in them. To this equalization in the world of commodities and money there springs up a corresponding trend toward equalization in the superstructural spheres of religion, law and politics.

No one has explained the organic descent of bourgeois ideology from the concrete historical conditions of capitalist production and exchange more probingly than Marx. In *Capital* he pointed out that the process of appropriating the surplus value created by the working class starts with the sale and purchase of its labor power. He then ironically expatiates on the inescapable consequences of the transaction whereby the wage worker alienated the sole commodity he owns:

"The sphere we are leaving, that of circulation or of the exchange of commodities, the sphere within whose confines the purchase and sale of labor power are effected is, in fact, a paradise of the rights of man. Here liberty, equality, property, and Jeremy Bentham, are supreme. Liberty, because the buyer and seller of a commodity, such as labor power, buy and sell at their own sweet will. They enter into bargains as free individuals, equals before the law. The contract between them is the final outcome of the expression of their joint wills. Equality, because they enter into relations only as owners of commodities, and exchange equivalent for equivalent. Property, because each of them disposes exclusively of his own. Jeremy Bentham, because each of the pair is only concerned with his own interest. The power which brings them together, which makes them enter into relation with another, is self-interest, and nothing more. Every one for himself alone, no one with any concern for another. Thanks to this, owing to the preestablished harmony of things, or under the auspices of an allwise providence, they work together for their mutual advantage, for the commonweal, on behalf of the common interest of them all."[4]

Here is the economic kernel, the innermost secret of the duality of such nuclear political categories of bourgeois democracy as liberty, equality and the rights of the individual. Their ambivalence stems from the formal equality of exchange relations which masks the real inequality of classes inherent in the capitalist mode of production. These economic relations contain a built-in contradiction between the abstract rights of the individual and the real power of the private-property owner.

On the surface, in the sphere of the circulation of commodities, there appears to be complete equality between the capitalist entrepreneur and the wage worker. In the process of production, however, the worker must give more than he gets by virtue of his capacity to create more value during his working time than he is paid for. The production of surplus value is the engine of the capitalist system which starts it up, keeps it going, slows it down or brings it to a halt.

These economic relations are reflected in the legal and political realms by the presumptions that all citizens are on an equal footing, have equal rights and thereby equal weight in deciding public affairs. In actuality, their monopoly of the means of production gives preeminent power to the rich over the poor, though the first is only a small fraction of the body politic compared to the toiling majority. The actual economic and political rights wielded by the capitalist preponderate over the "natural rights" supposedly shared by every individual citizen.

Alongside formal equality and natural rights, three other major constituents of the bourgeois-democratic outlook grew out of the characteristic relations of capitalism. These were individualism, nationalism and liberalism.

The spread of the idea of individualism, which is the most prized value in the bourgeois ethic, is coeval with the generalization of commodity relations. It issues at bottom from the dissolution of the bonds uniting the direct producers with their conditions of production in precapitalist formations. Originally, from tribal times through feudalism, men were an organic part of their material conditions of production and did not conceive of themselves as something apart from them. They began to be individualized, first in practice, then in theory, through the separation of their capacities for labor from the objective conditions of its realization, above all, the land. This divorce of the subjective agent from the objective conditions of production is consummated under capitalism where labor is free, that is, the proletarian is totally dispossessed of all the means of production and dependent for his livelihood upon the sale of his labor power, the only commodity he owns.

These economic processes gave rise for the first time to the prevailing concept of the isolated individual as the possessor of innate powers and rights and projected the ideal of free individual development as the aim of enlightened mankind. The emergence of individualism greatly promoted the emancipation of mankind. It has acted as a dissolver of archaic bonds and a powerful motivating force throughout the career of bourgeois culture. In Protestantism, in law, in philosophy, in economic and political theory, it affirmed the proposition that each and every person had an inherent worth, which did not depend upon birth, rank, wealth, race or national origin but solely upon the fact of belonging to the human race. He was endowed with certain inalienable rights that could not be denied, restricted or taken away by any authority against his will. Thus every individual had the right to an equal opportunity for the free and full development of his capacities.

The liberation of the individual from the limitations of the past and the devaluation of hereditary distinctions was most strongly broached in the Yankee republic where bourgeois customs and standards were well advanced at the end of the eighteenth century. In 1784 Benjamin Franklin stressed in his "Information to Those Who Would Remove to America" the fact that birth "in Europe has indeed its value; but it is a commodity that cannot be carried to a worse market than that of America whose people do not inquire concerning a stranger, What is he? but What can he do?"

However, upon its initial large-scale manifestation in history, the notion of free individuality acquired an extremely contradictory form. The essentially humanistic content of this conception was materialized in a dehumanized and distorted manner. While the features of competitive capitalism popularized the idea, it could flourish only among the most favored sectors of an exploitative society. Bourgeois individualism was tainted at the source by the callous egotism, self-aggrandizement and alienation which saturated it. The humanistic ideal it fostered was frustrated by the lack of sympathy and solidarity with fellow human beings fostered by its unbridled competitiveness.

These conflicting traits of individualism can be discerned in the positions of the most eminent antifeudal political the-

orists of the seventeenth century, whose views served as the
basis for all the subsequent ideas of the bourgeois economists and political writers. The institutionalized fiction of the
autonomous private personality was drawn from the conditions of the market economy where independent producers
were related to one another solely as owners of commodities
and money.

Hobbes, the Machiavelli of the English revolution, most
forthrightly translated these underlying economic relations into
political terms. For him the market, that is, the network of exchange relations, was the supreme regulator of the social structure. He pictured humanity as a pack of fiercely competitive
isolated units avid for power. All other human relations were
subordinate to the relations of exchange. A man's worth and
social standing were determined by what the purchaser would
give in the marketplace of public opinion. Man's innate desire and unlimited thirst for power, which meant command
over others, was the political equivalent of the unlimited thirst
for expansion of capital, which is command over the labor
of others. From this thoroughly bourgeois conception of human nature, Hobbes drew the political conclusion that an
absolute sovereign was essential as a coercive authority to
protect property and maintain order.

Hobbes did not see men as motivated by goodwill toward
others, as philanthropic liberalism is wont to do. For him,
self-interest was the engine of society. Men were impelled "either
for gain, or for glory; that is, not so much for love of our
fellows, as for love of ourselves."

His view that man is naturally a wolf toward man and
each is engaged in a struggle for power and aggrandizement
against everyone else was an extreme expression of the individualism engendered by a society dominated by exchange
relations of a capitalist type. He claimed to have deduced
that men are inclined to relapse into a natural state of civil
war from direct observation of the conduct of himself and his
neighbors.

He wrote in *Leviathan*: "It may seem strange to some man,
that has not well weighed these things; that Nature should thus
dissociate and render men more apt to invade, and destroy
one another: and he may therefore, not trusting to this In-
ference, made from the Passions, desire perhaps to have the
same confirmed by Experience. Let him therefore consider
with himself, when taking a journey, he armes himself, and
seeks to go well accompanied; when going to sleep, he locks

his dores; when even in his house he locks his chests; and this when he knowes that there be Lawes, and publike officers, armed, to revenge all injuries shall be done him; what opinion he has of his fellow subjects, when he rides armed; of his fellow Citizens, when he Locks his dores; and of his children, and servants, when he locks his chests."[5]

The clear-sighted and, some would say, cynical realism of Hobbes's reasoning shocked those who preferred to keep a veil draped around the facts of domination and servitude in class society. But his insights corresponded so closely to actual circumstances that they have continued to carry conviction ever since *Leviathan* was published in 1651 in the midst of the English civil war.

The Levellers who were his contemporaries were militant democrats and not bourgeois absolutists. Their version of human nature included the individual's natural right to certain civil, political and religious liberties. Yet they no less vigorously asserted the individual right to property. They equated liberty with the possession of property and regarded private ownership as one natural right among others. Thus John Lilburne insisted in 1648 that "they (the Levellers) have been the truest and constantest asserters of liberty and propriety (which are quite opposite to communitie and levelling) that have been in the whole land."[6]

The Levellers were petty-bourgeois individualists while Hobbes and Locke spoke from the standpoint of the gentry and merchants. The disagreements in their views and evaluations reflected the differences between the big and the little bourgeoisie, between men of riches and estates and the petty proprietors. The Levellers would not have extended freedom or the franchise to the unpropertied servants and alms-takers or women.

The category of the self-contained individual was one facet of the world view presented by the empirical philosophers of the seventeenth and eighteenth centuries which permeated all departments of bourgeois culture from religion to physical science. In the mechanical conception of nature, the universe was made up of atoms having only external relations with one another; in social theory, isolated individuals came together involuntarily through the mechanism of the market and more voluntarily through the social compact; in the Protestant theology, the solitary soul had direct communion with God without the mediation of any clerical hierarchy; in the mind, knowledge was compounded out of single self-sufficient sense-data, impressions or ideas. This metaphysical outlook of possessive individualism was translated into legal terms by making all persons formally equal in the eyes of the law, and into electoral terms by the rule of one-man, one-vote.

Locke derived all political rights and obligations from the interest, property and will of the dissociated individual. He had the same disdainful attitude toward the laboring poor as Cromwell, who had dismissed them in the Putney debates as "men that have no interest (in the Commonwealth) but the interest of breathing." Locke construed majority rule as the rule of the majority of property owners, the landed proprietors, merchants and moneyed men who had ascended to power through the Glorious Revolution. It must be remembered that the Whig victory in 1689 not only clinched the supremacy of Parliament over the monarchy but of the possessing classes over the plebeians, who were totally excluded from political participation. Locke, like Hobbes and the Levellers, allotted no political rights to either the employed or unemployed proletarians on the ground that they belonged to an inferior and irrational breed of men.

Thus during this pioneering period of the bourgeois revolution, the scope of the rights possessed by the free rational individual was very narrowly interpreted in theory and practice. Their extension to the majority of citizens came much later in the evolution of bourgeois democracy.

Nationalism was more deeply embedded than democracy in the bourgeois outlook because the framework of the nation-state was the most advantageous medium for the development of the productive forces under the native capitalist class. If the bourgeois revolutionists did not find that form of political organization ready-made, as in England and France, they had to create it, as in Holland, the United States and later Italy, by expelling their foreign overlords and amalgamating the dispersed and divided elements of nationality into a political, cultural and spiritual entity.

The nation-state represented a far more dynamic type of political formation than the loose imperial agglomerations and petty particularisms of medieval times. It was the indispensable lever for liberating Europeans from spiritual bondage to the Catholic Church and from political subjugation to alien masters. The struggle for national self-determination and independent sovereignty roused the common people from apathy at their lot, stimulated their energies and widened their connections and horizons.

From the sixteenth to the twentieth centuries, most of the advances in the Western lands were bound up with the formation and growth of the national state. This form of organization provided a shelter for the people in promoting their distinctive culture, achieving their self-identity, exploring and expanding their capacities and raising their collective pride and dignity.

Although its prerequisites had ripened over a longer time, modern nationalism is not much older than the second half of the eighteenth century. Under feudalism between the universalism of the Church and the empire and the localism of the city-states and rural manors or villages, nationalism had neither the need nor room to exfoliate. The framework of a centralized sovereign state was created by the absolute monarchies in France, England and Spain, but the content of specific nationality attached to it, by welding the people into a single homogeneous unit, was brought into being by the bourgeois-democratic revolutions.

On its democratic side, nationalism is bound up with the idea of popular sovereignty, of a fatherland which claims to represent the whole people, which grants and defends their liberties and gives the inhabitants a share in legislation and a conscious stake in its destinies. On its bourgeois side, political and civic liberties are linked with such economic freedoms as the rights of private property, freedom of trade and enterprise. These are the cornerstones of the bourgeois fidelity to nationalism.

The idea of a distinctive American nationality was hardly mentioned before 1776. This national identity was hammered out by the common experience of armed struggle against Great Britain, the winning of independence and the unification of the thirteen separate colonies into a constitutional republic.

From 1789 on, revolutionary France provided the exemplary embodiment of "the national idea." There the titanic conflicts with the royalists and the foreign interventionists, coupled with the development of the democratic dictatorship and the successes of French arms, filled a reservoir of national feelings to the brim. France, *la patrie*, was identified with the revolution, progress, enlightenment, popular rule and imperial grandeur. This fusion of revolutionary enthusiasm and patriotic ardor was later exploited for reactionary and imperialistic purposes by the bourgeoisie, the Bonapartes and the kings. Paradoxically, the patriotic fire that stirred the French soldiers ignited a counter-national consciousness among the Spaniards, Austrians, Prussians and Russians when Napoleon's armies invaded and occupied their countries.

Nationalism generated its dynamic force from both bourgeois and plebeian sources. The common folk saw in the democratic nation the fount of their freedoms, their best opportunities for self-development and for the cultivation of their own language, customs, literature and culture. The peasants, farmers and other small-property owners felt that they had a private share in the territory itself.

Nationalism involved a shift of allegiance from the Church and the crown to the nation-state which the Third Estate aspired to control at all costs. The bourgeoisie regards the nation-state as the indispensable economic, political, military and diplomatic instrument, which protects its home market from foreign competitors, keeps interlopers beyond the frontiers, extends its territorial domains and serves as a staging area for its international operations. For these imperative reasons, it is determined to acquire and retain possession of state power, come what may. It will join the insurgent masses and even rouse them in order to defy and displace ecclesiastical and monarchical opposition, repel invaders and strengthen its rule.

The bourgeoisie demands supreme loyalty to the nation so long as it retains command of the government. In their hands nationalism is a powerful sentiment to dupe the masses and dominate them. That is why the capitalist regime systematically fosters the cult of patriotism through such customs as mandatory salutes to the national flag, singing the national anthem and taking an oath of allegiance in the public schools.

However, the patriotism of the big bourgeoisie itself does not extend much beyond its profits and property interests. Like the royalists, this class will repudiate the devotion to the fatherland it propagates while in power when its supremacy is at stake. It can then ally itself with the worst enemies of the people, as the French bourgeoisie did through the Vichy regime after Hitler conquered the country in 1941.

Nationalism was a mighty force for overturning the old order and cementing the new one. In its heyday, the national-democratic movement was a potent generator of material, moral and cultural advancement for the people. To this day, it retains its progressive potential in backward countries and among nationalities which are economically and politically subject to foreign oppression or imperialist exploitation and have yet to achieve their democratic revolution.

Almost from birth the best of bourgeois nationalisms were disfigured by obnoxious features which in time tainted their worthier accomplishments. By making submission to the dictates of the regime the prime test of good citizenship, patriotism was a powerful sentiment in the hands of the classes in control of the state apparatus, to abuse as they pleased. Through the gospel of "my country, right or wrong," progressive patriotism and revolutionary nationalism could pass over into reactionary chauvinism, which justified abominable crimes in the name of defending the fatherland.

Bourgeois and petty-bourgeois nationalism fostered exclusivism at the expense of other peoples. The North Americans provided a conspicuous example of how a previously oppressed nationality could be transformed into an oppressor power — a phenomenon which was to be duplicated many times thereafter. During the nineteenth century, patriotic bigots at the head of the United States displayed national arrogance toward Mexicans, contempt for Indians, white-supremacist attitudes toward blacks and instituted discriminatory immigration policies toward Asiatics.

The bigger capitalist powers practiced a national messianism based on an arbitrary right to serve as a master-model for "lesser breeds." "The conquering republic" of the United States pursued a policy of aggression toward its weaker neighbors (Mexico, the Philippines, Cuba and Puerto Rico). England had long before justified its imperial aggrandizement as the bearing of Anglo-Saxon freedom and civilization to its dominions. France built its empire under the ensign of exporting the values of its cultural enlightenment to the natives. The patriotism which had once furthered democracy turned under imperialist auspices into chauvinism and became the corroder of democracy at home and the most vicious foe of the self-determination of other peoples.

If the idea of nationalism was predominant in the bourgeois revolutions, the broader ideal of internationalism was projected by their noblest spokesmen at the height of their revolutionary energy and enthusiasm. They identified the popular revolution with the general cause of liberty as an action undertaken for the good of all mankind in league with its most progressive forces. Thus John Milton envisaged the whole of mankind following the lead of the English revolution. "I now imagine," he wrote, "that, from the columns of Hercules to the Indian Ocean, I behold the nations of the earth recovering that liberty which they so long had lost; and that the people of this island . . . are disseminating the blessings of civilization and freedom among cities, kingdoms and nations." [7]

Tom Paine not only had a similar vision but carried it into

practice. After coming from England to help promote American independence, he went to France and then to England to champion the struggles of their peoples against tyranny as wholeheartedly as he had the colonial cause. I am a citizen of the world, he proclaimed, and to do good is my religion. "Where liberty is, there is my country," he is said to have proclaimed upon his departure from America. In theory and action, Paine was the foremost international revolutionist of the eighteenth century.

The leading French revolutionaries welcomed the participation of foreign revolutionaries like Paine and conferred honorary citizenship upon them. They announced sympathy and support for antimonarchical and antifeudal movements in the rest of Europe and set up "sister republics" under their protection so that liberated peoples could apply the "principles of 1789" beyond their borders.

However, these expressions of internationalism were exceptional, short-lived and uncharacteristic of the bourgeois era. Unlike the proletarian revolution, whose ideals and objectives were internationalist in essence, the bourgeois revolutions were encased in national boundaries and could not transcend these limits without negating themselves.

Liberalism designates both a specific phase in the evolution of bourgeois democracy and the ensemble of ideas and policies corresponding to it. Liberal democracy is a political product of postrevolutionary conditions when the militancy of the masses has subsided and the moderate bourgeoisie sets the tone of political life. It is a sequel and becomes a rival to the radical democracy of the plebeian type.

Historically, liberalism emerged from the bourgeois reaction against the "excesses" of the French Revolution during the rise of industrial capitalism, when the industrial and commercial bourgeoisie was consolidating its supremacy. It was a reformist and gradualist tendency whose spokesmen exalted evolution as the antithesis to disruptive revolution. Chateaubriand caught the essence of its temper when he said: "We must preserve the political work which is the fruit of the Revolution . . . but we must eradicate the Revolution from this work."

England became the classic home of both liberalism and parliamentarism. In the days of competitive capitalism when England was the workshop, banker and shipper of the world market, liberalism was the policy and outlook of the prosperous middle classes. Although the British bourgeoisie was hostile to any domestic revolutionary commotion, it could afford to dole out minor modifications of the old aristocratic order.

The Whigs and, after 1830, the Radicals, who espoused laissez-faire in commerce and in capital-labor relations, undertook to repeal the mercantilist laws that hampered the growth of manufacturing and trade. Their movement succeeded in repealing the Corn Laws and instituting free trade in 1846. The program of the first Liberal Party in England featured free trade, religious liberty, abolition of slavery, extension of the franchise and other reform measures.

The theoretical foundations of liberalism were laid down in law and ethics by the Utilitarian thinkers, Jeremy Bentham and James Mill, and in political economy by the classical school of economists from Adam Smith to David Ricardo. Its watchword was individual liberty. This was interpreted along different lines by opposing tendencies within the liberal camp. The left wing of the John Stuart Mill school identified liberalism with respect for the individual and his civil rights, which was extended as far as women's rights. The right wing around Herbert Spencer and his Social Darwinian disciples upheld unrestrained competition as the way to freedom and social progress.

The English liberals, backed up by sections of the labor movement, conducted campaigns to extend representation in Parliament, modernize municipal administration, improve legal procedures, reorganize the courts and create sanitary codes and a system of factory inspectors. These and other reforms were to be achieved exclusively through parliamentary legislation and constitutional revision.

In the twentieth century, the term liberalism has come to cover any ideological position on a bourgeois-democratic basis that occupies a middle ground between conservatism and socialism and seeks to mediate between the plutocracy and the proletariat. Liberalism could be hospitable to improvements effected through constitutional means and methods; it is obdurately opposed to direct mass action with revolutionary implications or to any measures which threaten the foundations of the parliamentary regime or the capitalist system. While liberalism reigned in the United States and England, its adherents tended to identify it with "democracy" as such, in sharp contrast with dictatorships of the right and the left, regardless of their class content.

The social theory of liberalism pivoted around a pluralistic analysis of the bourgeois order and the concept of countervailing powers. It assumed or asserted that capitalism was not divided into classes with antagonistic interests nor its states dominated by a ruling class. Society was made up of a congeries of contending groups with miscellaneous interests whose respective claims had to be balanced against one another to maintain social harmony and dispense justice.

The function of the state was not, as Marxists taught, to be the executive agency of the economically dominant class but rather the impartial arbitrator in the contention of the various groupings.

The liberals favored contests between the candidates and programs of rival parties so long as there were no irreconcilable clashes between opposing social forces. All differences were to be adjudicated within the existing economic system and parliamentary political institutions. The working out of such accommodations provided the guideline and goal of progressive political activity. Classical liberalism prized individual initiative above collectivism as the stimulant of progress in all spheres and extolled constitutional parliamentarism as the most rational and enlightened mode of representation and rule.

Liberalism did not become as strong on the European continent as it did in the Anglo-American world. In France, Spain and Italy, bourgeois liberalism was linked up with constitutionalism and anticlericalism in the struggles of the merchants and manufacturers against the guardians of obsolescent institutions.

Anglo-American middle-class liberalism was associated with sharp criticism of the plutocracy and a philanthropic sympathy toward the lower classes on the part of its intellectual representatives. John Stuart Mill, the mentor of British liberalism, and John Dewey, his later analogue on the other side of the Atlantic, even tried eclectically to combine their principles of individualism with a leaning toward certain socialistic ideas.

As capitalism grew over from its competitive to its monopolistic stage, the attitude of liberalism toward the role of the state underwent an ironic inversion. Laissez-faire liberalism had, in the name of individual liberty, opposed the interference of the government in economic activity or social affairs. However, capitalist development keeps widening the state's sphere of action and continually imposes new functions upon it, making more and more necessary its intervention in the economy and society on behalf of the large-property owners.

Twentieth-century liberals were obliged to take these irresistible trends into account. They consequently turned more and more toward the government, as the guardian of the middle classes and the poor, against the terrifying consequences of the automatic operation of corporate capitalism. Nonetheless, in both stages they regarded the state as the representative of the general public interest, not as the agency of the ruling class.

In addition to the standards of middle-class liberalism which presumed that equality regulated the relations of men in politics as in the commodity and labor markets, the bourgeois-democratic movement has felt the impress of the plebeian classes. As has been noted, the drive for popular rights started on a minimal footing with the demand for a measure of control from below over church practices and organization. It moved from there to the political structure where the disfranchised put in their claims for rights and representation. Thereafter, under pressure of the plebeian thrust and the labor movement, it transcended the precincts of the state and penetrated to the economic foundations of society, touching upon the nerve center of the material distinctions among its classes.

The constitutional reforms that wiped out the "estates" of feudalism and equalized individual rights did not eliminate all the de facto discriminations suffered by diverse sections of the population; racial, national, sexual and other privileges persisted under the most democratic bourgeois regimes. The representatives of the exploited and oppressed plebeians pressed for a far more sweeping equalization of rights than the limited proposals for purely legal and electoral equality.

The landless peasantry clamored for a redistribution of the land and the greater equalization of property ownership at the expense of the large proprietors. In the nineteenth century, the socialist sections of the proletariat fought for nothing less than the abolition of classes through the extension of equality to the social and economic spheres. Their call for a workers' democracy was the appropriate complement and logical consummation of political democracy.

This extremely radical application of democracy horrified the conservative upper classes and the moderate petty bourgeoisie. The capitalists viewed it as a dire threat to their domination and condemned it as the spawn of the devil. An equality which trespassed upon the sacred rights of private ownership of the means of production was going much too far.

Though these opposing class conceptions of equality could not be reconciled in the long run, the working-class demand for greater equality could not be totally ignored by the parliamentary bourgeoisie. It entered as an inharmonious and disturbing factor into the democratic ideology and took lodging there as a harbinger of the next stage of political development rather than an immediate reality.

All these variegated constituents of the bourgeois-democratic ideology shared one ineradicable characteristic. They were swathed in metaphysical mysticism. Kingship by the grace of God had enveloped monarchism with an aura which the theorists of representative government did their best to dispel. To them the bourgeois republic was the model of political rationality.

It was indeed a far more reasonable and equitable system than one based on the principle of dynastic succession. Nonetheless, the claim that the institutions and ideas of bourgeois democracy had a supraclass character invested this type of political thought and organization with an inherently formalistic and idealistic nature. Such absolutist abstractions as its principle of ideal equality were at variance with the fundamental facts of capitalist life. As the colonial wit observed:

> "All men are created equal,
> But differ greatly in the sequel."

The bourgeois-democratic ideology has been permeated with mysticism from its birth, owing to the glaring discrepancies between its pretensions of equality and the persistence of inequalities on all levels of social life. That false consciousness is encapsulated in its unscientific notion of the classless democratic regime. This key conception of the liberal school is a fraud and a fiction. All the historical forms of political democracy have had a multiclass basis and been dominated by some ruling class. The theory of socialist politics is founded on the recognition of that truth. But the bourgeois democrats refuse to acknowledge that the capitalist minority exercises its social dictatorship behind the screen of a formal equality in the juridical and parliamentary domains.

Its metaphysical traits were implanted in the foundations of bourgeois political ideology by its pioneer theoreticians. Locke's empirical theory of knowledge flowed from the denial of the existence of innate ideas and the affirmation that all ideas depended in the first place upon sensory experience. Yet in his *Two Treatises of Government* Locke discarded this cardinal tenet of his empirical philosophy by assuming that both natural rights and the law of reason were innate ideas. The existence of natural law, he wrote, was plainly "writ in the Hearts of all

Mankind." This was an obvious departure from his elementary philosophical principles.

Such a conflict between the cardinal assumptions of his theory of knowledge and his sociological and political premises was only one aspect of the multitude of incongruities in his philosophy. As Laslett, the editor of the most complete edition of his treatises, remarked: "Locke is, perhaps, the least consistent of all the great philosophers." [8]

The bourgeois-democratic regimes themselves contained as many inconsistencies as their ideologues. In Great Britain a monarchy, state church and House of Lords coexisted with the supremacy of the House of Commons and a Labour Party. Until the American Civil War, the Constitution of the model American democracy legalized slavery. The actual practices of every bourgeois democracy have violated the most elementary tests of equality. In the United States, women, who compose half the inhabitants, were not allowed to vote in national elections until 1920 and, half a century later, young men from eighteen to twenty-one, who could be conscripted to fight and die, were denied the franchise in most states.

For all its defects and contradictions, the bourgeois-democratic ideology secured a broader mass following than any other political doctrine or movement before the advent of Marxism. Its program, carried forward with the rise of bourgeois civilization, was a force for enlightenment and progress wherever the commercial, industrial, urban and rural classes came into collision with royal and ecclesiastical absolutism.

The ideas of bourgeois democracy became more than a political philosophy and program. They projected a world outlook, a view of historical development and an interpretation of human destiny that captured the minds and kindled the imaginations of successive generations of idealistic individuals. This secular faith came to acquire more force of conviction than any religious belief, serving as a substitute creed among the liberals who cherished it and the masses who clung to it. The tenets of abstract democracy were venerated as unassailable values, the premises of all rational political activity. While the devotees of liberalism derided credulous folk who still believed in the outworn Catholic theology, they had a comparable dogmatic attitude toward the shibboleths of bourgeois democracy. Its propositions appeared to them as impregnable as Euclid's axioms then appeared in plane geometry. Whoever dared question their universal applicability or desirability was regarded as an obscurantist, like those who thought the earth was flat.

Nowhere was this trust in the absolute virtues of bourgeois democracy so deeply rooted and stubbornly maintained as in the United States. The nineteenth-century American historian George Bancroft held up Yankee democracy as the goal toward which all other peoples were destined to move. Although his twentieth-century successors were somewhat more sophisticated and disenchanted, they did not doubt that the United States remained the paragon of "the free world" and its democracy superior to any other form of government projected or practiced on this planet.

Thomas Jefferson wrote that man's "mind is perfectible to a degree of which we cannot form any conception," and that they speak falsely who insist "that it is not probable that anything better will be discovered than what was known to our fathers." But the liberal devotees of the cult of Jeffersonian democracy fail to apply this notion of progress to the constitutional handiwork of the eighteenth century. They turn against the spirit of both Jefferson's evolutionism and revolutionism when they deny the prospect of "anything better" in political and social structures than what was known to the founding fathers.

7

THE EVOLUTION OF
PARLIAMENTARISM

Parliamentarism has been the standard type of democratic rule in the most highly developed capitalisms. This system crowned the historical process by which bourgeois forces reconstructed the old order from its economic foundations to its forms of governing. Parliamentarism enabled the new possessing classes to secure, maintain and wield power under a relation of forces most favorable to them.

Liberal supporters of capitalism esteem this kind of government as the supreme expression of self-rule. They believe that progressive mankind cannot pass beyond this peak of perfection in the fulfillment of democracy. However, a critical examination of the origins, evolution and chief characteristics of this institution does not confirm such a one-sided evaluation. Parliamentarism has been — and remains — an instrument of capitalist control which shares both the merits and faults of this phase of class society.

In politics, as in other fields, mankind does make substantial advances from one epoch to the next. This was demonstrated in the transition from medieval to more modern times. The outcome of the contests for sovereignty under feudalism constituted the starting point for the political activities of the bourgeois period. The medieval political systems and theories of Western Europe were polarized between the contending claims of the Church and the crown. An irreversible displacement in the axis of political conflicts occurred when the absolute monarchy prevailed over the papacy and went on to repudiate it under Protestant regimes.

Thereafter kingship vied less for supremacy with the priesthood than with parliament and, behind it, the people. These were not necessarily identical forces. The principal political issues to be fought out and thought out depended in large measure on which of these bodies — the crown, parliament or the restricted or enlarged citizen mass — was to be predominant in governing the country.

Parliament was not a creation of the revolutionary masses like the Paris Commune or the original soviets. It was gradually and slowly shaped as an instrument by the upper layers of the bourgeoisie, who were obliged to strive for supremacy against the absolute monarchy to their right and against the plebeians on their left flank. This struggle on two opposing fronts gave birth to the highly contradictory, two-faced nature of the parliamentary system.

The bolder leaders and ideologists of the bourgeois revolution had to bring forward the democratic doctrine of popular sovereignty as a counter to the monarchical dogma of the right to rule by the grace of God. This was necessary to discredit the sanctions of the old regime, validate their own claims to power, enlist popular support for their cause and establish the predominance of parliament. The essential principles of republicanism were first set forth in England during the Great Rebellion by Sir Henry Vane and others. They defined it as complete sovereignty by the people through the representative rule of a single assembly.

Later in the seventeenth century, the empirical philosopher John Locke, apologist for the consummated and conservatized bourgeois revolution in England, became the most influential exponent of parliamentary hegemony. In his *Two Treatises of Government* he set out to disprove the rationale for the divine and absolute right of the monarch and justify in its stead the claims of the bourgeoisie who aspired to make the throne subservient to the House of Commons.

Locke taught that, according to the laws of nature and reason, the people were the source and seat of power in society and the state. Both the throne and parliament were subordinate and responsible to them. The legislature is no more than the deputy of the people, who have the right to remove or alter it when it acts contrary to their mandate.

Locke endorsed the right of revolution as the guarantee of representative government. If representatives violate the confidence of their constituents, the power reverts to society. The people retain the right at all times to "erect a new form, or under the old form place it in new hands, as they think good."

To the question "Who shall be judge, whether the prince or legislative act contrary to their trust?" Locke forthrightly replied: "the people shall be judge; for who shall judge whether his trustee or deputy acts well, and according to the trust reposed in him, but he who deputes him, and must, by having deputed him, have still a power to discard him, when he fails in his trust?" [1]

These were explosive ideas. They permeated progressive political thinking throughout the eighteenth century and were used as powerful weapons by the most intrepid representatives of the revolutionary camp to oppose and overthrow the old regimes in the American colonies and France. Thus Rousseau maintained that sovereignty is inalienably vested in society as a whole, which retains its supremacy regardless of any temporary and partial delegation of powers.

Tom Paine argued that there are two irreconcilable modes of government: government by election and representation (republicanism) and government by heredity and succession (monarchy and aristocracy). The one is based on reason and equality; the other on ignorance and privilege. In a republic the people are sovereign and free; in a monarchy they are victims of superstition, despotism, bribery and corruption.

The democracy envisaged by the most radical political theorists and installed under the bourgeoisie was not a direct democracy like that of Athens, where the laws and decisions were made by the assembled citizens, who then participated in their execution. Except for the Swiss cantons, this sort of democracy by direct action and personal participation in public functions was revived and realized in the bourgeois era only at the height of revolutionary commotions, when plebeian insurgents entered en masse into the struggle and intervened as the decisive force in the determination of events.

But such assertions of direct democracy were exceptional and episodic; they flagged or were crushed with the subsiding of revolutionary energies and rightward shifts in the balance of forces. Where democratic institutions survived or were set up after the upsurges of popular rebellion were over, these took the form of parliamentary bodies which exercised the governmental functions as real or supposed agents of the people's will. The parliamentary system rested upon a more or less stabilized equilibrium of class forces which assured the continuance of capitalist domination and development.

In both its beginnings and further evolution as a mode of bourgeois rule, parliamentarism had an equivocal character. An appeal to popular sovereignty was indispensable to mobilize the masses for mortal combat against the monarchy and its upholders. Its legal consecration in a constitutional order legitimized the new regime. But this doctrine was risky for those large-property owners who sided with the revolution or reconciled themselves to it and profited the most from its results.

Democratic preachments held out the promise that the welfare of the majority should be paramount over the interests of any minority, that inequalities and injustices of all kinds would be eliminated and that the people would actually possess and use the power to decide all vital issues. The complete and consistent democracy logically entailed in the principle of popular sovereignty conflicted with the aims of the possessing classes and the realities of their rule.

To get rid of their precapitalist antagonists or lay them low, the more intransigent spokesmen of the democratic revolution felt called upon to proclaim all power to the people. But the big bourgeoisie were a small minority of society. As such they could not afford to hand over unrestricted sovereignty to the plebeian majority. They were caught in this dilemma: how, while appearing to comply with the formal requirements of popular sovereignty and democratic representation, could they reserve and preserve the substance of rule for the rich and prevent the masses from exercising power on their own behalf?

The solution to the predicament confronting the rising ruling classes was worked out empirically, step by step, over the centuries in the course of intense social and political struggles. Bourgeois parliamentarism, with or without a compliant monarchy, emerged from the laboratory of Western European history as the model for the domination of the owners of wealth over the rest of the nation through more or less democratic forms.

England, which became the most advanced of the first-born capitalist nations, was the mother of parliamentarism. Originally the English Parliament was not a popular body but a highly aristocratic assembly of the barons, who were summoned by the monarch on occasion to deliberate on their own affairs and especially on their financial and other obligations to the crown. It later admitted members of the wealthy urban bourgeoisie into its councils.

The sixteenth-century Reformation increased the power and elevated the status of both the House of Lords and the Commons because the break with Rome had been effected and the Church of England established by King Henry VIII through Parliament. The supremacy of Parliament came about through the revolutionary events of the following century, when the Presbyterian and Puritan bourgeoisie turned the tables and used Parliament as an agency in their contest against the crown and the Episcopal Church.

In the revolutionary and counterrevolutionary upheavals from 1640 to 1688, Parliament experienced many vicissitudes. It passed from the Long Parliament, which headed the opposition to the king and then beheaded him, through its purges and dissolution by Cromwell to its restoration by Charles II. The victory of the anti-Stuart forces in the Glorious Revolution of 1688 finally settled the prolonged duel with the monarchy by irrevocably affirming the constitutional sovereignty of the Parliament over the crown.

However, Parliament itself was not the major force in overturning the old order. That decisive role was played by the revolutionary army of Cromwell and his Agitators, who dictated to Parliament what had to be done. When its more conservative majority demurred, they swept aside the resistant members, and finally the body itself, as intolerable impediments to victory in the civil war and the remodeling of society and the state.

The postrevolutionary English Parliament of the eighteenth century did not pretend to be democratic. In fact, its representation was confined to the propertied upper classes, the ten thousand or so landed proprietors, merchants, manufacturers and bankers who held England in their hands. An Act of 1710 required members of the House of Commons to possess private incomes corresponding to some $25,000 a year today, and this had to come from ownership of land. From 1688 to 1832, England was governed by a bourgeoisified aristocracy.

The diffusion of democratic ideas following the American and French revolutions, the demands of the powerful new social forces brought on the scene by the Industrial Revolution and, especially, increased pressure from the working masses forced a reluctant aristocratic plutocracy to broaden parliamentary representation as the nineteenth century advanced. The extension of the franchise through the Reform Bills of 1832, 1867 and 1874 culminated in the granting of general suffrage in 1918, after the First World War and the Russian Revolution. This gradual expansion of the electoral basis of parliamentary rule went along with the shriveling of the prerogatives of the monarchy and the hereditary House of Lords until today the supremacy of the Commons is regarded as unchallengeable.

England provided the prototype for the parliamentary institutions of other lands. Her North American colonists were the most apt pupils. After an apprenticeship in the colonial assemblies and town meetings, they appropriated the ideas of the republican and democratic thinkers to organize and conduct their war of national liberation and then took the parliamentary system of the mother country as the model for their own political structure.

Parliamentarism found highly fertile soil for growth in the United States. Here, unlike its original home, it had no native royalty, hereditary nobility, state church nor, until the twentieth century, any powerful military establishment to incorporate or to contend with and no far-flung colonial possessions to dominate.

The Declaration of Independence, the charter of the first American revolution, enunciated ideas taken from Locke, Rousseau and other theorists of the radical bourgeoisie. The right of revolution is so unequivocally acknowledged and firmly embedded in this birth cry of the American nation that it has troubled conservatives and reactionaries ever since. The declaration asserted that governments derive their just powers from the consent of the governed and that "whenever any Form of Government becomes destructive of these ends, it is the Right of the People to alter or to abolish it, and to institute new Government, laying its foundation on such principles and organizing its powers in such form, as to them shall seem most likely to effect their Safety and Happiness."

The doctrine of popular sovereignty, under which the War for Independence was waged and won, inspired the struggle to cast off the despotism of the British crown. But once independence had been achieved, it remained to be seen how much that principle would be observed in the construction and operation of the new Republic.

At the time of its adoption, the Constitution of the United States of America was the most democratic and the government it set up the most representative in the Western world. Nonetheless, the conservative delegates of the capitalist-planter coalition who drafted the articles of state at Philadelphia in 1787 took pains to insure that their positions, property, power and privileges were given maximum protection against encroachments by unruly plebeian majorities.

To safeguard the interests of the rich against the poor, the participants in the Constitutional Convention incorporated three key devices into their ingenious setup. They inserted prohibitions into certain fundamental government powers such as the taking of private property without due process of law. To cushion the shocks of sudden onslaughts by popular majorities, they removed much of the governmental apparatus from direct or simultaneous election. The Constitution envisaged no parties, no national campaigns and no popular vote for president. The president was to be chosen by an electoral college derived from the state legislatures. Senators were elected for six-year terms with only one-third of its members chosen at one time. Federal judges were to be appointed by the president with confirmation by the Senate.

Finally power was dispersed on two planes: vertically between the federal and the state levels of government and horizontally among the executive, legislative and judicial branches. While the structural principles followed by the architects of the Republic were supposedly designed to protect the people against arbitrary centralized power, under the rule of the capitalists and planters, they largely served in practice to safeguard the interests of the well-to-do against the rights and welfare of the masses.

The theory of the tripartite division of powers in the state, which is so esteemed by liberals nowadays, was the handiwork of the constitutional monarchists in England and France. John Locke first suggested partitioning power into the legislative, executive and judicial. The idea was later developed by Montesquieu as a device for limiting absolutism and concentrating legislative power in the hands of the bourgeois representative institutions.

The division of the U. S. government into three separate and coordinate branches enabled the legislative to be checked by a powerful presidential executive, who assumed some of the powers of a monarch while in office. Both were restrainable by a Supreme Court whose members were appointed for life. The makers of the Constitution rejected a single chamber in favor of a double house, like the British system. Amendment to the Constitution was made difficult. Each revision had to be ratified by three-fourths of the states rather than a majority of the states or voters. Slavery was guaranteed along with all other forms of private property and made a basis for the representation of the states in Congress.

After hard-fought struggles, a Bill of Rights was appended to the Constitution as the price of its passage, to appease both the antifederalist forces and the distrustful plebeians. These first ten amendments modified the upper-class bias of the original draft without excising the numerous antidemocratic features from the basic structure of the Constitution.

During the nineteenth and the first half of the twentieth century, as the mass of people put pressures upon the political parties competing for their votes, some of the most glaring antidemocratic defects were eliminated from the federal structure even faster than in England. Property qualifications for the franchise were reduced or removed; slavery and its representation was abolished as the result of the Civil War; universal male suffrage over twenty-one years was granted. This latter measure remained restrictive in practice since poor whites who could not pay poll taxes and blacks, especially in the southern states, were effectively excluded from voting. Woman's suffrage was enacted after the First World War. Finally, under the influence of the civil-rights movement of the 1950s and 1960s, poll taxes were illegalized, the franchise was made more available to Afro-Americans and election districts were made more equitable.

Despite these reforms, the system of representation remains stacked in favor of the rich all the way from running for office (the presidential candidates of the major parties in 1968 reportedly spent $50 millions in running for office) to shaping and making decisions on domestic and foreign policy.

Apart from the Scandinavian countries, France has been the most important center of parliamentary government in Europe. Its political vicissitudes since 1789 have resulted in a variety of forms which range from constitutional monarchy and military dictatorship through the direct democracy of the Paris Communes to the parliamentary republic.

The Declaration of the Rights of Man, adopted by the Constituent Assembly on August 26, 1789, and embodied as a preamble to the French Constitution of 1791, has since served as a fundamental charter for most of the bourgeois-democratic movements and regimes. It guaranteed the rights to "liberty, property, security and resistance to oppression" and the rights to freedom of speech, of the press and of worship. It asserted the principles of the equality of men and the sovereignty of the people, "on whom the law should rest, to whom officials should be responsible, and by whom governors should be controlled."

The American Declaration of Independence and the French Declaration of the Rights of Man are the pivotal documents of the revolutionary democracy of the bourgeois era. They expound the subversive principles that all men are created equal; that all have a right to life, liberty and the pursuit of happiness; that the paramount purpose of government is to secure these rights; and that, if any regime fails to do so, citizens have the right and even the duty to dispose of it and make a new and better one.

However, the severity and ups and downs of class conflicts forbade the installation of a durable parliamentary system in France for almost a century after the revolution. France provides a convincing example of how the bourgeois-democratic parliamentary regime is founded upon a stabilized domination of the ascending capitalist ruling class, once the royalist and militarist contenders for political mastery have been shelved and the working masses subdued. This form of government was not securely established in that country until the last quarter of the nineteenth century following the Franco-Prussian War, the crushing of the proletarian bid for power in the Paris Commune of 1871 and the fading of the dangers of another military dictatorship or monarchist restoration.

Even though it was far more centralized, the democratic republic was never so solid and stable in France as in England and the United States. After it was installed under the Radicals in 1879, the republic remained susceptible to assaults from the right as well as upheavals from the left. Its history in the twentieth century shows how the absence of industrial democracy and social-economic equality is such a perennial source of discontent and unrest that they periodically threaten to unsettle the parliamentary system and eventually lead to its undoing.

This fragility was shown in the grave political crises of the 1930s, the Vichy regime of Marshal Petain under Hitler's occupation during the Second World War and, more recently, de Gaulle's assumption of personal power in his Bonapartist experiment for the years from 1958 to 1969.

In his last public letter, written in 1826 on the fiftieth anniversary of the Declaration of Independence which he had penned, Thomas Jefferson expressed the following hope. "May it be to the world, what I believe it will be. . . . the signal of arousing men to burst the chains under which monkish ignorance and superstition had persuaded them to bind themselves, and to assume the blessings and security of self-government. . . . All eyes are opened, or opening, to the rights of man. The general spread of the light of science has already laid open to every view the palpable truth, that the mass of mankind has not been born with saddles on their backs, nor a favored few booted and spurred, ready to ride them legitimately, by the grace of God."[2]

These were the aspirations of equality and enlightenment which attended the springtime of parliamentary democracy. The form of government Jefferson celebrated was an immense advance over monarchism, absolutism and clericalism. It is greatly preferable to any bourgeois despotism of a military, personal or fascist type. It popularized the merits of rule by the people, however much it fell short of attaining this goal. "The political rationalism of democracy," wrote Trotsky, who had the advantage of more historical background and insight than Jefferson, "was the highest achievement of the revolutionary bourgeoisie."[3]

The announced principles of the democratic creed — equality, liberty, the recognition of human and civil rights — which were forged as weapons against the older order, were not fictions or illusions. They had deep roots in the demands of social development. Even though they could be very inadequately realized under bourgeois conditions, they marked an epochal forward step in human progress.

Parliamentarism was a mighty school of experience for the masses. At least in theory, it involved them in the affairs of state hitherto reserved for ruling clans, bureaucratic elites, the wealthy and the well born. It taught the people that they are entitled to be the supreme power in the land and to exercise supervision and control over all its officials and institutions. Where bourgeois democracy lasted long enough to implant such conceptions deep in the general consciousness, they could not be rooted out, no matter how harsh repressions may have been or how great the loss of rights from a relapse into undemocratic regimes.

This conditioning of the popular mind to expect and insist on democratic rule and rights has been the most progressive aspect of parliamentarism. It took effect even where parliamentary government was incomplete even within its own limits. In England, for example, the House of Commons had to cohabit with an effete monarchy, a state church and an aristocratic House of Lords. The dominions and colonies had no representation there. The state apparatus was actually run by professional bureaucracies which perpetuated their authority through seniority and strategic placement.

In addition to such imperfections, the parliamentary system suffered from a built-in contradiction. It proclaimed the predominance of the people without providing the ways and means for them to exercise their supposed sovereignty. It promised far more than it ever performed in its palmiest days. The democratization of political life could not go very far so long as the economic foundations of the social order remained under the domination of property owners headed by the magnates of capital. Their control of the economy blocked and frustrated every attempt to bring national policy-making under the control of the masses.

Through the century between the close of the Napoleonic wars and the outbreak of the First World War, parliamentary democracy continued to gain ground and consolidate itself in the West. This institution was the prime political beneficiary of the colossal expansion of the capitalist productive forces which lifted the bourgeoisie to the heights and fortified their hold in the industrialized countries.

Political parties as a vehicle of national and class representation were a product of the bourgeois-democratic and industrial revolutions. The system existed in embryo in eighteenth-century England in the division between the Whigs and Tories, although these were contending ruling factions or cliques, rather than organized parties vying on the electoral arena for popular votes in the modern manner.

The founding fathers of the United States did not envisage political parties and they were unrecognized by law as late as 1907. This political institution was not mentioned in the Constitution. The party system was a genuinely original political creation which grew up unofficially as an indispensable cog in the mechanism of parliamentary democracy. The parties had to select candidates for office, run campaigns and raise money, manage elections, formulate policies and direct the government.

The North Americans shaped this instrument into the two-party system, which first emerged in the contests between the Federalists and Democratic-Republicans in the presidential election of 1800. Jefferson's Democratic Party is the oldest in the world. The party setup enabled differences among the property owners to be regulated and settled and permitted the masses to participate in political affairs without endangering or upsetting the foundations of capitalist power. It gave a legitimized place to an opposition and made possible the peaceful transfer of the administration from one segment of the ruling class to another.

While the major parties in a bourgeois state have all been heterogeneous combinations of social forces in their makeup, pretending to be all things to all men, they have had no unbridgeable principled differences. All, in their own way, have been subservient to the sectors of the ruling class they represented. Thus the Democratic Party was the favored political agency of the plantation owners before the Civil War; the Republican Party became the main instrument of the industrial capitalists; and nowadays both vie with each other in catering to the interests of big business.

Modern mass parties originated in the United States because this nation was the first to enfranchise sizable numbers of citizens. As late as 1866, only one adult in eight in England could vote. The party system was developed still later in the nineteenth century in most of the Western European countries, after they adopted secret voting along with manhood suffrage.

The socialist parties were the first to be built on ideological principles and clear-cut class programs. They also introduced the customs of having a regularized dues-paying membership and local party branches.

The ascendancy of the parliamentary system with its party contests, periodic elections and democratic liberties, which grew out of these specific historical conditions, depended upon a particular alignment of class forces. The commanding heights of national politics were occupied by trusted agents of the large-property owners. They manipulated all the levers of power from the banks and the stock exchanges through the higher government officials and the army to the press, the educational institutions and the church.

However, big business and high finance could not have governed effectively through the democratic mechanism without acquiescent support from important elements among the middle classes and sizable sections of the workers. The principal social prop of bourgeois hegemony came from the petty bourgeoisie of the city and country (farmers or peasants) who clustered around the parties of either a liberal or conservative stripe. These parties could garner the votes of the middle classes, thanks to steady improvements in their standards of life, and could retain their loyalty so long as the masses had faith that the bourgeois-democratic regime was going to fulfill their expectations.

The prosperity and imperialist aggrandizement of the wealthiest and most fortunate capitalist nations was the groundwork for the relative stability of their internal relations and the absence of revolutionary upheavals from the 1870s to 1914. This atmosphere facilitated the flourishing of the philosophy of gradualism which viewed the achievement of piecemeal reforms within the precincts of the parliamentary system as the ultimate realistic objective of progressive political activity. This outlook was the hallmark of Western political life in the half-century preceding 1914.

Almost every section of society cherished the belief that the fundamental problems in the development of the country and in the relations among classes could be resolved through the electoral process, the debates and votes in the national assembly, House of Commons or Congress, and in no other way. This glorification of bourgeois democracy was a boon to the capitalist rulers who used their control over the parliamentary governments and their parties to advance their interests in the most expedient fashion.

The widespread reverence for parliamentary methods to the exclusion of all others encountered very little criticism or opposition, even from socialist quarters. Indeed, the reformist moods and illusions about the omnipotence of pure parliamentarism were so pervasive and persuasive in the prewar period that they succeeded in penetrating the Social Democratic parties adhering to the Second International and ultimately in corrupting and conquering their leaderships. This process was manifest as early as 1899, when the French Socialist deputy Alexandre Millerand became minister of commerce in the bourgeois government of Waldeck-Rousseau. He was the first in a long list of opportunist socialists (and later Stalinists) who were to discard the independent program and positions of the socialist movement to participate in a capitalist cabinet.

The reformists justified the abandonment of the Marxist strategy of class struggle for class collaboration with left political agents of the bourgeoisie on various pretexts according to the given circumstances. Their underlying conception was that the joint exercise of political power with "progressive" bourgeois elements would protect the welfare of the working class and create more favorable conditions for the coming of socialism. They mistook the conquest of one or another cabinet post for so many steps toward the conquest of power by the workers.

In actuality, the entry of socialist leaders into coalition governments with the bourgeois politicians resulted, not in strengthening either the economic or political positions of the workers, but in aiding the capitalist rulers to thwart their aspirations, dupe them and weaken the drive toward power of the revolutionary masses. In no case has it led either to the political or the economic dispossession of the possessing classes.

There were ideological as well as grosser material reasons for the blindness of the reformists. Along with the bourgeois political theorists, they could not conceive that any form of government might be superior to parliamentarism and go beyond it. With all its faults, the parliamentary system appeared to them as the zenith of political organization.

This view was transmitted to socialists in other European lands which had yet to pass through their own democratic revolution. The most remarkable case of this kind was provided by the Russian Mensheviks and Social Revolutionaries.

From first to last, through thick and thin, the leaders of these two parties clung tenaciously and dogmatically to the parliamentary form of representation as the sole and unsurpassable model of progressive and revolutionary politics. In 1917 they proclaimed it to be the unique form of statehood, not simply for an enlightened bourgeois rulership, but even for a socialist society.

Despite the experience of 1905, these socialist parties could not foresee the popular soviets as the basis for an alternative to the parliamentary system. Trotsky conceived of such a substitution as early as 1906. But it was not until Lenin's April 1917 Theses that the proposal of the soviet power as a form of government opposed to bourgeois parliamentarism and destined to replace it was forcefully raised for consideration in the revolutionary camp.

Until 1914 the moderate socialists regarded the direct revolutionary struggle of the workers for the seizure of power as antiquated and superseded or as relegated to an indefinite future. In assessing the life prospects of parliamentarism, such explosive events as wars, revolutions, social crises and economic catastrophes were not included in the calculations of either liberals or socialist reformists. Whatever they declaimed on holiday occasions, the latter thought it unlikely, and even undesirable, that the workers and their allies would succeed in overthrowing capitalism by direct revolutionary action and then establish a mode of government essentially different from the parliamentary state.

They were shocked when this actually occurred in a country which had not experienced any democratic revolution and where parliamentarism existed only as an adjunct to the bureaucratic monarchy. Russia completely skipped over the formal democracy which had crowned the previous bourgeois revolutions. In its stead the victorious workers and peasants led by the Bolsheviks set up the Soviet system which embodied a new and higher form of political democracy.

Unless one views the October 1917 revolution as utterly retrogressive and its chief political creation as a horrible relapse into totalitarian darkness, the establishment of the first soviet form has epoch-making significance. It sounded the knell of parliamentarism as the last word in political democracy. It presented a living challenge to the pseudodemocracy of the bourgeois exploiters and oppressors which was counterposed to it both in theory and in practice.

The advent of a new creative revolutionary force on the stage of world history had brought with it the creation of a new type of democracy based upon the supremacy of the working masses, the abolition of capitalist property and the conscious collective eradication of the inequities and evils bound up with class society. It marked the beginning of a new stage in the evolution of the forms of popular representation which went back to the Greek city-states.

It became clear with the arrival of its successor that the parliamentary democracy of the bourgeois era was no more everlasting than its precursors of ancient and medieval times. It had emerged and established itself as the political product of a constellation of historical factors belonging to a rising and robust capitalism. As world capitalism decayed, the process of disintegration found political expression in a concomitant weakening of the type of rule suited to its prime. The sharpening of the class struggle not only made it difficult to bring new parliamentary democracies into existence in countries with a retarded development but it shook the supports of traditional democratic institutions.

Thus, in the protracted period of transition from unchallenged capitalist supremacy to workers' power, the parliamentary regimes found themselves threatened from two opposite sides: the most rabid counterrevolutionary forces on the right and the mobilization of the revolutionary masses to the left. The squeeze of bourgeois democracy between these extremes was to shape global political developments from 1917 on.

8

PARLIAMENTARY

DEMOCRACY IN CRISIS

Every state, whether democratic or autocratic, maintains its rule in two ways: through its organized instruments of repression (the army, police, paramilitary forces, courts, prisons, assassination of opponents, exile) and through the spiritual, moral and ideological influences emanating from the ruling class. The bourgeois-democratic regime is distinguished from more restrictive forms of government by the extent of its reliance upon indoctrination through the church, family, educational institutions, the communication media and artistic and cultural channels. Its perpetuation depends in no small measure upon the ability of the capitalists to retain the faith of the masses in the merits of their regime.

The people's allegiance to a democracy need not come from blind confidence in the justice and beneficence of the powers-that-be. It is based upon the strength of a sentiment that the social system offers broad possibilities of progress and is measurably moving ahead. The bulk of the working population that creates the country's wealth must believe that the existing organization of society is superior to any available alternative and can in good time give them and their children a better life. Where this conviction is firmly held, the masses, especially in the earlier stages of capitalist development, will put up with manifold shortcomings in many domains.

The sturdiest democratic regimes maintain their internal cohesion through such a pervasive psychological cement. At the same time, the agencies of coercion, which are built into the most democratic of republics, are kept in reserve for the master class to call upon in case of emergency. The most liberal bourgeoisie has not hesitated to use official repression against one or another segment of its own people, especially against the wage workers, whenever it faces a serious threat to its property rights or hegemony.

However, resort to repression is exceptional and episodic under normal circumstances. Whereas dictatorial regimes rest upon naked force, the bourgeois-democratic state relies upon the force of persuasion, fortified by habit and inertia. Just as religion was used by the crown and Church to sanctify feudal regimes, so a liberal political order in a bourgeois society is sustained by a secular faith in the beneficent state.

The solidity of such a democracy is a function of its class relations. The big-property owners must not only feel sure of their supremacy but have the resources to grant concessions to the masses that will smooth accommodation to prevailing conditions. Political democracy presupposes the preservation of a relation of mastery and subordination between the upper and the lower classes, which is maintained in a delicate equilibrium of forces. When this balance is upset from either side, a social or political crisis can easily ensue.

The considerable role of conviction and conciliation in the maintenance of the democratic form of rule lends exceptional importance to the ideological factor in upholding the status quo. Experienced bourgeoisie like the English and American understand the necessity of making their views and values a common possession of all social layers, from the haughtiest to the humblest, and utilize every means of persuasion to that end.

That is the mission of mystification assigned to what Brooks and Henry Adams called "the democratic dogma" in its diverse representations. The capitalist class is obliged to keep its ruling ideas intact and shield them from challenge and criticism, especially from the left. If trust in the validity of its ideological defenses crumbles, one of the mainstays of its political power becomes gravely impaired.

Liberal ideology fares best in fair weather. Bourgeois democracy enters into crisis whenever the relations between the contending class forces are severely strained and the hold of its illusions upon the minds of the dissident strata of its citizens is loosened. As the vicissitudes of the system and the shocks of class conflict strip the political structure of the mystical veils which obscure the realities of capitalist domination, pure liberalism is soon beset from the right by Bonapartist, clerical-reactionary or fascist contestants, or from the left by socialist forces. The ensuing furious confrontation of ideologies and tendencies is a telltale sign that the authority of liberalism is on the wane.

The loss of faith in class conciliation which places liberalism in peril horrifies and puzzles its adherents. In their perplexity they attribute its appearance to malevolent and demonic forces. Yet the phenomenon has material causes which grow out of the historical crisis in the life-span of the capitalist system.

So long as capitalism kept advancing and was able to dispense reforms and material improvements to the more favored segments of the population, as it did in Europe from the 1870s to 1914 and still does in North America, its democratic representatives maintained their rule without much trouble, despite periodic interruptions of prosperity by the fluctuations of the business cycle. They commanded the allegiance, or at least the toleration, of the mass of workers and above all of the middle classes: the shopkeepers, professionals and craftsmen in the cities and the farming folk in the countryside. A reformist democratic regime is most powerful when it rests upon a firm alliance of big business with the middle classes that can pull the proletariat in its wake.

A bourgeoisie which is sure of its authority can be flexible and moderate, if it has the resources and wealth enabling it to bend under pressure. By combining reforms and demagogy, its agents can exploit the democratic shibboleths to keep the masses docile. Such was the political role performed under a robust and ascending capitalism by the Radical Socialists in France, the Liberals in England and Canada and the Catholic Center in Germany, and still played by the Democrats in the United States. (When their credit among the masses is expended, that function can be taken over by the Labor, Social Democratic or Communist parties.) The paramount task of such parties is to keep the clashes of divergent class interest within the safe and secure boundaries of the established parliamentary system.

The whole art of conservative politics in the twentieth century, wrote Aneurin Bevan in his book, *In Place of Fear,* has consisted in the following: "How can wealth persuade poverty to use its political freedom to keep wealth in power?" [1] That has likewise been the art of liberal and liberal-labor coalition politics.

Liberalism was buoyed up and kept afloat by two illusions. One was the belief that the parliamentary type of representation was the *ne plus ultra* of political systems and the predestined goal toward which all political progress tended. The other was the pretension that bourgeois democracy impartially served the entire people and its elected officials heeded the demands of all strata of the nation.

In reality, parliamentary democracy has for the most part been confined to those countries of Europe and North America where capitalism had its earliest and most luxuriant growth and favored beneficiaries. Bourgeois democracy was not a hardy enough plant to take deep root and thrive under difficult conditions. It required special historical preconditions for its emergence and endurance. These included an impetuous development of the productive forces under bourgeois auspices; powerful new social forces ready and able to wrest command of society and the state from the traditional ruling orders; a successful mass revolutionary thrust against the ancient regime; an extensive agrarian reform which bound the peasants or farmers to the renovated bourgeois order; and extensive and comfortable layers of the middle class. This constellation of conditions came together during the ascent of capitalism only in the more advanced countries, though even in their best days the parliamentary regimes were liable to be upset, as France and Germany demonstrated.

Liberalism not only exaggerated the geographical scope of the democratic republic under capitalism, but also misrepresented its essential function. The main mission of the parliamentary system was not to execute the will of the people or defend their rights but to promote and protect the rights of capitalist private property. That has been its prime purpose, which the partisans of liberalism seek to camouflage and keep hidden.

But the parliamentary regime carries out this assignment in a particular way and by specific means. Unlike other modes of bourgeois domination, it keeps the masses under control, not by force and terror, but through illusion and deception. Bourgeois democracy is two-faced and demagogic by its very nature, because it must pretend to serve the welfare of the majority while actually committed to obeying the mandates of the rich.

The capitalists face this dilemma. They are the most powerful economic class, yet form a tiny minority within the social structure. The stability of their rule therefore depends upon the amount of support they can secure from the other parts of the population, who constitute the majority of the nation. The decisive force in making up and maintaining a liberal democracy is the petty-bourgeois masses.

The big bourgeoisie was neither the primary promoter nor the principal upholder of democracy. Most of the parliamentary regimes were established before the industrial proletariat became a large-scale social and political force.

The original source and support of democracy in bourgeois society has been the petty bourgeoisie of the city and country. The first popular democratic movements, led by the Levellers, the Jacobins and the Sons and Daughters of Liberty, were based upon such elements. The conceptions of rights and representation they expressed were especially suited to small agrarian communities without gross distinctions in wealth or prosperity among the inhabitants, as in the Swiss cantons or the small towns and rural areas of the United States.

The parliamentary regime as such did not appeal so much to the polar classes of industrial capitalism, the capitalists at one end and the wage workers at the other, as it did to the small shopkeepers, craftsmen, professionals and peasant proprietors. The complicated and indirect mechanism of ruling through a parliamentary system is bothersome to the men of money, who lean toward some authoritarian method of government where the decision-making powers are centralized in a small core of trustworthy liegemen and lieutenants or even in an autocrat.

For their part, the workers gladly embrace a bourgeois democracy in preference to any sort of monarchical, clerical or dictatorial domination and accept it as the starting point for their political activities and self-determination. Outside the United States, universal franchise was *everywhere* conquered or granted after a campaign undertaken by the working-class movement rather than by the liberal bourgeoisie.

At the same time, the realities of the struggle against the bosses sooner or later drive home its fraudulent character and limitations to the more advanced members of the class. As its consciousness is clarified, its independence and organizations grow and Marxist ideas become widely influential, the working class seeks a more authentic form of democratic representation.

However, history does not provide a wide range of choices to the constituent classes of the bourgeois order at turning points in their political development. When the petty bourgeoisie casts its weight in the balance, both the capitalists and the workers have been obliged to adjust themselves to constitutional democracy and to seek to utilize its institutions for an extended period to further their own class objectives. Thus the stability and longevity of the bourgeois-democratic regimes have depended to a great degree upon the political disposition of the intermediate layers of capitalist society.

In *The Only Road for Germany,* written in 1932 just before Hitler came to power, Leon Trotsky set forth the dialectical development of the relationships among the big bourgeoisie, the petty bourgeoisie and the proletariat in connection with the rise and decline of democracy. He observed that the political evolution of the petty bourgeoisie in capitalist history has passed through three broad stages. ". . . at the dawn of capitalist development when the bourgeoisie required revolutionary methods to solve its tasks; in the period of bloom and maturity of the capitalist regime, when the bourgeoisie endowed its domination with orderly, pacific, conservative, democratic forms; finally, at the decline of capitalism when the bourgeoisie is forced to resort to methods of civil war against the proletariat to protect its right of exploitation.

"The political programs characteristic of these three stages: *Jacobinism,* reformist *democracy* (social democracy included) and *fascism* are basically programs of petty-bourgeois currents," he wrote. "This fact alone, more than anything else, shows of what tremendous, rather, of what decisive, importance the self-determination of the petty-bourgeois masses of the people is for the whole fate of bourgeois society." 2

By its plebeian methods, the radical petty bourgeoisie enabled the liberal bourgeoisie to dispose of feudal, monarchical and ecclesiastical power in the period of its rise. The acquiescence of the petty bourgeoisie was the main adhesive holding parliamentary democracy together and keeping the capitalists and workers from a direct measuring of their independent strength.

However, in times of social and economic stress, the exasperated petty bourgeoisie can be transformed from a shock absorber into an intensifier of social frictions. Then its feverish attitudes can introduce extreme instability into the democratic order.

The most serene period of bourgeois democracy was bound up with the vigorous flourishing of world capitalism which lasted until the First World War and the Russian Revolution. The weakening of its supports has coincided with the evaporation of confidence in bourgeois authority and the intensification of class conflict rooted in the economic development of the system. Whereas competitive capitalism and the alignment of class forces within it fostered the expansion of democracy in

the richest countries, the advent of the monopolist stage has
led to its contraction and corroded the symbiosis of capitalism
with democracy that was established at an earlier stage.

The democratic forces were strongest under competitive capitalist conditions. This is the kernel of truth in the contention
that democracy flourishes best under free enterprise. The predominance of small proprietors in the towns and villages provided a broad social base and propitious political atmosphere
for petty-bourgeois democracy.

By the turn of the twentieth century, small-scale production
had given way to large-scale production in the industrialized
countries. The giant banks, corporations, insurance companies
and trusts dominated the economy and controlled the bourgeois
parties. The capitalist aggregations of the major powers vied
for mastery of the world market, areas of foreign investment,
seizure of colonies, spheres of influence and sources of raw
materials. As the monopolists struggled by all means at their
command to eliminate their rivals on the world arena and
crush their competitors at home, their imperialism trampled
upon the democratic rights of subject nations, large and small,
and chipped away at democracy within their own borders.

Capitalism began to decline as a world system as its units
sought to keep the immense social productive forces created
by modern science and technology pent up within the confines
of the nation-state and the framework of private property. The
ungovernable periodic outbursts of imperialist war were proof
of the dangers and difficulties of this impossible endeavor.
These interimperialist conflicts signalized the convulsive efforts
of the contending states to change the balance of forces and
the distribution of wealth and resources to their advantage at
the expense of their rivals. They were not only thoroughly
reactionary in their aims but also inimical to democracy. The
preparations for wars and the waging of them strengthened the
forces of militarism and imperialism in the aggressor and belligerent countries. Monopolistic capitalism, wrote Lenin, meant
"reaction all along the line."

A representative democracy is alien to the economic tendencies
of corporate capitalism. The advent of monopoly rule not only
halts the extension of new freedoms but also brings about the
contraction of already acquired rights of the people. Imperialism accentuates the contradiction, which existed from the first,
between the coexistence of the power, profiteering and property
of the capitalist rulers and political democracy. It inescapably
fosters antidemocratic forces and trends because the heightened

centralization of command, required by the operations of big business in both production and political life, conflicts with the dispersion of power among the voters and parties on which the parliamentary system rests.

This underlying incompatibility has not been made visible all at once. As a rule, political developments do not keep step with economic changes but limp on crutches behind them. It has taken decades for the antidemocratic essence of imperialism to manifest itself in full panoply. In fact, this tendency has come into plain sight at very variable rates and measures in different countries since 1914.

The turning point in the political evolution of bourgeois democracy in the advanced capitalisms came with the First World War. Its decay has passed through three stages since and is by no means near its end.

In the preliminary period from 1914 to 1929, Germany, Austria-Hungary and Russia, the three great defeated European states with monarchs at their head that had not previously gone through a bourgeois-democratic transformation, were shaken by revolutionary convulsions. These had very different results. After an abortive proletarian uprising, imperial Germany gave birth to the rickety Weimar Republic. Austria-Hungary followed suit after 1919. On the other hand, the first workers' state was established in the Soviet Union. In the camp of the victors, Italy's parliamentary regime crowned with a monarchy was overturned by Mussolini's brownshirts in 1922.

Thus the postwar history of the European continent displayed all three main variants in the spectrum of political options open to its peoples: on the extreme right, the fascist dictatorship of big capital; in the center, brittle parliamentary regimes torn by class strife; and on the left, a workers' state produced by the socialist revolution.

The 1929 world economic crisis of capitalism opened a second stage in the deterioration of bourgeois democracy. The political life of the 1930s was overshadowed by the conquests of fascism, which spread like a black stain over Europe and obliterated democracy in Germany, Austria-Hungary and Spain. This posed the gravest threat to democratic liberalism in its entire career. For a while it looked as though classical bourgeois democracy was on its last legs in the original homelands of capitalism.

Although parliamentary democracy was salvaged, refurbished and given a new lease on life in the next decades, the attacks did disclose its fragility and mortality. As subsequent chapters will set forth, the same set of international factors which led to the strangling of parliamentary democracy in the most vulnerable capitalisms simultaneously facilitated the crushing of Soviet democracy by the Stalinist bureaucracy in the isolated USSR. These symmetrical political developments were terrible punishments inflicted upon mankind for the failure of the workers to take power in the industrial countries.

While Hitlerism rode like a steamroller over the remaining democracies on the European continent, democratic institutions were damaged to one or another degree in all the anti-Axis belligerents during the Second World War. Besieged England under Churchill was governed by a Tory-Labour coalition cabinet in a national union which by agreement suspended parliamentary elections while the war against Germany lasted.

Just as President Wilson proclaimed that the First World War was waged to save the world for democracy, so his successor Roosevelt announced that the Allies were fighting to protect "the four freedoms." The defeat of the Axis was going to assure the future of democracy for all. Indeed, the most barbarous form of capitalist domination was crushed and democracy restored in Western Europe. This came about less through the will of the imperialist victors than through the resurgence of the working class, which was stopped short of revolution but managed to regain some of its rights, organizations and positions, snatched away by the fascists.

Except for the Iberian Peninsula, where Spain and Portugal kept the black banner aloft, the debacle of its German and Italian embodiments has discredited fascism for decades on the European continent. With the aid of American arms and money and the collusion of the Social Democratic and Communist parties, parliamentary democracy was rehabilitated and given a reprieve.

Nevertheless, all has not been well with bourgeois democracy. It has been unable to regain the robust health it enjoyed before 1914. If the fascist menace has been removed for the time being, the weaker parliamentary regimes have had to grapple with the potential prospect of socialist revolution to the left or the danger of replacement by "the strong state." The postwar history of France is a graphic illustration of this instability.

The takeovers of the more coercive ruling-class agents following the collapse of the democratic order show that the capitalists can ensure their hegemony by very different political methods in different situations. The maintenance of a democratic regime requires a prosperous economy, a docile working class, a more or less contented petty bourgeoisie and a successful foreign policy. It can be placed in jeopardy in the absence of any one or more of these decisive factors.

The state power of the bourgeoisie can survive without the familiar attributes of the parliamentary game: party contests, elections, congressional debates, etc. In the showdown its supremacy can be maintained by its entrenched bureaucratic apparatus, the police, army, and stock exchange and by its ownership of the means of production, dispensing with democratic institutions and practices.

To be sure, the change from one form of rule to another is fraught with peril for the possessing classes, since the political upheaval risks calling forth a revolutionary response from the workers. But a beleaguered bourgeoisie in an otherwise insoluble predicament can be impelled to try and navigate the dangerous passage from parliamentarism to more forcible forms of rule.

The precarious state of a parliamentary regime is the mark of a revolutionary situation where the conquest of power by the workers and fascist reaction are counterposed as the polar prospects of political development. Spain in the 1930s provided a clear example of this choice.

On April 14, 1931, over a year after the downfall of King Alfonso, a republic was proclaimed. This feeble regime failed to satisfy a single one of the demands of the masses. It lurched through a liberal honeymoon from 1931 to 1933, a turn to the right from 1933 to 1935 and then a new radicalization, culminating in the election victory of the People's Front in 1936.

The showdown was precipitated by the refusal of the possessing classes to accede to the verdict of the polls. Their generals, shielded by the Popular Front government, launched a coup d'etat that sought to check the offensive of the masses, provoking the civil war. The workers spontaneously rose up against the military conspirators in every industrial center, took over the barracks and factories, armed themselves and started to produce under the control of their committees. Peasants and agricultural workers took similar revolutionary steps.

This promising and powerful thrust toward the conquest of power by the workers was not just suppressed by the military might of the Spanish fascists and their German and Italian backers and starved out by the blockade by Blum's Popular Front government in France. It was throttled from within by the false and cowardly line of the workers' parties that subordinated themselves to the liberal bourgeoisie in the republican camp. This coalition in defense of private property refused to give land to the peasants or freedom to the Moroccans or to ratify the proletarian possession of the means of production.

These counterrevolutionary policies of the Popular Front were fatal to democracy and socialism alike. By depriving the workers of their gains and stifling their socialist aspirations, the republic proved incapable of smashing the fascists or saving constitutional democracy. The Spanish experience demonstrated that, when the chips are down, the struggle for revolutionary socialism is the only realistic and viable alternative to capitalist despotism.

The same lessons have been driven home by the infirmities of parliamentary democracy after the Second World War, despite the prolonged economic boom and the passivity of the working class. The tendency to augment the executive power of the heads of the capitalist state at the expense of the prerogatives of parliamentary bodies and the rights of the electorate has gained strength in virtually all the advanced capitalisms from West Germany to the United States. This is an irrepressible outgrowth of the overwhelming influence exerted upon the government by big business.

Alarmed by the conduct of the White House in the Vietnam war, Chairman Fulbright of the Senate Foreign Relations Committee warned in 1969 that the United States is "already a long way toward becoming an elective dictatorship." He noted that the constitutional system was being eroded in all the Western parliamentary democracies as the centralization of power in the executive continually increases. A report by his committee on April 16, 1969, stated that the U. S. president "now exercises something approaching absolute power over the life or death of every living American — to say nothing of millions of other people all over the world." It warned that, in consequence, the American people are threatened with "tyranny or disaster."

Big business feels increasingly hampered in conducting its affairs within the limits of parliamentary democracy and is striving to step over or cast off its constraints. This course involves whittling down the democratic rights of the people and ultimately dispensing altogether with parliamentary institutions.

The big bourgeoisie, a small and superprivileged minority, rarely governs in its own name. It must have recourse to one or another form of indirect rule in which its actual domination is disguised and carried out by intermediary agencies. Parliamentary democracy, based upon the mandate of the citizens, periodically renewed or revised by national elections, is one such means. When this type of rule can no longer guarantee its hegemony and property, the capitalists will jettison the norms of constitutional democracy and go over to more authoritarian forms of governance.

The democratic order is placed in jeopardy when the reformist parties become bogged down in hopeless difficulties, are manifestly impotent to cope with the most urgent problems and appear to be leading the nation to disaster. The extreme restlessness of the masses prevents the parliamentarians from mitigating class collisions as the country heads towards a state of civil war.

The turmoil incites each of the classes to search for a new political road to defend its welfare and save itself. National political activity undergoes a radical reorientation. The contending forces tend to bypass the regular parliamentary channels, which play a more and more recessive and auxiliary role. The axis of the class struggle shifts to the streets, the neighborhoods, the factories and workplaces, where it asserts itself in a violent and undisguised manner.

The capsizing of the class equilibrium upon which the parliamentary regime reposes brings about a prerevolutionary situation in which the question of power is sharply posed. Each section of society musters the resources and mobilizes the forces at its disposal to settle this all-important issue in its favor. The petty bourgeoisie cannot play an independent role. It can either cast about for some demagogic savior in the service of capitalism to rescue itself from ruin — or it can look for a way out through the leadership offered by the working class.

When parliament can no longer regulate class relations, the further political destiny of the nation has to be decided by extraconstitutional means and methods, of a revolutionary or counterrevolutionary character. Either the insurgent working class will go forward with its allies to overthrow capitalist power and property and set up a workers' democracy — or else in the interests of self-preservation, the capitalists will proceed through one way or another to scuttle democracy and install their dictatorship in its stead.

The 1967 coup of the colonels' junta in Greece is the latest instance of the suppression of constitutional democracy by military dictatorship in "the free world." It has been calculated that today junta governments outnumber those where some kind of elective democracy is in force.

This fundamental alternative has confronted one democratic capitalism after another throughout Western Europe since Mussolini seized power in 1922. Because of the defaults of the socialist-reformist, Stalinist and anarchist leaderships of the workers' organizations, they have invariably ended in perpetuating the supremacy of the capitalist class. Yet these situations continue to recur, as they did in France in May 1958 and then again in May-June 1968.

There is a deeper meaning to these recurrent upsets of parliamentary democracy. They signify that on a broad historical scale the reign of bourgeois democracy has passed its zenith. Just as the power of absolute monarchy drew to a close as the bourgeoisie ascended, so the rise of the working class, with the challenge it presents to capitalist domination, portends the decline of parliamentary democracy.

That was from the outset a highly contradictory type of government, combining the socioeconomic domination of the capitalist exploiters with the forms and appurtenances of popular representation. The contradiction could be muffled so long as class relations remained stabilized. But whenever class conflicts are exacerbated in the imperialist epoch, the basic choice more and more comes down to victory for the proletarian revolution or some sort of capitalist reaction.

There are three reactionary variants: Bonapartism, military dictatorship and fascism. While all involve the scuttling of parliamentary power, each rests upon a different combination of social forces and represents differing degrees of the displacement and destruction of democracy.

9

BONAPARTISM, MILITARY

DICTATORSHIP AND FASCISM

The movement to the right, away from the parliamentary regime, can assume diverse forms. These reactionary replacements range from Bonapartism through unconcealed military dictatorship to fascism. The latter is the most terroristic system of monopoly-capitalist domination.

Which of these methods of rule may be adopted depends upon the actual circumstances in the unfolding of the class struggle and the specific distribution of power among the contending forces. Parliamentary government, with its constitutional guarantees, democratically elected majorities, contesting factions and periodic party campaigns, becomes a liability to big capital when the middle classes are radicalized, the workers take the offensive and the country appears to be slipping out of its control.

In the drive undertaken against an aging parliamentarism, the big bourgeoisie seeks to revert to the more carefree and unhampered power it wielded when parliament was young. Parliament did not come into being, as many believe, to provide adequate national representation for the masses, but rather primarily to regulate the affairs of the propertied classes and adjudicate the claims of the diverse elements among the ruling order. In England it was originally monopolized by the landed aristocracy. James Mill, writing in the *Westminster Review* in 1834, estimated that the House of Commons was effectively chosen by some two hundred families.

The execution of its main function of serving the rich encountered growing difficulties as the franchise broadened and gave the lower orders greater representation and influence in the national assemblies through the nineteenth and twentieth centuries. From an institution which arbitrated the divergences

within the ruling circles, parliament tended to become transformed into an arena for conciliating the lower classes.

The contradiction between these two functions of parliament
grew still more acute as universal suffrage and the growth of
the labor movement put an increasing number of deputies of
the working-class parties into parliamentary seats. Big capital had multiple means at its disposal to tame and bridle
labor's political representatives: flattery, bribery, lucrative posts
and sinecures, absorption into the upper crust, etc.

Speaking from long personal experience in English politics,
Aneurin Bevan described in his book *In Place of Fear* how
"the atmosphere of Parliament, its physical arrangements, its
procedure, its semi-ecclesiastical ritual" are calculated to over-
awe susceptible Labour M. P.s and bring them to their knees
in prostration before the past and the establishment. "Parliamentary procedure neglects nothing which might soften the
acerbities of his class feelings," he pointed out. "In one sense
the House of Commons is the most unrepresentative of representative assemblies. It is an elaborate conspiracy to prevent the real clash of opinion which exists outside from find-
ing an appropriate echo within its walls. It is a social shock
absorber placed between privilege and the pressure of popular discontent."[1] Any maverick who threatened to get too far
out of line or too militantly defended the welfare of the workers was liable to be red-baited, witch-hunted and even accused
of treason.

However, when social tensions tighten to the breaking point,
parliament is less and less able either to settle the disputes
at the top or to act as a buffer between the power of property
and the wrath of the masses. General disappointment with
its performance plunges bourgeois parliamentarism together
with its parties into a period of acute crisis. The resolutely
reactionary forces in the ruling class thereupon conspire to
get out of their bind by shunting parliament aside and going over to a more exclusive method of rule.

The moneyed men are propelled in an antiparliamentary
direction by still another powerful factor. Under the domination of monopoly capital, the actual centers of economic and
political decision shift away from the chambers and corridors
of parliament. The executives of the corporations, banks, insurance companies and huge financial groups negotiate face
to face with the most highly placed government officials and
military chiefs on the matters of vital concern to them in domestic and foreign affairs. Private consultations of this kind

go on continually in clubs, restaurants, residences and resorts. Lobbying conveys the wishes and advice of the wealthy and powerful to their compliant political henchmen.

Such informal pressures have acquired incomparably greater importance as the corporate complexes have taken over direction of the national economy and government intervention in economic life has swollen to gigantic proportions. In the competitive race it has become a matter of survival for the mammoth corporations to know what the administration intends to do and to ensure that its decisions help and do not harm their corporate interests. Billions can be at stake in the drafting of a tax law, a clause of the military budget or a fiscal change.

As the parliamentary mechanism becomes more unreliable, big business casts about for some other political instrumentality which can guard its material interests better than a broken-down parliamentary system. The question then comes down to this: What sort of regime can do the job?

Bonapartism

The first step away from a decrepit parliamentarism is Bonapartism. This is a bureaucratic-military dictatorship born of a deep-going but incompletely resolved confrontation of openly antagonistic class forces.

Unlike the parliamentary order which bases itself upon a (presumably) democratically elected majority and its party representation, the main props of a Bonapartist type of regime are to be found in the police, the army and the administrative apparatus.

Bonapartism carries to an extreme the concentration of power in the head of the state already discernible in the contemporary imperialist democracies. All important policy decisions are centralized in a single individual equipped with extraordinary emergency powers. He speaks and acts not as the servant of parliament, like the premier, but in his own right as "the man of destiny" who has been called upon to rescue the nation in its hour of mortal peril.

Whether the "man on horseback" usurps authority through extraparliamentary force or under a legal cover, he exercises it by decree. His regime need not immediately dismantle or wholly discard parliamentary institutions or parties; it renders them powerless. These may be permitted to survive, provided they play merely supernumerary and decorative roles. Whether they rubber-stamp or resist the mandates from on high, these prevail as the law of the land.

The dictator may pay a hypocritical homage to the tradition of popular consent by means of occasional plebiscites in which the people are asked to endorse some proposal desired by the government. But this purely formal consultation is usually carried out in an atmosphere of intimidation wherein the propagandists of the ruling clique predict the direst consequences unless the proposition is confirmed.

The Bonapartist regime makes a big show of total independence from special interests. Its head invariably claims to be above the brawling party factions which have misruled the nation and led it to the brink of ruin, from which he has providentially snatched it in time. He parades as the anointed custodian of the eternal values, the true spirit of the people who have been victimized by selfish warring cliques or threatened by alien and subversive mischief-makers.

Actually, the "man of iron" is mandated to defend the social interests of the magnates of capital by blunting the class conflicts which created the opportunity for his despotism. He can exact a heavy price from the property owners for performing these salutary services. He demands a larger percentage of the emoluments of office for his entourage and retinue of followers than a more docile subordinate would be entitled to. Though the big bourgeoisie may clench its teeth at the overhead cost of the Bonapartist experiment, it prefers to pay up lest worse befall it.

Despite its show of force, Bonapartism is flawed by serious weaknesses from birth. The extraparliamentary personal dictatorship rests on a narrow social base. It need not be warmly supported by the agrarian or urban middle classes or be welcomed by any but the most backward workers. Its vigor is derived, not from any enthusiastic allegiance of the populace, but from the major agencies of coercion in the state, the military, the police and the bureaucracy. Since it takes power as the agency of a single faction of the possessing classes and not the capitalists in their entirety, the regime is subject to sniping and undermining by other competitors for first place. Having climbed to the heights by neutralizing the mutually antagonistic forces of the proletariat and the exploiters, Bonapartism can start to tumble once these irreconcilable camps overcome their paralysis and again come to grips with each other.

Regimes of the Bonapartist type have a long historical lineage in the Western world. Their embryonic appearance can be traced back to the tyrannies in the commercial city-states of ancient Greece. The tyrants took advantage of the turmoil of class conflicts to combat the kings, nobles and plutocrats, place themselves at the head of the commoners and take over the state. The regimes of these self-made autocrats, who were often heroes of the populace, were progressive in many respects.

These prototypes had one feature which all subsequent Bonapartisms shared. They had no traditional or constitutional legitimacy. The tyrant took power by force and held it by virtue of superior strength against all other claimants. This form of sovereignty was an intermediate and transitional formation in the political evolution of the Greek city-states. The tyrannies breached the rule of the aristocracies or oligarchies and paved the way for the democratic revolution of the middle classes, which proceeded in many cases to get rid of the tyranny itself.

Caesarism was the Roman precursor of Bonapartism. Julius Caesar, a man of patrician birth allied with the popular party, used his legions to overthrow the Roman Senate, destroy the republic and establish his dictatorship. This conquering general became sole master of the state in a slave society torn by seemingly interminable conflicts between the patricians and plebeians and cutthroat rivalries among the contestants for supremacy. He put an end to internecine warfare and inaugurated the long reign of the empire by suppressing these social and political commotions.

Since the French Revolution, that country has been the classic home of bourgeois Bonapartism. The "man on horseback" enters the scene, writes Trotsky, "in those moments of history when the sharp struggle of two camps raises the state power, so to speak, above the nation, and guarantees it, in appearance, a complete independence of classes — in reality, only the freedom necessary for a defense of the privileged."

The dictatorship of Napoleon the First fulfilled these requirements. The little Corsican concentrated supreme power in his hands by overthrowing the Directory through the coup d'etat of the eighteenth of Brumaire (November 9), 1799, during the recession of the French Revolution. As first consul and emperor, he waged war and directed the affairs of state with a firm hand in his own name — and to the greater glory of the French bourgeoisie.

The legend of his triumphs helped make his far less talented nephew president and then emperor after the bourgeoisie had crushed the insurgent masses in the Revolution of 1848. Napoleon the Little outmaneuvered the representatives of the royalists, the bourgeois republicans and the democratic petty bourgeoisie at odds with one another, and overturned the constitutional republic with the aid of the army, police and state apparatus and the support of the reactionary countryside. The industrial bourgeoisie in particular saluted the coup of December 2, 1851, which dissolved the Legislative National Assembly and sealed Napoleon's monopoly of executive power. The second Bonaparte wrested political power from the bourgeoisie only to protect them against the masses. Under the Second Empire, their economic affairs prospered exceedingly — until the top-heavy edifice collapsed in 1870 as the result of defeat in the Franco-Prussian War.

The role of a Bonapartist regime in the epoch of imperialism and the decline of capitalism is no different from that in the period of its rise. It intervenes to head off a potential state of civil war in a divided nation by referring all disputed issues to a supreme arbiter invested with exorbitant power. The master of destiny seeks to use his authority to reduce social tensions and stabilize class relations for the benefit of the threatened property owners.

The longevity of Bonapartist rule depends upon the measure of success attained in these efforts. Whether it be of brief or protracted duration, contemporary Bonapartism, as a regime of crisis, has perforce a transitional character. This was plainly manifested in the political evolution of Germany between the disintegration of the Weimar Republic and Hitler's triumph. The interim Bonapartist governments of Bruening, von Papen and Schleicher had a short life and fell quickly.

The Achilles' heel of Bonapartism lies in its lack of a broad mass base. Since it does not represent a significant social force, it is precariously poised and highly vulnerable to the shocks of setbacks at home or abroad. It provides a halfhearted solution to the crisis of the bourgeois order, because it does not carry through the civil war of big capital against the workers or the demolition of democracy to the very end. It can come to grief when the class antagonisms that it temporarily but not totally annuls flare up anew.

After the Second World War, a kindred version of Bonapartism has come forward in certain European countries in the shape of "the strong state." The terrible discrediting of fascism, the prolonged economic boom and the wariness of the workers made it virtually impossible for big capital to bring the forces of fascism back on the scene. Faced with grave civil convulsions, neocapitalism has arrived at the alternative political solution of "the strong government" which elevates the executive power above parliament. It has not hesitated to abrogate the constitutional liberties of its citizens and suspend parliamentary institutions in order to impose an emergency power upon the nation.

Gaullism, which displaced the Fourth Republic in 1958, has been a characteristic case of this type of development. The political solution of the Fifth Republic was improvised by French capital to find its way out of the crisis caused by the Algerian war and the danger of a military coup from the extreme right. General de Gaulle bypassed parliament, which surrendered most of its powers. He ruled largely by decree for eleven years, until he was sent into retirement as a belated consequence of the unparalleled upheaval of the May-June 1968 general strike. Whatever happens to Pompidou's substitute Gaullism, parliamentary democracy in that country has been but a shadow of its old self since the early 1930s.

Military Dictatorship

A Bonapartist government may contain elements of a military despotism and be barely distinguishable from it in many respects. As the example of General de Gaulle shows, the prestige of an army career and the power of military command can be very helpful to any aspirant for Bonapartism. But it is not indispensable. A Bonapartist regime may have a civilian at its head, just as a democratic republic can elect a general like Eisenhower to be president. Napoleon the Little had no military victories to boast of, although he could not have usurped power without the army. In Germany, Bruening and von Papen were civil servants, and although Schleicher was a general, he did not come to power through a coup d'etat.

A standing army, and especially its officer caste, has been an ever-present danger to any kind of democracy through the ages. The more privileges it has, the more separated its personnel are from the people, the closer its ties with the ruling class — the more menacing it is.

Military men are indoctrinated with the idea that the defense of the fatherland and the security of the nation depend in the last resort upon them. The armed forces are put on the alert and summoned in all emergencies, foreign and domestic. Thus its commanders are easily persuaded that they should become rulers in their own right. This conviction becomes almost irresistible whenever they feel that the civilian politicians are making a mess of things and the workers may threaten to rise up.

At that juncture, either on their own initiative or spurred by one or another faction of big capital and the landed proprietors, the generals, colonels and even lower officers can plot to set their forces into motion, chase the civilian ministers and presidents out of office and take charge of the government.

The success of their coup depends largely upon what kind of reaction it meets from the workers and their leaders. They are the sole force strong enough and strategically well enough placed to frustrate these designs. Thus the German workers blocked the putsch of General Kapp in 1919 by means of a general strike. Failing such vigorous counteraction by the working masses, the odds favor the militarists. The reformist parliamentary leaders usually put up little, if any, resistance of their own, since they fear to call upon the masses to act or arm themselves in a direct struggle to defend democracy.

Latin America is the classic continent of military takeovers. During the single decade of the 1960s, nine countries there, including the two largest, Brazil and Argentina, fell under direct military rule. In 1969 Bolivia had its 185th coup in 144 years of independence, when General Ovando ousted and exiled President Siles; it experienced two more the following year.

The instability of constitutional government and the necessity for constant intervention by the military "gorillas" on that continent can be attributed to the situation of a weak, belated and divided bourgeoisie in a poorly developed economy, caught between the domination of foreign capital and the desperate misery of the workers and peasants, without the cushion of a sizable middle class to attenuate class antagonisms.

Even where it has not directly encouraged the militarists, finance capital readily accommodates itself to a dictatorship of the army which is, after all, the ultimate prop of its domination, even under parliamentary democracy. However, regardless of the social demagogy of its propagandists, the military state based on naked coercion is so widely unpopular and palpably reactionary that its service to the ruling class is necessarily limited and temporary. A contemporary case in point is the government of the colonels in Greece, which in 1967 threw out parliament and later forced out the king. This dictatorship of mediocrities and torturers is so hated and isolated in the nation and the world that it is more of a liability than an asset to the Greek capitalists and their NATO patrons in Washington.

Recognizing the limitations of military rule, the bourgeoisie often tries to give the government some civilian cover or convince the generals to hold elections and go back to constitutional forms. If they refuse and hang on to the end, the downfall of a military dictatorship can be a period of extreme emergency for the ruling class, since it reopens the problem of power and offers the workers and their leadership another chance to come forward and redirect the fate of the nation.

Fascism

Bonapartist and military regimes have a major shortcoming from the standpoint of subduing the class struggle in a given country. Military dictatorships can be as ferocious as fascist ones, as the massacre of 500,000 Communists and oppositionists by the Suharto regime in Indonesia illustrates. But they do not necessarily carry the suppression of oppositional forces through to the very end. They may leave standing certain party organizations, parliamentary bodies and constitutional liberties belonging to bourgeois democracy, as well as trade unions and other organizations which are the nurseries of proletarian democracy. These may subsequently serve as springboards for the revival of mass actions and a comeback of the labor movement.

Unlike other forms of antidemocratic rule, which represent differing degrees of bourgeois reaction, fascism spearheads a political counterrevolution. It thoroughly extirpates all institutions of both bourgeois and proletarian democracy and all independent forces. It binds the masses hand and foot, gags them, atomizes the working class and thrusts the nation into a totalitarian straitjacket.

If parliamentarism is the most characteristic political product of the rise of capitalism, fascism is the distinctive outgrowth of the decomposition of bourgeois society in its monopolist phase. This is indicated by its generic name, derived from Mussolini's dictatorship, which took power in Italy in 1922 and lasted until July 1943. His blackshirt regime provided the model perfected by Hitler's National Socialism and Franco's tyranny in Spain.

A fascist formation is engendered by a state of intolerable social crisis in an advanced capitalism which shakes up all classes and threatens the customary norms of bourgeois domination. The relations of such a movement to big business are ambiguous and complex and have often led to one-sided and incorrect conclusions.

When fascism entered the political arena and proclaimed its will to power in Italy and Germany, it was not welcomed or supported by all sections of the capitalist class. Indeed, the capitalists in general would prefer, if possible, to maintain the appearance of a more representative and less repressive regime. Fascism is a last desperate resort for them.

Initially the fascist movements were subsidized largely by the magnates of heavy industry in iron, steel and mining, while the makers of consumer goods in light industry retained more liberal inclinations and affiliations. These differences in political outlook had economic roots. The enterprises engaged in heavy industry have a far greater investment in fixed capital (plants, machinery, real estate, etc.) and consequently much heavier overhead charges than those producing for the consumer market. Their operations are also subject to much wider fluctuations. In periods of depression, these industrialists have to cut costs through massive layoffs and by slashing wages and social gains to the bone. The resistance of the workers and their organizations to these attacks upon their living standards impels the industrialists to seek more drastic ways and means of removing these barriers to their further exploitation.

Such capitalist magnates encourage the fascists out of governmental considerations as well as economic motives. The prosperity of the heavy industries relies upon a steady flow of military orders from the state. If the government or parliament is controlled by political forces reluctant to follow an aggressive foreign policy, which holds armaments down to low levels, the industrialists and their bankers are pressed to get rid of these obstructions once and for all.

However, in its origins and makeup, fascism is much more than a hireling of big business. Fascism differs in one decisively important respect from other political expressions of reaction. It is a mass movement based upon the activity of a particular social force, the dispossessed and despairing petty bourgeoisie. Unlike Bonapartist and military dictatorships which are imposed from above, the fascist movement surges up from below. It has a plebeian composition, impetus and leadership.

Fascism attracts to its banner the most discontented elements from the battered and bruised intermediate layers of bourgeois society. Its following embraces shopkeepers, professionals, white-collar workers, small artisans and functionaries in the cities and towns, and small landholders in the countryside. It recruits its shock troops from the lumpenproletariat, the unemployed and the most demoralized and backward toilers. It can make strong appeals to jingoistic war veterans who feel out of place and unrewarded in civilian life, to misled youth and to alarmed pensioners beset by inflation and insecurity.

The capitalists cannot smash the workers and shatter the parliamentary system by themselves alone. They require the services of a far more formidable organized mass force and popular political movement to act as a battering ram. They find this agency in fascism. Through collusion with its top leadership, often unbeknownst to the ranks, they take hold of this seething social movement, which demands radical changes and has a momentum and aims of its own, and ultimately bend it to their purposes.

These two opposing characteristics of fascism — a popular base and a plutocratic purpose — are inextricably intertwined. This duality endows the formation with a two-faced demagogic nature. It moves on two planes at one and the same time, presenting itself as one thing, a radical plebeian movement, while acting as quite another, a tool of the big bourgeoisie against the workers. Fascist gangs can be strikebreakers and bodyguards for the bosses, as Mussolini's blackshirts were in their early days, while their publicists rave against the plutocracy.

In contrast to Marxism and even bourgeois democracy, fascism has no systematic theory. What is left of the social and political doctrines of the European fascists twenty-five years after their shipwreck? The heterogeneity of its social base and composition, the duplicity of its aims, the hodgepodge of its ideas, the confusion of its feelings and the unmitigated opportunism of its leadership and program forbid the development of any consistent doctrinal justification for its existence. Its organizers and patrons are intent on capturing power through any expedients and alliances. They will unscrupulously latch on to anything that will promote that end.

Mussolini, who, as an ex-socialist, had a somewhat greater bent for theorizing than Hitler or Franco, spoke frankly of "the pragmatic veins in Fascism." He and his blackshirts seized power in 1922 without benefit of any ideology other than unabashed nationalism. After consolidating his supremacy, he felt a need for some rationale as a fig leaf for his naked personal dictatorship on behalf of the Italian capitalists and landowners. Il Duce decided in 1929 that fascism must "provide itself with a body of doctrine." He accordingly instructed his official philosopher, Giovanni Gentile, to have one ready in two months "between now and the National Congress of the party."

Hitlerism had more power but fewer philosophical pretensions than its Italian precursor. In the domain of ideology, the Nazis made do with a nationalistic and racial mysticism buttressed by suppression of all independent and critical currents of thought from liberalism to Marxism.

In place of any thought-out philosophy, fascism exploits whatever is obscurantist, backward and reactionary in the traditions, customs and psyches of the masses: racism, superstition, antisemitism, xenophobia, ultrachauvinism, mysticism, messianism, etc. The fascist hordes are animated and held together, not by reasoned convictions, but by furious anger against the status quo and its upholders and by mystical trust in the supreme leader. The words of Il Duce, der Fuehrer and the Generalissimo are law and must be blindly believed and obeyed. The leader is always right and any doubt of his omniscience is impermissible. The fascists enforce monolithism within their ranks before they clamp it on the state and nation.

The wrath of the discontented is directed against a motley group of scapegoats from bloodsucking bankers to Jews, foreigners, liberals, Marxists and Communists. Among the mainsprings of fascism is the illusion of the petty bourgeoisie that it is out to combat big business. In rallying its adherents on the road to power, fascism caters to the anticapitalist sentiments of the masses. Its propagandists rage against "the fat, corrupt bourgeois, slack, sloppy and accommodating." Many of its followers are sincerely duped by this ranting. But the imprecations against the rich are as hollow as the fascist protestations of solicitude for the workers and occasional offers of support to the trade unions.

Leon Trotsky explained this paradoxical process in *Whither France?*, which he wrote in 1934 at the onset of the antiparliamentary offensive in that country: "The despairing petty bourgeoisie sees in Fascism, above all, a fighting force against big capital, and believes that, unlike the working-class parties which deal only in words, Fascism will use force to establish more 'justice.'. . . The petty bourgeoisie is economically dependent and politically atomized. That is why it cannot conduct an independent policy. It needs a 'leader' who inspires it with confidence. The individual or collective leadership, i. e., a personage or party, can be given to it by one or the other of the fundamental classes — either the big bourgeoisie or the proletariat. Fascism unites and arms the scattered masses. Out of human dust it organizes combat detachments. It thus gives the petty bourgeoisie the illusion of being an independent force. It begins to imagine that it will really command the state. It is not surprising that these illusions and hopes turn the head of the petty bourgeoisie!" 2

What gives fascism its big opportunity is not primarily its ideas or program, its mass strength, its pugnacity or the behind-the-scenes backing of big business. It is above all the default of the proletariat and its organizations. It is a historical law, Trotsky observed in the last article of his life, that "fascism was able to conquer only in those countries where the conservative labor parties prevented the proletariat from utilizing the revolutionary situation and seizing power."

He gave this concise sketch of the background which enabled the fascists to conquer. "Both theoretical analysis as well as the rich historical experience of the last quarter of a century have demonstrated with equal force that fascism is each time the final link of a specific political cycle composed of the following: the gravest crisis of capitalist society; the growth of the radicalization of the working class; the growth of sympathy toward the working class and a yearning for change on the part of the rural and urban petty bourgeoisie; the extreme confusion of the big bourgeoisie; its cowardly and treacherous maneuvers aimed at avoiding the revolutionary climax; the exhaustion of the proletariat; growing confusion and indifference; the aggravation of the social crisis; the despair of the petty bourgeoisie, its yearnings for change; the collective neurosis of the petty bourgeoisie, its readiness to believe in miracles, its readiness for violent measures; the growth of hostility towards the proletariat, which has deceived its expectations. These are the premises for a swift formation of a fascist party and its victory." 3

Though the fascists have no fear of violence, their leaders prefer not to clash directly with the official repressive forces of the state. They maneuver to acquire power legally if possible. They succeeded in doing so in Italy and Germany with the complicity of liberal and conservative politicians alike. Mussolini was invited by King Victor Emmanuel and Hitler by President Hindenburg to form cabinets. Once the existing state authorities had turned over the reins of office to them, the fascists proceeded, with some delay under Mussolini but forthwith under Hitler, to suspend all parliamentary liberties, exterminate the workers' organizations and install their regime of undisguised terror.

Fascism makes a clean sweep of everything that stands in the way of its monopoly of power. The state flings its forces of repression first of all upon the working class as the main enemy. It imprisons and executes their leaders, outlaws their organizations and destroys their rights, pitilessly punishing the least resistance to repression. Distinctions among the diverse tendencies in the labor movement are disregarded, since the mission of fascism is nothing less than the subjugation of the entire working class, from the most moderate to the most revolutionary opinion.

While it treats Marxism as the greatest of evils and the spawn of the devil, fascism assails liberalism as corrupt and corrupting, impotent at home and abroad and fit only for the junk heap. It is almost as implacable an enemy of parliamentary democracy (liberalism) as it is of workers' democracy because it sees the former as the protector of the latter. The authoritarian state it sets out to construct allows no room for either.

Many liberals and reformists failed to reckon with the totalitarian exclusiveness of fascism. They tried to come to terms with its leaders, who cast them contemptuously aside and crushed them in short order. The fascists were interested not in parliamentary combinations but in doing away with parliamentarism entirely and erecting their despotism on its ruins. Social Democratic union leaders, like Leipart in Germany, likewise mistakenly believed and hoped they might save their posts and organizations through agreement with the fascists and collaboration with their government, as they had done with previous capitalist regimes.

The fascist dictatorship insists on expelling the old political servitors of the bourgeoisie and concentrating all instruments of power in its own hands. Because of this political counter-revolution, it is widely believed that fascism abolished the power of capitalism. Nothing in the records of its Italian, German or Spanish varieties substantiates this view. While the plebeian parvenus expropriate the big bourgeoisie politically, they not only leave its property and possessions intact, nationalizing much less than many reformist regimes, but also institute economic, social and international policies which strengthen big capital and enable it to operate more profitably.

Though the fascist state regulates the economy, the big corporations continue to direct the state as they did under liberal auspices, but "by other means." The fascists restore total authority to the industrialists in the factories where the workers have been stripped of all defenses. They adopt an inflationary monetary policy and launch programs of public works and stepped-up arms expenditures which benefit big business. Their actions abroad are charted in accord with the imperialist ambitions of the magnates of capital.

Ironically, if the rich are the sole beneficiary of fascist policies, the lower middle classes become its victims as well as the workers. The most radical wing of the plebeians speedily discover this when they demand payment on the anticapitalist promises of their leaders. They are mercilessly put down when they plan a "second revolution" against the exploiters. Thus on June 30, 1934, on order from his financial backers, Hitler shot down his closest collaborators among the storm troopers, including their chief-of-staff Ernst Roehm, Gregor Strasser and others. Mussolini also had to purge his party several times of those troublesome partisans who urged and took drastic measures against the privileged.

Fascism tends to shed its plebeian features as it consolidates and exercises its power. Its state becomes transformed step by step into a bureaucratic military-police dictatorship of a Bonapartist type. This evolution was especially marked in the cases of Italian and Spanish fascism, which had longer life-spans than their more explosive German counterpart. The policies of the fascist state, which favor big capital over small business, the large landowners over the peasants and the chain stores over the small shopkeepers, sorely disappoint the hopes for improvement expected by the middle classes. The regime seeks an outlet for their frustration and aggression in a frenzied nationalism and an adventurist foreign policy that serves the objectives of the imperialists.

While fascism saved capitalism from the socialist revolution in Italy and Germany and Spain, it did so at tremendous cost to the working class and all humanity. The West German workers have still to recover from the demoralizing defeat they suffered. Yet it also proved costly to the European bourgeoisie itself. Within less than a decade, the expansionist aims of German imperialism collided with the resistance of France and England and precipitated the Second World War. After its first round of victories, the Axis powers succumbed one after the other to the hammer blows of the Allied armies and their own loss of morale. Mussolini was the first to go; he was strung up by his heels. Then Hitler took poison in the smoking ruins of Berlin. Franco, who acquired power with their help, hung on long after their end, thanks to the utter exhaustion of the revolutionary forces in Spain and the aid forthcoming from Washington.

The whole historical setting of the period following the Second World War has been extremely unfavorable for the fostering of fascist tendencies. After the horrible consequences of the first experiments with this bloodletting remedy for social revolution, even big capital is wary of its resurrection. This does not mean that fascism cannot revive in the advanced industrial countries, no matter how democratic their traditions. The causes of its development are deeply embedded in the decay of monopoly capitalism and have not been removed with the deaths of Il Duce and der Fuehrer. Its germs circulate within the capitalist organism and can have a malignant growth in the event that capitalism again experiences a mortal crisis.

Although every fascist formation has pronounced national peculiarities, it is not simply a localized European but an international tendency. The same factors that brought fascism to the fore in Europe between the First and Second World Wars can reproduce this ferocious political phenomenon.

It is impossible to foretell what the specific circumstances of its recurrence would be. But should fascism again take over any major capitalist power, it would very likely have from the first the most menacing belligerence. In addition to the workers' organizations and socialist forces within its own domain, it would take as its targets the workers' states arrayed against imperialism. Hitler's anti-Communism and invasion of the Soviet Union prefigure the dynamic of any future fascist dictatorship.

The grim experience of the first large-scale coming of fascism teaches that, in times of crisis, the workers must go ahead to win power in struggle against the capitalists for socialism first — or else the fascists will, with the aid of big business and the disillusioned middle classes, be lifted into the driver's seat, where their state can ride ruthlessly over the prostrate bodies of the working class.

It also teaches the folly of relying upon any alliance with the leaders of bourgeois liberalism to stop the fascists. Confronted with the offensive of ultrareaction, the liberals and reformists either prefer to conciliate and negotiate with the fascists or are powerless to combat them.

The working class has only one effective way to eradicate the sources of reaction, win over the intermediate sections of society, defeat the threat of fascism and prevent it from reemerging and conquering. That is by persevering in a strategy of revolutionary struggle leading to the overthrow of capitalism.

The various forms of antidemocratic rule in the era of imperialism are not separated by impassable partitions. The lines of demarcation between them are often blurred and one can in the course of time grow over into another. A "strong government" can readily give rise to Bonapartism. A Bonapartist regime can yield to a military dictatorship or bow before fascism, as happened in Germany in 1932-33.

The political history of France over the past forty years most strikingly illustrates what political transformations can be generated by the continuing crisis of bourgeois society. Since the early 1930s, this country has passed through a succession of upheavals in which the political structure has changed numerous times.

After the failure of an extreme right-wing coup in February 1934 and the downfall of Premier Daladier, the tottering parliamentary republic passed into the hands of the reactionary Doumergue government. In a sharp lurch to the left, it went over to a Popular Front coalition, coinciding with the massive factory occupations of the workers in 1936. Then its crippled parliamentarism underwent an abrupt shift to the right, culminating in the overturn of the Third Republic and the establishment of the Bonapartist Vichy regime of Petain after Germany occupied most of France. The Fourth Republic set up immediately after the war was replaced by de Gaulle's personal dictatorship in 1958 and the vicissitudes of the general's Fifth Republic have by no means been ended by his retirement.

Such sharp oscillations from one method of rule to another within the framework of private property must persist as the relations of class forces within each country and the external situation of the nation are altered and so long as no definitive settlement of accounts takes place between big capital and the working class.

What is decisive in determining the nature of a given government is not the listing of separate traits, any formal designation or abstract definition, but the actual alignment of class forces and the amount of liberties salvaged from the wreckage of liberal democracy. This has to be ascertained concretely in each case and at every turn in the evolution of the political regimes.

Although uninformed radicals and reckless ultralefts may put them all in the same sack, not all forms of bourgeois domination are the same. There are important differences between the democratic method of rule and its rivals — and there are significant differences among these latter. The exponents and leaders of the different forms of bourgeois rule can not only be in league against the working class but also enter into fierce competition with one another in the struggle for power. A vigilant revolutionary leadership must be aware of these cleavages so that its tactics may take full advantage of them.

While all the modes of bourgeois domination are arrayed against the interests of the proletariat and must be combated, some are more dangerous than others because they hold out

a greater immediate threat to the existing rights and organizations of the working class. Some offer wider latitude for
action and reaction by the masses. From this standpoint a
bourgeois democracy is preferable to any dictatorship — and
certain milder forms of Bonapartism retain better conditions
for the recuperation of lost ground by the workers than fascism,
as the relation of forces in Gaullist France demonstrated.

In the case of civil war, it is imperative to distinguish between
the camp of overt counterrevolution and any sections of the
bourgeoisie and petty bourgeoisie which actually take the field
to fight the fascists. It is permissible and may be imperative
to effect a practical alliance with such elements.

However, there are vitally important conditions attached to
such a united front. It has to be made without confusing the
political programs and aims of the different classes, without
entering any political coalition with the bourgeois liberals
which subordinates the class struggle to their stipulations and
restrictions, and without teaching the workers to trust in the
reliability of the temporary ally. The Spanish civil war was
lost and its chances of socialist revolution ruined precisely
because the workers' parties disregarded these conditions as
the price of maintaining a political bloc with the republican
liberals.

The most costly example of indiscriminately applying the
label of fascism to any type of bourgeois rule was furnished
by the false positions of the German Communists from 1930
to 1933. They not only characterized the prefascist governments
of Bruening, von Papen and Schleicher as fascist but even
placed the Social Democrats in the same category. This was in
line with Stalin's assertion that the Social Democrats were not
the antipode but the twin of fascism.

"Fascist dictatorship is in no way opposed in principle to
bourgeois democracy under whose cover the dictatorship of
finance capital also prevails," declared the resolution of the
German Communist Party Central Committee following the
Second Plenum of the Executive Committee of the Comintern
in May 1931. In many powerful polemics from 1929 to 1933,
Trotsky refuted this senseless refusal to recognize any differences between democracy and fascism or social democracy
and fascism.

Here are two passages from his pamphlet *What Next?*, written
in 1932: "A contradiction does exist between democracy and
fascism. It is not at all 'absolute,' or, putting it in the language
of Marxism, it doesn't at all denote the rule of two irreconcilable

classes. But it does denote different systems of the domination of one and the same class." [4]

"In order to try to find a way out, the bourgeoisie must absolutely rid itself of the pressure exerted by the workers' organizations; these have to be eliminated, destroyed, utterly crushed.

"At this juncture, the historic role of fascism begins. It sets on its feet those classes that are immediately above the proletariat and who are ever in dread of being forced down into its ranks; it organizes and militarizes them at the expense of finance capital, under the cover of the official government; and it directs them to the extirpation of proletarian organizations from the most revolutionary to the most conservative.

"Fascism is not merely a system of reprisals, of brutal force, and of police terror. Fascism is a particular system of government based on the uprooting of all elements of proletarian democracy within bourgeois society." [5]

The confusion spread by the Stalinists in the name of Marxist policy had the most catastrophic results. If fascism had already taken power, what need was there to summon the workers to prepare for mortal combat against Hitler's thugs? It could only be a variant of the same power. And, if the Social Democrats were nothing but "social fascists," it was obviously impossible to try and unite forces with them in a common front of struggle against the Nazis. The whole world and the cause of socialism paid a terrible price for the blunders of political analysis committed under the aegis of Stalinism in Germany, which helped Hitler come to power.

The essential nature of political democracy, and of bourgeois democracy in particular, cannot be grasped without understanding the connection between the socioeconomic substance and the varying forms assumed by the state power. Economics is more decisive than politics in determining the essence of a regime.

The true class character of the state can be ascertained, not simply by the legislation it enacts, the kinds of war it conducts or the categories of citizens it represses, but above all by the type of property ownership it protects and promotes. Every state is the organ of a given system of production based upon a particular form of property, which invests the state with a class bias and social content. Every state is the organized expression and instrument of the will and welfare of the dominant class, or the strongest section of it.

The class nature of a state is not determined by its political form, which can vary considerably from time to time according to the changes in historical conditions and the alignment of class forces, but by the productive relations and property rights its agencies defend. In the course of its evolution, bourgeois society based upon capitalist ownership of the means of production has been governed by absolute and constitutional monarchies, oligarchic republics, parliamentary democracies, military regimes and fascist dictatorships.

Conversely, if dissimilar modes of political rule can be erected on the same economic foundation, a single form of sovereignty can in its mutations have very different socioeconomic roles. Political democracy, as has been noted, has grown up in a sequence of historical formations since the rise of commercial city life. First came the democracy of the petty republics of Greece followed by the medieval urban communes; then the democracy of bourgeois times which is weakening but still with us; and after that the still mutilated and immature workers' democracy which has emerged in the twentieth century.

These successive forms of democratic government have rested upon different economic foundations and different combinations of social forces. Ancient democracy was rooted in small-scale commodity production, trade and slavery, medieval democracy in the feudal commercial and craft community, bourgeois democracy in capitalist property relations, and workers' democracy in nationalized property, centralized planning and the state monopoly of foreign trade.

They have likewise been dominated by different ruling classes. Greek democracy was the instrument of large and small slaveholders, the medieval communes of the merchant and craft guilds. Parliamentary democracy has been the instrument of big and little businessmen and those in their tow, while socialist democracy is the product of an anticapitalist revolution headed by the industrial wage workers.

The connection between the political and sociological aspects of state power acquires great practical importance when the democratic structure is shaken and imperiled and has to give way to another type of rule. The preservation of the property of the capitalists in the shift from one to the other demonstrates how the same ruling class and its mode of production can exercise its domination in very different ways at different points in its evolution, as the Italian and German capitalists have done.

The capitalist class, which originally made use of the monarchy to further its economic interests and then adapted to parliamentary democracy, is more and more impelled in its twilight years to resort to authoritarian methods of rule to save its property and power from confiscation. Yet, through all the substitutions of one political regime for another, the economic foundation of its rule in the private ownership of the means of production persists. That is why the principal objective of the socialist movement in its struggle for democracy is the expropriation of the capitalist owners.

SECTION III

THE DEVELOPMENT

OF DEMOCRACY

IN THE UNITED STATES

10

TWO TRADITIONS
OF AMERICAN DEMOCRACY

July 4, 1976, will mark the two hundredth anniversary of the Declaration of Independence. This assertion of national self-determination can be taken as the birthday of democracy for the American people.

The longevity of the governmental structure set up thirteen years later — the federal republic is the oldest constitutional regime in the world — has buttressed the belief that the development of democracy in the United States has been a seamless process. The original content of popular democracy, it is assumed, was deepened and expanded but has not undergone any significant alteration over the past two centuries.

The course of American democracy has not been that smooth and simple. The democratic movement under bourgeois auspices is divided into two major historical stages, each lasting almost a century. The first extended from the upsurge of the masses and the opening of the armed struggle for national liberation in 1774-75 to the close of the Reconstruction period in 1876. The second covers the decades since that time.

The struggles of the democratic forces during the first period, which were mainly directed against precapitalist formations, comprised two successive stages of the unfolding and triumph of the bourgeois-democratic revolution. They were essentially different from the post-Civil War crusades against the plutocracy in power because they culminated in colossal armed conflicts which resulted in the crushing of the counterrevolution and the creation and reinforcement of democratic rights and institutions. In contrast, the movements under the banners of Populism and

Progressivism, which followed the consolidation of the economic
and political supremacy of the capitalist class after the Civil
War, were conciliatory and reformist. They made only slight
modifications in the system of bourgeois democracy and in the
end left the magnates of capital more securely entrenched in
their positions.

The political evolution of the United States has proceeded
from one of these forms of democratism to the other, from
revolutionary democracy to a liberal-reformist regime. Although
academic historians do not distinguish between the two, they
represent polar types of democratic movements within the framework of bourgeois society.

The war of liberation from Great Britain was interlaced
with a civil war in the colonies between the Tories and patriots.
The committees set up by the insurrectionary masses in the
localities, crowned by the Continental Congress, were instrumental in shattering the royal authority and serving as pillars
of power for the revolutionary cause. The frictions and conflicts
within the coalition of classes which made the revolution were
on occasion very sharp, but they did not produce such overturns of the revolutionary regime as occurred during the French
Revolution.

The heterogeneous components of the colonial side managed
to submerge their differences and hold together until peace was
signed with Great Britain. No sooner had they won home rule
than contests broke out between the patricians and plebeians,
in almost every state of the confederation from 1783 to 1787,
to decide who should rule at home and how. The results of
these encounters, which came to a head with Shays's rebellion
in Massachusetts, were codified in the U. S. Constitution and
its Bill of Rights and in the constitutions of the thirteen states.

Though new native ruling classes, composed of the merchants
and other big-property holders in the North and planters in
the South, took over the reins of power from the British officials, the revolution initiated a process of internal democratization which overrode resistances from the rich and gave more
liberties to the unenslaved common people than any other
nation then enjoyed. These democratic features, to be sure,
fell far short of later standards. All the original state constitutions, for example, limited suffrage to free, white, adult, Protestant, propertied males.

The reasons for these restrictions were frankly stated by
eminent spokesmen for the upper classes. When the French
statesman Turgot chided the Americans for copying European

models rather than setting up simple democratic governments, John Adams, who was to be the second president, wrote in 1787-88 a three-volume answer entitled *A Defence of the Constitutions of Government of the United States Against the Attack of M. Turgot.* He there asserted: "It is essential to liberty that the rights of the rich be secured; if they are not, they will soon be robbed and become poor, and in their turn rob the robbers, and thus neither the liberty or property of any will be regarded. . . ." [1]

A third of a century later another conservative, Chancellor Kent, speaking at the constitutional convention of New York in 1821 against removing suffrage qualifications, declared that "the tendency of universal suffrage is to jeopardize the rights of property and the principles of liberty. . . . France has upward of four, and England upward of five millions of manufacturing and commercial laborers without property. Could these kingdoms sustain the weight of universal suffrage? The radicals in England, with the force of that mighty engine, would at once sweep away the property, the laws and the liberties of that island like a deluge." [2] The jurist feared a like calamity if general manhood suffrage were adopted in New York.

Nevertheless, the forces favoring further democratization were so strong that white males in the United States secured the franchise much sooner than in Western Europe.

The elementary conditions and institutions of democracy were established and the basic ideas of popular sovereignty disseminated during this pioneer period of the bourgeois revolution, which was the springtime of democratic thought and activity in the United States. As the young nation prospered and expanded its territory, the democratic ideology permeated the minds of the American people and became the conventional form of political discourse. These ruling ideas were appealed to not only by those who governed but by the governed, though rulers and ruled gave widely different interpretations of their concrete applications.

The democratic credo born of the first American revolution sufficed to meet the requirements of the leading forces of the ascending bourgeois society. This was confirmed when they came into headlong collision with the most formidable of all their domestic adversaries, the southern cotton nobility. The slave power had stood from the birth of the nation in flagrant contradiction to the principles of democracy and freedom even from the bourgeois standpoint.

Nonetheless, that anomaly embedded in the Republic had been legitimized by the Constitution while its representatives shared control of the country. This social tumor did not call for radical surgery until the slavocracy embarked on a counterrevolutionary uprising and the southern states seceded from the Union. The war against the Confederacy demanded the defense of all the democratic gains of the American people. It involved a reaffirmation of the ideals of bourgeois democracy and their extension to the chattel slaves, not their replacement by a more advanced set of political principles.

The defeat of the South awarded a total monopoly to the democratic doctrines. Who could doubt their superiority and merits when these had been proved by their invincibility in war, their truth in national life, their ability to withstand the most violent aggression? The sweeping triumph of the bourgeois forces and ideas made it impossible for any alternative social and political views that looked beyond the immediate stage of national development farther into the future to get a hearing from the masses or find a firm foothold in the American environment.

The alignment of social forces following the conquest of supremacy by the capitalists favored the remodeling of the existing political structures rather than a search for radically new foundations for political theory and action. The opponents of the plutocracy from the middle and lower orders tried to improve their situations within the capitalist system by reasserting the traditional democratic values and turning their still sharp edge against "the malefactors of great wealth." The two victorious democratic revolutions, the prodigious expansion of capitalism on a national and world scale, the relative stability of social relations and the immaturity of the labor movement gave liberalism an almost impregnable hold upon American politics after 1876.

There has thus been an extraordinary uniformity in the mainstream of social and political thought in the United States since the days of Thomas Jefferson. Despite wide variations in their conditions of life and labor, all classes appealed to the basic premises of bourgeois democracy. Even spokesmen for the slaveholders tried to twist this tradition for their own benefit by picturing themselves as "Athenian democrats"—who were likewise slaveholders.

C. Wright Mills pointed out that the "power elite" of the United States has not needed to create any special conservative ideology to sanction its domination. Its defenders have continued to use "the liberal rhetoric which is the common denominator of all proper and successful spokesmanship. . . . They have not had to confront any opposition based upon ideas which stand in challenging contrast to the liberal rhetoric which they employ as standard public relations." [3]

The historian Louis Hartz offered a quaint rationale for the vitality of petty-bourgeois democracy in *The Liberal Tradition in America: An Interpretation of American Political Thought Since the Revolution.* He argued that American liberalism "is what Santayana called, referring to American democracy, a 'natural' phenomenon. But the matter is curiously broader than this, for a society which begins with Locke, and thus transforms him, stays with Locke, by virtue of an absolute and irrational attachment it develops for him, and becomes [as] indifferent to the challenge of socialism in the latter era as it was unfamiliar with the heritage of feudalism in the earlier one. It has within it, as it were, a kind of self-completing mechanism, which insures the universality of the liberal idea." [4]

This notion that the American people have "an absolute and irrational attachment" to John Locke's conceptions of constitutional government and an automatic mechanism which awards a perpetual monopoly to "the liberal idea" is reminiscent of the political theorists of the royalist era who taught that the monarchy would last forever.

Hartz is typical of those doctrinaire liberals who may have abandoned belief in survival after death but retain full faith in everlasting life for bourgeois democracy in the United States. Their arguments are primarily aimed against critics to the left who may unhinge this absolute attachment by replacing Locke and Jefferson with Marx and Lenin. They brandish the traditions of American democracy against the Marxists and misinterpret them in order to justify the politics of gradualism and reformism. They seek to annex American democracy to their own territory and set up a "no trespassing sign" excluding revolutionary socialists from any rightful share of its heritage.

The liberal ideologists base their claim to a monopoly of the democratic tradition by tracing a direct and unbroken line of succession from Jefferson through Lincoln to themselves. They represent themselves as the sole heirs and legitimate continuators of these illustrious creators and champions of American democracy.

John Dewey, the noted instrumentalist philosopher, was an outstanding theoretician of this viewpoint which he expounded in many works on sociology, politics and ethics. In *Freedom and Culture,* published in 1939, he polemicized in defense of democratic liberalism against the capitalist reactionaries on one side and the revolutionary Marxists on the other, in the name of the distinctively American democratic tradition originating with Jefferson. Jefferson "was the first modern to state in human terms the principles of democracy," he wrote. ". . . I believe that only one who was attached to American soil and who took a consciously alert part in the struggles of the country to attain its independence could possibly have stated as thoroughly and intimately as did Jefferson the aims embodied in the American tradition: 'the definitions and axioms of a free government' as Lincoln called them." [5]

This conception of a straight line of descent of democracy from Jefferson to Deweyism has a serious flaw. It leaves out of account the role of revolution, which separates the mass democratic movements associated with Jefferson and Lincoln from the liberalism of Dewey, and makes them two essentially different stages in the evolution of bourgeois democracy. The dividing line between these two schools was drawn precisely at that point where liberalism takes issue with Marxism: the use of revolutionary methods to secure the rights of the people.

Though all were democrats, Jefferson and Lincoln incarnated one tradition in this respect; Dewey another. Jefferson in the first American revolution and Lincoln in the Civil War led movements which were not only progressive in their aims and democratic in their programs but also revolutionary in their methods and achievements. Although they were not so consistently militant as Sam Adams or Wendell Phillips, both belonged in the same camp of *revolutionary* democracy.

Dewey belonged to a later tendency which grew up after the Civil War in the form of various Populist-Progressive movements. These were democratic and plebeian but not revolutionary in temper. They were liberal, aiming to modify the established economic and political structure by gradual reform. Whereas the older tradition created, protected and promoted American democracy by revolutionary resistance against the hosts of reaction, the Progressives sought to defend and extend democracy against the plutocracy by gradualist means and measures. The two are not the same.

The root of the differences between these two phases of bourgeois democracy is to be found in the place they occupied in the development of American capitalism. Jefferson and Lincoln headed mass movements which had to engage in revolution and civil war in order to clear away the obstacles thwarting the expansion of our national capitalism, which in their times was the mightiest accelerator of economic and social progress. The revolutionary democrats of the eighteenth century abolished

British domination and Tory feudalism; their nineteenth-century descendants overthrew the slavocracy.

Dewey and his fellow Progressives of the twentieth century had no precapitalist forces to combat. They confronted the exclusive tyranny of the capitalist class itself. But they did not seek to abolish the capitalist system or dispossess its beneficiaries. They tried to improve the conditions of life and protect the liberties of the people without injuring a capitalism which had become monopolistic, imperialistic, parasitic and increasingly reactionary. Their means were not suited to realizing their ends.

The liberalism of this school occupied the center of the political stage after the bourgeois-democratic revolution had already been consummated in the United States and before the revolutionary working-class movement had come forth on the arena. Although Dewey's childhood had been lit by the flames of the Civil War (he was born in 1859), he felt, as did most of his contemporaries, that the United States had left its era of revolutions behind forever and outgrown such antiquated methods of social and political change. The rest of his long adult lifetime (he died in 1952) seemed to bear out this conclusion. Although the capitalist system was somewhat shaken from time to time, there were no radical upsets in established class relations. This highly stable national environment conditioned Dewey's social and political thinking far more than he and his admirers knew, if indeed they were at all aware of its influence.

He would never admit that revolutions have any lawful or necessary place in the development of class society, although they have erupted whenever and wherever long-standing social antagonisms have reached the breaking point. This happened twice in our nation's history.

In his arguments on the avoidability of revolutionary actions, Dewey did not bother to analyze the causes of the two great revolutions in his own country. In reply to his critics in *The Philosophy of John Dewey,* for example, he referred to the France of 1789 and the Russia of 1917 but not to the North America of 1776 and 1861. However, these revolutionary periods of our own national development deserve primary attention not only from any theoretician of social conflict but also from any supporter of democracy. For the democracy which he worked so hard to uphold was the offspring of these revolutions.

Such gaps in his thought, which it is tempting to psychoanalyze, are characteristic. While he extolled and analyzed Jefferson's conceptions of democracy at length in *Freedom and Culture,* he said nothing about Jefferson's forthright defense of the popular right to revolution. "I hold it, that a little rebellion, now and then, is a good thing, and as necessary in the political world as storms in the physical," Jefferson wrote to James Madison from Paris on January 30, 1787, in regard to Shays's Rebellion. [6]

Jefferson here sounds more like a Marxist than a Deweyan. Indeed, there is a world of difference between the two types of democrats. Jefferson was the spokesman for a *revolutionary* democracy. Dewey was the philosopher of a *liberal* democracy that abhorred revolution. The Virginian proclaimed and led a revolution. The man from Vermont sought to persuade his countrymen that revolutions were completely outmoded. To Jefferson periodic rebellion, at least once every twenty years, was "a medicine necessary for the sound health of government." [7] To Dewey revolution was poisonous to the "body politic," even though that capitalist body had entered into decay.

The same distinction can be made between Lincoln and Dewey. Although by temperament and training a moderate Republican, Lincoln did not hesitate to uphold the right of revolution in general and to lead one in particular when he found it necessary. Dewey, on the other hand, argued that revolution as such was wrong. He carried forward the *democratic* tradition of Jefferson and Lincoln, but discarded their *revolutionary* positions.

Dewey assigned to philosophy the duty of "auditing of past experiences and programs of values." In his own audit of our national experience, he failed to give enough positive value to revolutions. This led him into an inadequate assessment of American history, and especially the mainsprings of American democracy itself.

In *Freedom and Culture,* Dewey wrote that "the source of the American democratic tradition is moral." [8] This is an extremely shallow observation. The real source of democracy in the United States was the revolutionary struggles of its people. In 1776 and 1861, when the further growth of the nation required a new road and the forces of reaction barred the way and tried to curb and crush the oncoming progressive classes, the revolutionary democrats took up the challenge. They armed the people, conquered the upholders of the old order in battle and created a new social and political regime. The distinctive ideas, demands, institutions and customs of democracy were forged in these revolutionary furnaces.

Dewey gratefully accepted the fruits of these revolutions, from the democratic republic to free public education, and did his best to improve upon them. But he failed to understand the necessity for the ways and means by which these gains were actually secured. This was an awkward theoretical position for an instrumentalist philosopher whose cardinal principle asserted that the end and the means had to be interdependent and inseparable!

Dewey did not, of course, deny that past revolutions had beneficial consequences. What he contended was that the subsequent advance of science, technology, education and a superior understanding of method had rendered such barbaric upheavals unsuitable or unnecessary in democratic countries like the United States.

In this denial of the need for any further revolutionary action, the liberal philosopher unexpectedly found himself in the company of extreme conservatives who shared the same view. They were willing to use the agencies of their government to suppress the mere expression of revolutionary ideas. Dewey protested whenever they did so. This did honor to his concern for democracy, though it did not testify to the validity of his position.

Moreover, by adhering so rigidly to his antirevolutionary doctrine, Dewey actually violated the spirit of his own instrumentalism which taught that no means to an end was to be ruled out in advance of the consummation of the process. Although he did not ban resort to revolution under all circumstances, for all practical purposes — and that is what counts in reality, as well as in pragmatic theory — he did not give it any weight as a means of progressive social action in the future of America.

What basis is there for this liberalistic prejudice against revolution? Let us acknowledge that revolution is an unusual method for purging the social organism of poisonous elements. Such convulsions do not happen every decade in the life of a great nation. In the United States they have come along only once a century.

But these extraordinary events do not occur without sufficient reason. Their underlying causes are lodged in economic developments which sharpen the conflicts among opposing classes. No people takes the road to revolution when easier and more conventional ways of remedying their ills and reaching their objectives appear available to them. Jefferson correctly pointed out in the Declaration of Independence: "All experience has shown that mankind are more disposed to suffer while evils are sufferable than to right themselves by abolishing the forms to which they are accustomed." So long as they can, they try to confine their contests and solve their problems within the bounds of the established order.

Revolutions and counterrevolutions erupt only when the burning issues at stake between the contending classes can no longer be adjudicated by conciliation. Tom Paine recognized this early in 1776 when he proclaimed that after Concord and Lexington, the issues between the patriots and the crown had to be referred "from arguments to arms." Senator Seward of New York recognized this after the Dred Scott decision in 1857 when he spoke of "the irrepressible conflict" developing between the slaveholders and the North. These radicals were far more realistic than the liberal Dewey whose general argument was that social disputes must invariably be subject to negotiation and compromise.

The American people have twice been compelled to embark upon revolution after they had already tried the methods of conciliation many times and found that they failed to work. They were pushed to the point where they had either to submit to outright tyranny by a minority or adopt the most radical measures to ensure that the will of the majority prevailed. Both times they undertook the revolutionary way in order, as Jefferson wrote in the Declaration of Independence, to "throw off absolute despotism" and "provide new guards for their future security."

When gradualists recommend the adjustment of grievances by mutual compromise as a panacea to cure the revolutionary itch, they overlook the fact that a revolutionary crisis comes about precisely because the methods of compromise have become played out. People approach the road to revolution hesitantly, by way of successive approximations. They do not adopt the most militant forms of action until the most advanced among them have become convinced by considerable experience that their urgent interests cannot otherwise be safeguarded.

Our forefathers were no less peace-loving, intelligent and inclined to moderation than the American people of today. They did not want or expect revolution, nor did they welcome civil strife. Is it reasonable to believe that they finally embraced the alternative without sufficient reason?

In fact, they were driven to take up arms by historical circumstances beyond their control and independent of the good or ill will of the participants on either side. The propelling factor in both cases was the initiative of the counterrevolution. When King George's troops occupied and blockaded Boston and threatened other provinces with similar treatment, when the Confederacy split the Union, fired on Fort Sumter and ran up the flag of proslave rebellion, the American people saw there was no room for retreat or compromise. It was "liberty — or death!"

The masses of the American nation twice became revolutionized, not by preconception, by desire or by accident, but through the harsh necessities of their class struggles. They made the transition from the stage of conciliation to that of intransigent battle under the whiplash of reaction. They arrived empirically at the conclusion that they had to defend their rights and their future by revolutionary means because the aggressors of the old order were using the most desperate and deadly means to hold on to their privileged positions. This pragmatic course of development of all great revolutions, including our own, provides the most telling refutation of the dogmatic warnings of the pragmatic liberal philosophers against recourse to revolution.

These revolutions, which appear to obtuse conciliators aberrations in the course of our national development, find their logical and scientific explanation in this dynamic of the class struggle. However irrational the climactic phase of the class struggle may seem to the liberal mind, it has nevertheless been the inescapable outcome of long-simmering social antagonisms which finally reached the boiling point and exploded. Revolutionary action became the only reasonable and realistic alternative to the threat of enslavement and national retrogression.

The present-day liberals who contend that tyranny may be combated to the point of revolution but not beyond part company with the militant democrats of the eighteenth and nineteenth centuries and repudiate the most precious part of the democratic heritage. Jefferson and Lincoln did not shrink from proclaiming the right of revolution as the ultimate guarantee of all other democratic rights and they followed through in action with the Declaration of Independence and the Emancipation Proclamation.

That is where the Marxists clasp hands with Jefferson and Lincoln. Although these earlier Americans promoted capitalism and the Marxists fight for socialism, all three stand together in recognizing the organic link between democracy and revolution. Jefferson and Lincoln belong among the revolutionary democrats of the eighteenth and nineteenth centuries. The Marxists are the genuine revolutionary democrats of the twentieth century.

That is why the tradition of the militant defense and expansion of democracy is continued, not by the liberal pretenders who have turned their backs upon the next American revolution, but by the Marxists who are faced toward it and preparing for it.

11

THE REALITIES OF

AMERICAN DEMOCRACY

The American liberal abides by two articles of faith. One is the belief that he lives under a genuine democracy which, for all its imperfections, is still the freest and finest in the world. The other is the conviction that this form of government is here to stay and will never be superseded by a better. How do these propositions stand up to critical examination?

The United States unquestionably has all the attributes of a capitalist democracy — a Constitution, a Congress, political parties, regular elections, legal rights for its citizens enforced by the courts, freedom of publication, etc. In addition, the North Americans have deep-seated traditions of popular sovereignty which go back to the founding of the Republic. They have long been taught that the right to determine national policy belongs to the majority of the people, not to any plutocratic elite. They are quick to resent and resist flagrant abridgments of their rights.

What most Americans fail to see are the major contradictions in their political structure. Historically, as we have sought to show, democracy has been a form of rule accessible only to rich and privileged states which directly or indirectly exploit and oppress other peoples. Athens, the most celebrated democracy of antiquity, was a fiercely imperialist power. British democracy rested upon the plundering and subjugation of its dominions.

The prevalence of dictatorships in the colonial world is organically linked with the presence of democracies in the metropolitan countries. Democracy, like so many other things within the orbit of capitalism, is by and large a luxury reserved for the wealthiest countries who enjoy it at the expense of poorer peoples.

The foreign relations of the United States since the end of the Second World War have conformed to this pattern. Washington has sought support from the most repressive forces in order to strengthen its international positions and curb or contain actual and potential anticapitalist revolutions. Its network of antidemocratic allies extends from Franco Spain and the NATO dictatorship of the Greek colonels through South Africa to the military governments of Indonesia, Pakistan and South Korea. Vietnam shows to what lengths the American imperialists are ready to go in propping up native hirelings and denying the right of self-determination to a small nation.

It has become widely recognized that the democratic principles professed by the partisans of "the free world" conflict with their military aggressions and complicity with autocracy abroad. It is not yet so clear that they are contravened by the realities of American life. The nominal equality of all citizens is at odds with the actual inequalities of American society; the owners of wealth wield far more power than the rest of the population; they constitute an oligarchy which exercises a social tyranny behind the facade of a representative democracy.

It is a law of civilization that political predominance inevitably falls into the hands of that class or combination of classes that commands the processes of production. Before the Civil War, the slaveholders were the decisive force in American politics because their cotton crop was the principal export of commercial United States. This gave enormous economic leverage and political weight to the representatives of the cotton barons in the national capital.

The regime of the southern states in the early nineteenth century showed how democratic forms can be combined with outright slavery. The democratic system since the Civil War has been rooted in a more subtle and disguised type of servitude. That is the exploitation of the wage workers by the capitalist proprietors of the economy, combined with the racial oppression of the bottom layers of the labor force.

The concentration of economic power in the mammoth corporations and financial institutions — and the political hegemony that goes with it — has accelerated decade by decade. According to a study by the Federal Trade Commission, the two hundred largest manufacturing corporations in 1968 controlled about two-thirds of all manufacturing assets — a proportion of total assets that was equal to the share held by the thousand largest corporations in 1941. This increase in power came at a time when the volume of industrial assets was growing very rapidly. A. A. Berle, the former State Department official, wrote in 1957:

"In terms of power, without regard to asset positions, not only do 500 corporations control two-thirds of the nonfarm economy, but within each of that 500 a still smaller group has the ultimate decision-making power. This is, I think, the highest concentration of economic power in recorded history." [1]

This power embraces the entire capitalist system. By 1960, United States foreign investments accounted for almost 60 percent of the world total. The gross value of American enterprises abroad is greater than the wealth of any country except the United States and the Soviet Union.

A number of economists and sociologists, such as C. Wright Mills, Paul Sweezy and E. Digby Baltzell, have published studies of the anatomy of the U. S. ruling class in recent years. Their findings have been amplified by G. William Domhoff in *Who Rules America?* He estimated that in the early 1960s nearly one million persons belonged to the upper class, or 0.5 percent of the population. On the basis of the empirical evidence cited in his work, he concluded that this small minority controls the major banks and corporations and therewith the American economy; the presidency and the executive branch of the federal government; the federal judiciary; the military; the CIA and FBI; the regulatory agencies; the foundations; the elite universities; the largest of the communication media; and the important opinion-molding associations. This upper class, he concludes, owns a disproportionate amount of the country's wealth, receives a disproportionate amount of the country's income and contributes a disproportionate number of its members to the controlling institutions and key decision-making groups of the country.

If it could be said of England in 1832 that the members of the House of Commons were chosen by about two hundred landed families, it is no less true of the U. S. government today that its top echelons are directed and staffed by stewards of the two hundred largest corporations. Of the thirteen men who have been secretary of defense or secretary of war since 1932, eight have been listed in the *Social Register*. Of the last four tenants of this key cabinet post, two were formerly heads of the biggest auto manufacturers, General Motors and Ford, and their successors were closely associated with the largest military contractors.

The methods by which the possessors of wealth enforce their supremacy in deference to and defiance of the forms of democracy are devious and complex. They have been worked out over many decades of experimentation with the techniques of domination in a dollar democracy.

The main mechanism through which big business maintains control over the country and suzerainty over a large part of the planet is the two-party system. The Republican and Democratic parties are utterly committed defenders of the capitalist order, though their representatives may serve rival interest groups within it. The ruling class itself utilizes both political machines for its purposes, just as its counterpart in Canada relies on the Conservative and Liberal parties.

If the capitalist parties see two sides to every question, these are not the cause of the poor versus the rich. Their paramount concern is whether they are in or out of office. Though they do not have fundamental differences, the candidates of the two organizations joust avidly with one another, sparing no demagogy in appeals to the voters in order to win election. Once in office, they pursue the same bipartisan foreign policy and both take good care of the needs of the well-to-do.

Those who pay the piper call the tune in the shaping of government policy and the administration of its affairs. Campaigning is very expensive. Robert Kennedy spent two million dollars to win his New York senatorial seat in 1966. If they do not have inherited wealth like the Kennedys and Rockefellers, candidates must hold out their hats to the wealthy for finances. Lyndon B. Johnson set up a President's Club whose members paid $1000 apiece to receive communications — and presumably favors — from the White House.

The Committee for Economic Development reported in December 1968 that "according to the best available estimates at least $140 million was spent on all political campaigns in 1952, $155 million in 1956, $175 million in 1960 and $200 million in 1964. The preliminary figures for 1968 exceeded $250 million."

Most of this money came from the corporate rich. It enabled them to pick, promote or drop candidates on all levels from the local districts to the highest executive posts and sway their decisions. In his book *My Brother Lyndon,* Sam Houston Johnson bluntly declared: "When a candidate has to raise many thousands from a single fat cat, can anyone seriously believe those big contributors are merely interested in good government? There isn't a single mayor, councilman, state legislator, governor, congressman, President or any other election official in this country who hasn't gotten a contribution from some fat cat expecting a Government contract somewhere down the line." [2]

The scandal of political fund-raising is only one aspect of the irremediable corruption at the core of bourgeois politics.

Revelations of the venality of public officials in the municipalities, state administrations and federal apparatus periodically break into the press — and but a small fraction of the cases are uncovered and publicized.

Politics is itself big business in the United States. It involves millions of jobs and appointments, the awarding of lucrative contracts, franchises and concessions, the administration of justice, the incidence of taxation. The vast sums at stake make the political trough a cesspool of legal and illegal corruption.

That is only one side of the situation. The big business of politics is inextricably linked with the politics of big business. These two merge at the summit in the White House and its cabinet, Congress and the Pentagon. The Defense Department, presided over by former presidents of General Motors and Ford during the Eisenhower, Kennedy and Johnson administrations, is by far the largest spending agency in the country, with a budget of up to eighty billion dollars a year.

Since 1946 American taxpayers have contributed more than a trillion dollars to maintain the industrial-military complex. Each year the federal government spends more than seventy cents of every budget dollar on past, present or prospective wars — and to sustain the profits of the Pentagon clients. The costs of the garrison state diminish the real wages of the workers through inflation and spiraling taxes and cut into all programs of public welfare.

Influence-peddling, behind-the-scenes pressures and interlocking directorates between the military and the contractors ensure that political figures comply with the requirements of the rich. The National Association of Manufacturers, the Committee for American Development, the Business Advisory Council, the National Advertising Council, the U. S. Chamber of Commerce and similar associations, together with special representatives of the military contractors, assiduously contact the right officials in the right departments to do the right thing for the right company — and the upper class as a whole.

The poor have neither the time nor the money to participate in government sessions and keep track of what is going on. The corporations and financial houses not only retain lobbyists to look after their interests but hold legislators and judges in leash. Just as the railroads, lumber and mining companies had senators on their payroll in the nineteenth century, so the oil and natural-gas tycoons, the utilities, the banks, insurance and mortgage companies and arms makers have congressmen whom they have bankrolled for election at their beck and call.

This is more openly done in some countries than others. In England it is less direct than in Japan where the eight factions in the ruling Liberal-Democratic Party can each count on receiving $30,000 a month from big business. This is called "rice money." Though the forms of collusion differ, the practice is general. Sherman Adams, Eisenhower's chief aide in the White House, was cashiered for taking favors from a New England manufacturer. He tells in his *Memoirs* that the president was reluctantly forced to fire him because some big contributors complained he had become a liability, injuring Republican chances in the next election.

The Democrats and Republicans resort to diverse devices to lessen the political rights of the masses. They restrict the franchise. Strict literacy tests, force and fraud prevent numerous blacks and poor whites from voting in some southern states. Until 1970 in all but a few states, youth from eighteen to twenty-one, who are old enough to be drafted, were ineligible to vote. A sizable percentage of the lower classes do not register for fear they may lose income if called for jury duty or if they come to the attention of the tax collectors. A quarter or a half of the registrants may not cast ballots on election day, out of distrust or disgust with the choices offered them. Of the forty-seven million Americans who did not vote in the 1968 presidential election, nearly one-half were disfranchised by strict residency laws, and many others had never bothered to register.

The basis of electoral representation for Congress and the state legislatures was grossly inequitable until recent Supreme Court "one-man, one-vote" decisions somewhat rectified the maldistribution. Rural areas were accorded parity with urban districts, though they may have had as few or fewer than one-tenth the inhabitants.

The most potent means of molding and manipulating public opinion is given to the ruling class through its grip upon the major media of communication — TV, radio, movies, the press and educational facilities. In theory, a free press is available to all. In reality the view of life and versions of events suited to the powers-that-be are disseminated in millions of copies by the daily press, the newsweeklies and the monthly magazines while nonconforming journals of anticapitalist opinion can reach only a few thousand readers for lack of financial resources and advertising.

Poverty snatches away from the dispossessed even those rights which capitalist democracy accords them on paper. Though they have the same formal rights, the rich and the poor do not get equal justice in the law courts, if only because of the delays and expense. Census Bureau studies have indicated that, at any given time, as many as one-half of those in many jails are there because they could not pay fines. And their skins were most likely to be black.

To uphold their political monopoly and prevent voters from having a distinct alternative to the capitalist candidates and programs, Republican and Democratic legislators make it exceedingly difficult, and in some states virtually impossible, for minority parties to get on the ballot. The 1969 New York City mayoralty race provided a typical act of exclusion. The incumbent mayor, having lost in the Republican primaries, ran under Liberal and an improvised Independent party designations. In order to secure two places on the top line of the voting machine instead of one, his henchmen successfully petitioned a subservient Board of Elections to declare invalid the petitions of the Socialist Workers and Socialist Labor parties, which would otherwise have occupied the mayor's chosen line on the machine. This cynical move helped return him to office.

Even if the electoral and governmental processes functioned more fairly, under monopolist domination the capacity to determine their own destinies would still be withheld from the American people. Democracy must have not only a political but an economic and social dimension. It must extend beyond the ballot box, which permits qualified voters to decide every so often which servitor of the status quo will take office, and beyond legislatures vassalized to the propertied interests. The most full-blooded capitalist democracy is no more than skin-deep, since it does not control the economic foundations of society or enable the masses to have a say in the most decisive areas of their lives.

Physical survival is the most fundamental of all human rights. The right to life for the worker and his family is the right to work. Without access to the means of subsistence and development, all the rest can be rendered meaningless.

By virtue of their ownership of the means of production, the employing class has the power of life and death over the working class. The worker can earn his daily bread only by selling his labor power to an employer. Yet, under the system of private ownership, he is not guaranteed a job or even a minimum subsistence. The power to give work, restrict it or take it away belongs to the profiteers. The imperatives of the accumulation of capital, not the vital needs of the workers, dictate who shall go to work, how they shall work and even whether or not they shall have work at all.

"Every hour of every day decisions affecting if and when

they shall work, what goods or services they shall or shall not obtain, are made by private individuals whose names never appear on the ballot the people mark in their voting booths," wrote Leo Huberman. "Americans — not all of them, as the registration drive for Negroes in the South amply proves — have the right to elect the men and women who make the political decisions affecting the country, but they do not have the right to elect the men and women who make the equally important economic decisions affecting every aspect of their lives." [3]

There is not the slightest democracy within the capitalist enterprises. Private businesses in industry, commerce, finance and agriculture are autocratically directed. The bosses and supervisors decide what is to be done without consulting the wishes of the hired hands. In their hierarchically administered division of labor, the capitalists give the orders and the workers must carry them out. The existence and influence of the unions are the sole check upon the arbitrariness of the employers, who resist all encroachments on their managerial prerogatives. A corporation has full legal right to shut down a plant or shift its location without consulting its workers and without regard to the adverse effects upon the community.

The gyrations of the stock market and the variations of the business cycle are more powerful factors in shaping the fortunes of the people than the election returns. The capitalists run their businesses autocratically, yet they do not have mastery over their own economic system, which operates blindly and convulsively. Even in boom times, several millions cannot find jobs. Recessions and sudden crises throw more millions out of work and spread misery. In addition to periodic interruptions of production, the growth of mechanization, automation and cybernation brings about chronic structural unemployment.

A presidential commission which studied the problem of poverty for twenty-two months stated that "at the end of 1968, there were twenty-five million poor Americans as measured by the Federal Government's poverty index." Millions go hungry and malnourished in a country bursting with agricultural surpluses. In 1969 there were almost a million individuals on the relief rolls in New York City alone. The commission observed that "most persons who depend on earnings for their incomes face the risk of losing that access to prosperity through accident, disability, loss of a breadwinner, or obsolescence of skills." [4]

If the mass of workers do not have either economic equality or security, neither are they assured of peaceful relations with other nations. Foreign-policy decisions involving issues of peace or war are not submitted for consideration to the voters or even to the Congress. They are usually made in secret by the chief executive and his entourage of advisers.

Although the Constitution says Congress alone has power to declare war, American presidents have disregarded this provision. Theodore Roosevelt and Woodrow Wilson sent troops to Central America, the Caribbean and Mexico without congressional authorization. Franklin D. Roosevelt entered into limited naval hostilities against Germany and Italy and agreed with England to fight against Japan in advance of a congressional declaration of war. Truman fought the Korean "police action" without congressional permission. In 1958, after Secretary of State Dulles by his own admission conferred with representatives of the big oil companies whose installations were threatened by the revolt in Iraq, Eisenhower dispatched troops to Lebanon. Kennedy imposed a quarantine on shipment of Soviet missiles to Cuba without reference to congressional resolutions. Lyndon B. Johnson, who had led the people to believe he was opposed to widening the Vietnam war in the 1964 campaign, escalated the war in 1965 on the basis of the flimsy Tonkin Gulf resolution. The unauthorized use of armed force whenever the White House and Pentagon see fit has become standard operating procedure.

On October 28, 1968, Senator W. J. Fulbright, chairman of the Senate Foreign Relations Committee, asserted that the Pentagon was engaged in a clandestine war in Laos without the knowledge or consent of Congress. The CIA has conspired to overturn governments in Iran, Guatemala, Cuba and elsewhere that were hostile to the monopolists and militarists.

Finally, one individual, the president of the United States, has the legal right and political sanction to press the button unloosing enough nuclear warheads to wipe out mankind. According to his brother Robert, the Kennedy war council was ready to wage nuclear war in the missile crisis of October 1962 if the Soviet leaders did not back down.

The usurpation of the war-making powers by the White House is the outstanding aspect of a broader phenomenon common to all the constitutional capitalist regimes in the West, that is, the irrepressible trend toward the reinforcement of the executive at the expense of representative parliamentary bodies. This is as strong in England as in the United States. Monopolist pressure is the principal factor in this process.

Having disposed of free competition in the economy, the big financial combines seek to cut down on the competition in the governmental domain which results from universal suffrage.

They require a centralization of political decision, conformable to their centralization of economic power, to counteract the consequences of party rivalries and popular clamor which may impede their designs and infringe on their interests. The White House and Pentagon also require the utmost centralization of military decision to carry out their plans — from the collection of intelligence, the overthrow of recalcitrant heads of state and the assassination of popular leaders like Che Guevara, to the invasion of Cambodia.

So long as the parliamentary system is maintained, the corporate capitalists accomplish their ends in two ways. They make obedient instruments out of such permanent institutions of the state as the army, the secret police, the top administrators of the government departments (the bureaucracy) and the judiciary, which are most removed from the influence of the electorate. They also work to shift the actual centers of decision in the most crucial matters from Congress and the voters to the executive branch, staffed with members of the ruling class. Carried to its logical limits, this trend leads to Bonapartism.

A system in which the people do not control the most important decisions and actions of the government, their economy, their welfare or the course of their lives can hardly be considered genuinely democratic. It can be more precisely defined as a plutocracy dressed in democratic disguise.

This was the opinion of the sociologist C. Wright Mills. "The United States today I should say is generally democratic mainly in form and in the rhetoric of expectation," he wrote. "In substance and in practice it is very often non-democratic, and in many institutional areas it is quite clearly so. The corporate economy is run neither as a set of town meetings nor as a set of powers responsible to those whom their activities affect very seriously. The military machines and increasingly the political state are in the same condition."[5]

Many less informed and articulate Americans have come to a like conclusion: that they have the forms but not the substance of democracy. This is expressed in a sense of individual powerlessness, the feeling that the major factors governing their lives are far beyond their reach. Instead of being the makers and masters of their destinies, they have become helpless and often hopeless victims of inscrutable and uncontrollable forces. They are not wrong. Their lives are determined not by them but for them by an economic and social system which is operated not for the welfare of its members but for the profits and privileges of the corporate rich.

Up to this point we have been considering the conditions of the American people as a whole, without distinction among them. This is insufficient. The state of democracy is most accurately measured, not by the freedoms enjoyed by those at the top and in the middle sectors of society, but by the circumstances of the very bottom layers. By this criterion, U. S. democracy has fallen short and failed from the beginning of the Republic.

It has largely been limited to the white majority. Numerous oppressed national minorities have been excluded from its benefits, and still are. American Indians have been decimated, dispossessed, herded into reservations and brutally maltreated; Mexican-Americans have been callously exploited; Japanese-Americans were detained in concentration camps during the Second World War; Puerto Ricans are refused their independence. The whole world recognizes that the greatest mockery of the pretensions of American democracy has been the discrimination practiced against the millions of Afro-Americans who, as Malcolm X said, have been denied not simply civil rights but the most elementary human rights.

While women have many of the same political and legal rights as men, they do not enjoy social and economic equality. In most cases working women receive less pay for the same work, if they can obtain such jobs. If they are not barred from entering certain professions, they are kept from advancing on a par with male practitioners. There are only a few women in top policy-making positions in Washington or the corporate world. This discrimination against half the population, so vigorously challenged by the women's liberation movement, is in itself indicative of the undemocratic structure of the most advanced neocapitalism.

In argument against the Marxists, who view these phenomena as logical consequences and structural characteristics of imperialist democracy, spokesmen for the ruling order contend that they are incidental and passing defects that time will diminish, rectify and abolish. This makes it necessary to ascertain the direction in which the political system has been developing. What are the real prospects of democracy in America? Is it contracting, or expanding — giving a fuller measure of rights to more and more citizens? Does capitalist rule ensure its improvement and continuance, or does it contain grave dangers to its survival?

It would seem that the world's richest country at the height of its power during the most prolonged prosperity in capitalist history could easily have broadened the freedoms of its own people, especially since the ruling class could count on a conservatized, docile and politically subservient labor movement. The contrary has been the case. Since the close of the war that was ostensibly waged for "the four freedoms," the democratic rights of the American people have been eroded rather than expanded. The sole exception is the paltry civil-rights legislation granted as a token concession to the Afro-American movement for emancipation.

The cold war witch-hunt, initiated and carried through by the highest agencies of the government, generated an atmosphere of intimidation which affected the liberties of the most diverse categories of citizens. The Smith Act, invoked against the Socialist Workers and the Communist parties, aimed to outlaw Marxist ideas and suppress minority parties on the left. The loyalty purge proscribed scores of organizations and penalized their members and supporters by arbitrary administrative action, solely because of their opinions and associations. American history had no precedent for such an official blacklist which was borrowed from the "thought control" arsenal of totalitarian states.

Congress set up inquisitorial investigating bodies like the House Committee on Un-American Activities and the Subversive Activities Control Board. The FBI and CIA grew into omnipresent secret-police agencies employing a swarm of informers and provocateurs. Sweeping conspiracy laws were enacted and applied. Congress passed harsh antilabor legislation, such as the Taft-Hartley and Landrum-Griffin bills.

Though victimizations may be heavier under one administration than another, repressive measures of this sort are not transitory phenomena. None have been repealed or annulled, though Supreme Court decisions have moderated some of them. More are added to the statute books from time to time. This formidable arsenal of punitive instrumentalities is a permanent feature of the present phase of capitalist development. The trends toward thought control and a police state spring from deep necessities of the monopolist and militarist masters of the United States.

The drive of the American monopolists toward world empire leads not only to recurrent armed assaults upon recalcitrant small nations but also to attempts to curb the expression of dissent at home. The immediate aim of the witch-hunters is to intimidate and isolate the opposition to unpopular policies and practices; their ultimate objective is to stamp out all possibility of organized protest. However, this requires a far different set of circumstances and relationship of forces from those that exist at the present juncture in the United States. Meanwhile, the forces of reaction nibble bit by bit at the traditional liberties of the American people.

The prodigious growth of the military octopus is a source of immense danger to the future of constitutional government. Antimilitarism was once exceedingly strong in the United States and until 1941 the professional army, though not the navy, was relatively small for a great power. That has been totally transformed over the past quarter-century.

The U. S. now has a military establishment of unprecedented size, with enough firepower to pulverize the planet and overkill all mankind. There are almost 3 million men in uniform. The Department of Defense employs over a million more civilians. The Pentagon maintains about 400 large and 3,000 smaller bases in 30 countries. A million troops are stationed in these bases, as well as 500,000 dependents and some 250,-000 indigenous employees. It costs from $60 to $80 billion a year to pay for all this.

The ever-widening influence of this colossal military machine is felt throughout the nation. Top officers are consulted daily by the White House and Congress on a range of diplomatic problems encompassing all the continents and also, in times of internal commotion connected with Afro-American upheavals and antiwar demonstrations, on grave domestic issues. The Joint Chiefs of Staff have become a weighty force in shaping foreign policy, as the intervention in Vietnam and the prolongation of military activities in Southeast Asia have demonstrated.

The military's multibillion-dollar annual budget makes it a dominant factor in the economy. Extensive lobbies, working on a single service or a weapons system, operate in Washington, seeking a bigger portion of the pie for their clients. A House Armed Services subcommittee found that more than 1,400 retired officers, including 261 generals and admirals, were employed by the hundred leading defense contractors.

In 1961 almost two out of every three congressmen had government military installations in their districts. The presence of these, together with the enterprises of private military contractors, exerts almost irresistible politico-economic pressures upon legislators to support arms appropriations and imperialist policies.

In 1969 President Johnson appointed a blue-ribbon panel to serve as a watchdog over the Pentagon. But, according to Wisconsin Senator William Proxmire, eight of its members have interests of more than a billion dollars in defense-related industries. "A sham," he called it, "and an indication that the Pentagon has become so powerful that it is able to control those who would criticize it."[6]

Even conservative political personages have taken alarm at the proliferating power of the military-monopolist partnership. In his farewell speech on January 17, 1961, former President Eisenhower warned: "In the councils of government we must guard against the acquisition of unwarranted influence, whether sought or unsought, by the military-industrial complex. The potential for the disastrous rise of misplaced power exists and will persist. We must never let the weight of this combination endanger our liberties or democratic processes."

The Pentagon is a hotbed of reaction. A number of generals and admirals, active and retired, are sympathizers or members of ultraright organizations. They fume at civilian officeholders who are "too soft on Communism" and champion the most belligerent policies, including the use of nuclear weapons.

So long as social and political stability prevails, the brass hats can be kept under civilian control and within parliamentary bounds. But the "warfare state" now contains a gigantic organized force which is capable of extraparliamentary action and a military takeover if a section of the ruling class, faced with a grave social crisis at home or an intolerable setback by the anticapitalist forces abroad, should decide that constitutional government has to be supplanted by a more authoritarian method of rule.

The attrition of democracy is a signal warning of what the future holds for American democracy under imperialist auspices. The traditional way of life is not by itself strong enough to offset the dominant drives of monopolist capitalism which have delivered such devastating blows to parliamentary democracy elsewhere. The unparalleled concentration of economic, political and military power in the gigantic aggregations of private wealth and the exclusive command over the decisive spheres of national life sought by the monopolists run counter to the preservation or extension of democratic rights and institutions.

One of the objects of the anti-Communist crusades instigated by big business, which keep pointing to the imaginary threat to American democracy posed by the Soviet Union, China and Cuba (not to speak of Vietnam!), is to distract attention from the very real dangers to democracy emanating from the ruling circles of the land.

If bourgeois society in its fight against feudalism and later under the conditions of competitive capitalism promoted the development of democracy, then capitalism in its monopolist stage restricts and strangles it. This qualitative change in the historical relations between capitalism and democracy will apply with full force to the United States. The contradiction between the popular aspirations for equality and private-property rights, which was a source of friction even in the most radical and progressive periods of capitalism, becomes accentuated and laid bare by the class conflicts of the imperialist epoch.

The political system of the United States, which gives formal sovereignty to the masses while the actual powers of decision are vested in an oligarchy of great wealth, is an anomaly which can hold together in fair weather but cannot indefinitely endure. Just as Lincoln declared that a nation cannot endure "half-slave and half-free," so contemporary America cannot go on being semidemocratic and semiplutocratic. The conflict between its political superstructure and the economic reality must sooner or later be resolved one way or the other. This is the major issue underlying all the other social and political problems of the American people.

Every capitalist ruling class has been highly sensitive to the dynamic of democracy: that the masses keep striving to bring the whole of society into consonance with the professed principles of equality. "If any one conclusion can be reached from a study of the results it is that democracy will lead, sooner or later, to socialism," observed the British conservative scholar C. Northcote Parkinson in his work on *The Evolution of Political Thought.*[7] He reasons that if the poor, who are in the majority, exercise their political power, they will proceed to confiscate the property of the wealthy minority.

Adolf Hitler had a similar appraisal of democracy. "Democracy, as practised in Western Europe today, is the forerunner of Marxism," he wrote in *Mein Kampf.* "In fact the latter would not be conceivable without the former. Democracy is the breeding-ground in which the bacilli of the Marxist world pest can grow and spread."[8]

An American historian, Forrest McDonald, discerns a continuity from the Declaration of Independence to the revolutions of the twentieth century. "The American Revolution was only a beginning in teaching men the process, but once it was done — once the vulgar overstepped the bonds of propriety and got away with it—there was no logical stopping place. *Common Sense* led unerringly to Valmy, and Valmy to Napoleon, and Napoleon to the Revolution of 1830, and that to the Revolutions of 1848, and those to the Paris Commune of 1871, and that to the Bolshevik Revolution, and that to the African and Asian Revolutions in expectations, and those to eternity."[9]

The most vigilant and aggressive guardians of monopolist domination are aware of this logic of democracy. That is why they seek to hold democracy down to the minimum both abroad and at home. And, when the survival of their supremacy and property are at stake, they will not hesitate to scuttle any and all democratic institutions.

Is this an imaginary fear bred by Marxist doctrinairism? Let us hear what U. S. Supreme Court Justice William Douglas had to say at the beginning of 1970 on the direction being taken by the American Establishment. In his book *Points of Rebellion*, he charges that "The Pentagon has a fantastic budget that enables it to dream of putting down the much-needed revolutions which will arise in Peru, in the Philippines and in other benighted countries." The justice asks: "Where is the force that will restrain the Pentagon?"

"At the international level we become virtually paranoid," he writes. "Indeed, a black silence of fear possesses the nation and is causing us to jettison some of our libertarian traditions.

"Truman nurtured that fear, Johnson promoted it, preaching the doctrine that the people of the world want what we have and, unless suppressed, will take it from us."

Revolution may prove to be the only honorable alternative to oppression, says the justice. "George III was the symbol against which our Founders made a revolution now considered bright and glorious. . . . We must realize that today's Establishment is the new George III. Whether it will continue to adhere to his tactics, we do not know. If it does, the redress, honored in tradition, is also revolution."

Whether that revolution proves violent depends on how wise the Establishment is, the justice concludes. "If, with its stockpile of arms, it resolves to suppress the dissenters, America will face, I fear, an awful ordeal."[10]

12

HOW CAN DEMOCRACY BE
DEFENDED AND EXTENDED ?

In view of the shrinkage of democratic rights and the possibility of ultraright offensives against constitutional government, the question is posed: how can the existing democracy best be defended? This issue sharply divides liberalism from revolutionary Marxism. While adherents to both can agree that democracy must be protected from attack and together can resist this or that specific violation of civil liberties, they part company on two major points: what forces can be counted on to fight most vigorously for democracy and how is that struggle to be conducted?

Liberals want to preserve both democracy and private property, freedom and "free enterprise." Marxists contend that these aims are contradictory and a policy of combining them is unrealistic. In order to achieve genuine democracy and safeguard the established rights of the people, the power, privileges and property of the capitalist minority have to be abolished. These positions, and the opposing perspectives of reform and revolution flowing from them, are basically incompatible and lead to entirely different strategies in the fight for the enlargement of freedom.

Proceeding from their central conception of a classless state, liberals look to "all people of goodwill," regardless of their class positions and interests, to unite against aggressions upon democracy from any quarter. Marxists do not deny that constant pressure has to be exerted upon the capitalist regime to protect the liberties of the people. But they propose to promote this aim by different agencies and methods. They call upon the organized working class to take the lead in the fight for democracy on all issues, in alliance with the oppressed minorities and progressive elements. Through the successive stages of such a militant and independent movement on the industrial and political fronts, the working masses will in the end come to the conclusion that their rights cannot be assured or their fundamental interests satisfied without replacing capitalist rule with their own power.

This line of class struggle, pushed to its conclusion, is wrong and must be rejected, say the liberals. Whatever good revolutions have done in the past, there are no justifiable reasons for that pattern to be repeated in the future. The American people now have enough knowledge, unity, maturity and good sense to settle conflicts of social interests by more reasonable means and to advance step by step, hand in hand, toward a better life for all.

This gradualist outlook hinges upon two big assumptions about the prospects of American capitalism. One is that the American people will receive an increasing measure of peace, security, liberty and material benefits from the powers that be. It must be admitted that the urge for revolutionary change would then be minimal.

On top of this, the liberals pile a greater assumption. Even if serious social crises do occur, they expect the financial magnates to be sensible and self-sacrificing enough to renounce their power and privileges and permit the people to come into their own. In that event, the methods of social action and political reform they advocate would have to be acknowledged as warranted.

However, both hypotheses rest upon shaky foundations. Capitalism is no longer expanding and progressive. It is a retreating and increasingly reactionary social system on a world-historical scale. Sooner or later, even its most highly favored American sector will be hard hit by the accumulated effects of this decline.

When the shocks administered by these crises set the workers into motion, will the American monopolists, who have so much to lose, prove to be more enduringly wedded to democracy than to the defense of their profits and property? Such a presumption can find no precedent either in our national past or in the conduct of similarly situated capitalist regimes elsewhere. The British overlords and the Tory landed proprietors of the eighteenth century, and the southern slaveholders of the nineteenth century, furiously resisted the loss of their sovereignty and property. And when the capitalists of other countries have been threatened with dispossession in the twentieth century, they have invariably resorted to military or fascist dictatorships or embarked as a diversion upon imperialist military adventures.

The capitalist rulers have invariably subordinated concern for the rights of the people to the protection of their material interests — and in any clash between the two, democracy is sacrificed. Yet the liberals count on the wealthy to respect the institutions and claims of democracy when their entire existence is at stake! The point is that, as soon as democracy tends to negate its narrow class character and become converted into an instrument for the welfare of the population, the democratic forms are set aside by the bourgeoisie and its state representatives.

The liberals are blind to the fact that the ties between capitalism and democracy have grown weaker and not stronger in the epoch of imperialism. In the eighteenth and nineteenth centuries, the revolutions which gave national supremacy to the capitalists propelled democracy forward at the same time. From the Declaration of Independence to the Emancipation Proclamation, the ascendancy of capitalism was compatible with the progress of democracy.

As the monopolists have concentrated political, economic and social power in their hands, democracy has stagnated. From the 1880s onward, the forces of Progressivism, captained by liberal reformers, waged many battles to protect democracy against the plutocracy. Despite all they have done over these decades, American democracy has limped along and its future is overcast.

It is one-sided to interpret the rampaging reaction associated with McCarthyism as the result of the cold war alone. The witch-hunt was not simply the product of international conditions and of the confrontation between the United States and the Communist countries. It also had deep roots in class tensions at home. The restrictions upon freedom are the reflexes of a more and more militarized monopolist regime that is unsure of wholehearted allegiance from its own citizens. They are symptoms of an organic trend toward despotism among the ruling class. Though they have not been used, the establishment of six detention camps for dissidents under the McCarran Act betokens the intentions of the government. The repressions against the Afro-Americans struggling for self-determination and the attempts to silence, red-bait and jail the most militant opponents of the Vietnam war show how much big business fears the dissidents among the people.

The erosion of democracy is not a passing phenomenon. It indicates that democracy and capitalism, which once went hand in hand, are more and more at odds with each other. The republic of Jefferson and Lincoln was, on the whole, a guardian of democracy. The Democratic and Republican administrations from Wilson and Roosevelt through Truman, Kennedy and Johnson to Nixon have been the underminers of democracy. World imperialism combined with domestic politics keeps throwing the capitalists into the embrace of reaction.

The big-property owners were not the chief custodians of democracy even in the most progressive days of U. S. capitalism. They tolerated the institutions of democracy while manipulating and restricting them to their advantage. The backbone of democracy was constituted by the middle and lower classes of the population.

Nowadays the urban and rural middle classes have receded in economic and social importance; the small-property owners no longer have enough independent strength to withstand concerted assaults upon democracy. There exists only one social force with enough power to defend democracy against "the clear and present danger" of capitalist reaction. That is the working class, which comprises the overwhelming bulk of the population. The white workers, the Afro-Americans and Third World peoples, the radical youth, the women rebels against their status as "the second sex" and the dissident intellectuals and professionals form a phalanx of forces which have to be united in a common front to defend democracy.

In order to salvage, strengthen and reshape American democracy, a new socioeconomic foundation is required, backed up by a system of political rule really representing the majority of the people. The democracy of the past was tied up with the advancement of capitalism. Now that its achievements are threatened by the retrogression of capitalism, the democracy of the future is necessarily bound up with the progress of labor and the program of the socialist movement.

It took two revolutions to make the United States as democratic as it has been and to keep it that way. It will take a third to make this country thoroughly and securely democratic. Just as the establishment of democracy in the United States involved the abolition of foreign domination and of feudal and slave property, so the preservation and extension of democracy demands the removal of the equally outmoded power and property of the financial and industrial moguls. Bourgeois democracy has to be supplanted by the higher form of workers' democracy.

This socialist program is abhorrent to the conservatives who are determined to defend capitalism, come what may. It likewise displeases and disturbs the liberals who want to repair and rehabilitate capitalism. They look upon anyone who proposes to revolutionize the present system through working-class action as a deluded victim of doctrinaire Marxism.

How can democracy be transferred from a capitalist to a socialist basis, the liberals argue, when not only the capitalists oppose it but most of the American people, workers included, do not accept this idea nowadays or even know about it? Wouldn't it be more reasonable to try to expand democracy without overstepping the existing economic and political framework?

This argument shows how little the gradualists grasp the dynamics of the class struggle for democracy in our time. For that is precisely what the American people can be expected to do for an extended period of indeterminate duration. The question is: what will be the outcome of their efforts to enforce their claims and obtain their just rights by exerting increased pressure upon the capitalist regime?

The liberals stake their position upon the capacities of the capitalists to respond to the appeals and satisfy the escalating demands of the people, white and black. The Marxists have no such confidence. They predict that the harder the masses press and the more concessions they exact, the more obdurate and tyrannical the financial oligarchy will become. The sharpening of their differences will ultimately force a showdown on the issue of democracy in a revolutionary way, as happened in 1776 and 1861.

But the alignment of social forces and the objectives of the struggle will be quite different. The people will not combine with progressive capitalists against the upholders of the old order but against the capitalist attempts to impose their naked despotism upon the nation. The workers and their allies will discover in the course of their defensive actions that, in order to bring about a broader democracy and smash the dictatorship of big business, socialist measures will have to be taken under their own independent power.

The consciousness of the new fighters for freedom will be transformed as the struggles between capital and labor, and between the white power structure and the blacks and Chicanos, proceed from one stage to the next. Regardless of their mutual relations at any given stage, the mass of workers will approach and appraise a maturing revolutionary situation in a different way from the socialist vanguard. By virtue of their scientific

insight into the necessary development of capitalism, Marxists are able to connect the beginnings of the conflict between
capital and labor with its culmination. In each successive phase
of their collisions, they foresee the growth and ripening of their
irreconcilable antagonisms and consciously prepare for the
showdown.

The broad masses, on the other hand, move along from
one landmark to the next, testing their strength, improving
their positions and increasing their understanding without as
yet grasping the whole line of development and its logical
goal. The basic revolutionary significance of their actions becomes disclosed to them only at its denouement, when it crashes
down upon them in full force, demanding the most drastic
decisions.

The empirical conclusions they embrace at this decisive turning point then coincide with the theoretical and programmatic
positions envisaged and previously formulated by the Marxists. They likewise repudiate in practice the conservatism of
the short-sighted liberals whose horizon is bounded by the
established order.

This conception of the development of the internal struggle for democracy is vehemently repudiated by liberalism.
Although some of its more radical exponents see that capitalism is more and more hostile to the perpetuation of democracy and may even have to yield at some time in some
way to socialism, they unite in asserting that revolution is
not — and should not be — that way. They forbid the contest
for national supremacy between capital and labor to go beyond the boundaries they prescribe, although the essence of
all forward movements in history is that they break through
the customary limits laid down in the past.

Though revolution did bring greater democracy to America in the distant past, it cannot do so in the future, insist
the opponents of socialism. Even worse, the specter of a workers' revolution would imperil democracy because it would pro-
voke a counterrevolutionary dictatorship by the more powerful capitalist rulers. The future of democracy therefore depends
upon diminishing class feelings and class actions, not upon
developing and organizing them. How this is to be done without abolishing exploitative relations and class differences in
our society, the liberals do not tell us.

Nonetheless, the meaning of their message is plain. Unless
the workers and the oppressed renounce their struggle for
emancipation and stay within the status quo, their masters
will punish them by scrapping democracy. This is a formula

for passivity and capitulation which can only serve to embolden the worst reactionaries and lead in the end to the destruction of democracy and the labor movement, as prefascist Italy and Germany demonstrated.

The liberal insistence upon maintaining the existing balance of class forces ignores the implications of the fact that the development of capitalist society in the twentieth century has brought about a profound and irreversible change in the situation and prospects of democracy. So long as the bourgeoisie, big or little, was a force for social, economic and cultural progress, it could further the cause of democracy. Now the economic, political and military necessities of that class not only preclude such a role but make the imperialists the deadliest foe of democracy at home and abroad.

Thus the struggle for the preservation and promotion of democracy has passed to other hands. According to Marxist analysis and the test of events in this century, the leadership in the next forward thrust of democratization belongs to the antithesis of the capitalist exploiters — the working class and its allies among the oppressed sections of the population.

The most powerful and important of these forces within the United States is the millions of Afro-Americans who are waging so persistent a battle for their self-determination. The movement for black liberation has a twofold character. It combines a democratic struggle for the self-determination of an oppressed nationality with a proletarian thrust against the capitalist regime. This explosive mixture has a highly revolutionary potential because the possessors of power cannot satisfy either the democratic demands for an end to discrimination and for community control, or the working-class demands for living wages, adequate housing, education, social and medical services, etc.

Afro-Americans have been the principal victims of the profit system at all stages of its development in North America. Despite their formal emancipation from slavery, they have never enjoyed equality. Their revolt against the deprivation of civil and human rights is the most crucial struggle for democracy going on in the United States today.

This is widely recognized. But their movement involves much more than that. The bulk of the black people, concentrated in the biggest cities and the key industries and services, belong to the most exploited sections of the working class. Their status as the poorest of the poor imparts a special direction of development to the struggles of the blacks. Their confrontation with the capitalist ruling class that denies equality, upholds white supremacy, segregation and discrimination and profits the most from these abominations, sharpens the revolutionary edge of their struggle and gives it an anticapitalist character, regardless of the consciousness of its participants and the views of many of its current leaders. The same considerations apply to the nationalist movement of the Chicano population.

The anticapitalist momentum of the struggle of the Afro-Americans, Chicanos, Native Americans and other oppressed peoples for national liberation is a built-in feature of every popular movement for democracy in our age. In earlier centuries the struggle for democratic rights was primarily aimed against precapitalist institutions and rulers. Nowadays, whether it breaks out in the colonial or the industrialized countries, it is willy-nilly directed against capitalist sovereignty and imperialist domination. Any serious mass movement for the acquisition or protection of democracy becomes more and more overtly anticapitalist and flows into socialist channels.

This logic of the permanent revolution, whereby the national people's revolutions which started on a democratic basis went forward to consciously socialist aims and achievements, characterized the armed struggles which overturned capitalism in Yugoslavia, China, North Vietnam and Cuba. The same line of development from originally democratic to more and more consciously anticapitalist demands, objectives and leadership is bound to assert itself in the Afro-American movement. As the struggle for basic human rights and power to control their own destiny deepens and widens, as the breach between the representatives of the capitalist power structure and the black masses becomes more and more unbridgeable, the drive for national liberation will merge with the struggle for full social liberation.

The propagandists for the ruling class stand many things on their head. They advertise Washington as the watchman over "the free world" while utilizing a retinue of despots and stamping upon the independence of brave peoples like the Dominicans, Guatemalans and Vietnamese. They systematically misrepresent the Marxist positions on democracy by counterposing themselves as ardent defenders of democracy to the revolutionary socialists who are lumped together with Stalinists and caricatured as totalitarians. Sanctimonious liberals add to this confusion about the real roles of the adversary camps.

The civil-liberties record is the most convincing refutation of this inversion of the real state of affairs. Who has defended and who has endangered democracy in the United States over the past twenty-five years? In thousands of cases, the capitalist authorities have wielded the legislative and legal machinery they command to deprive others of their rights. This is an indubitable fact.

On the other hand, the revolutionary Marxists have been in the forefront of the struggle to ward off attacks upon civil liberties and labor's rights. They were far more consistent than numerous craven liberals who refused to speak out for the 110,000 Japanese-American deportees herded into detention camps during the Second World War or failed to uphold the constitutional rights of the Communists indicted under the Smith Act. Contrast these defaults with the principled attitude of the Socialist Workers Party which rallied to the support of the victimized Stalinists, even though their leaders had defamed the Trotskyists and endorsed the frame-up of Trotskyists under that same law during the Second World War.

The Marxists have defended the rights of all victims of reactionary persecution, whether these were Jehovah's Witnesses, pacifists, anarchists, Afro-Americans or other Third World peoples. They have opposed all forms of discriminatory legislation from the antilabor Taft-Hartley and Landrum-Griffin acts to the restrictions upon minority parties. They have condemned any attempt by the authorities to take away any person's freedom of expression.

These actions conform to the traditional Marxist positions on democracy. Socialists consider that the specific guarantees in the Bill of Rights — freedom of religion, freedom of speech, freedom of the press, freedom of assembly, the right to petition for a redress of grievances, freedom from arbitrary arrest — are precious acquisitions of past struggles. However much they may be restricted or infringed upon, all these liberties must be cherished and safeguarded. They are essential to the well-being of the people and facilitate the efforts of the working class to better its conditions and move forward to a new order.

Marxists uphold the democratic republic over all other modes of rule in class society and fight for the utmost expansion of popular rights within it, because that kind of state is most advantageous to the education and organization of the working masses and their preparation to take power and direct society. Militant struggle for democratic demands can accelerate the advance of the class struggle by stimulating the autonomous activity of the masses, dispelling their illusions about the capitalist regime, radicalizing their consciousness and increasing their self-confidence.

Marxism diverges from liberalism, and goes far beyond it not over the duty to defend civil liberties but over the attitude to be taken toward the capitalist regime and its pseudo-democratic pretensions. Liberals and reformists look upon bourgeois democracy as the ultimate means of transferring power to the people. They rely upon the capitalist government to live up to its professed allegiance to democratic principles and thereby propose to confine the struggle for democracy within the limits of the established order. This permits the plutocratic possessors of power to lay down the ground rules for the conduct of that struggle.

Marxists take a fundamentally different approach to the problem. They regard bourgeois democracy not as an end in itself but as one stage in the evolution of popular sovereignty whose progressive achievements have to be preserved. However, these conquests continue to be imperiled by the ever-more reactionary rule of the rich during the decay of capitalism. They can be maintained and expanded only through the independent action and organization of the working masses and all the oppressed against the monopolists and militarists, which should ultimately lead to their dispossession from power.

In the light of the world contest for supremacy between capitalism and socialism, which has dominated twentieth-century history, parliamentary democracy in the United States as elsewhere can no longer count on a secure and stable future. Imperialist reaction and militarism represent a rising trend in the present phase of capitalism while bourgeois democracy moves in a descending line.

There are plenty of signs in the United States today of the mobilization of the forces of ultrareaction and the polarization of social and political tendencies to the right and to the left. These tensions will be accelerated and exacerbated by any economic decline or social shake-up. The intensifying conflicts within its organism contain the sources of the disruption and undoing of bourgeois democracy.

The irrepressible antagonism between the dominant monopolists and the strivings for equality, social justice and even for life itself among the masses of the American population holds out two opposing lines of long-range development for American politics.

One is the road to a socialist democracy. The other is the road marked out and being traversed by the corporate rich whose "warfare state" is dragging the nation toward political reaction. This second process inexorably heads toward the enfeeblement of liberal democracy and its dispossession by some mode of open dictatorship. Bourgeois democracy, like bourgeois society itself, creates its own gravediggers.

With the immense resources at its disposal, U. S. capitalism may stave off the total collapse of its constitutional democracy in the short run. There can be multiple variants of political development before the most vicious agents of capitalist reaction come to grips with the representatives of the working masses. But whatever the intervening phases may be, one or the other of these opposing class forces must become the successor of the traditional political power.

Both of these alternatives that would emerge from the disintegration and collapse of bourgeois democracy appear remote and unthinkable to the ordinary Americans who regard the existing state of affairs as unalterable and everlasting. They are unaware that the earlier revolutionary upheavals and epochs in our national life broke forth unexpectedly and caught the people by surprise, forcing their minds to catch up with the acceleration of events in a hurry. Moreover, it was not the offensive of the revolutionaries but the intolerable encroachments of ruling-class reaction upon the rights of the people that precipitated the final conflict between the contending camps.

Democracy is an overhead expense for the capitalist rulers which they are willing to pay for only so long as they can afford it. Whenever the monopolists observe that sections of the oppressed aggressively utilize democratic rights and institutions to promote their welfare, when they see the workers and their organizations strongly challenge their supremacy, they feel that the democratic bodies and norms are becoming too dangerous a threat and hasten to restrict and eventually do away with them entirely.

The aim of their resort to authoritarianism is not merely to cripple and destroy such democratic prerogatives as the power of parliament, contesting parties, regular elections, the right to vote, a free press and other general rights. Their class objectives go further than that.

Bourgeois democracy harbors valuable elements of workers' democracy, such as the trade unions, that first-line defense of the toilers' incomes; the labor political parties; the labor and socialist publications; the educational, cooperative and social-welfare agencies. These achievements can serve as levers for the conquest of proletarian power. The prime function of bourgeois dictatorships is to break up and outlaw such institutions in order to terrorize, atomize and paralyze the anticapitalist forces.

In order to protect all such democratic institutions, Marxists are ready to fight, arms in hand if need be, against ultra-reactionary movements aiming to erase them. For the sake of self-preservation, the working class is duty-bound to combat would-be military dictators and fascists from their first appearance and prevent their legions from growing strong enough to seize power. This lesson, driven home by the experiences of the working class during the rise of European fascism, applies to the counterrevolutionary tendencies at work in the major imperialist power, as it is being driven back by the advancing forces of socialism on other continents and confronted by increasing mass opposition within its own borders.

However, it is not enough, and indeed it would be a losing game, to confine the struggle for greater democratization within the bounds of a capitalist regime which keeps on spawning ultrareactionary movements. Such a purely defensive posture for the democratic and proletarian forces in the confrontation with capitalist reaction is conservative and self-defeating. While it is imperative to resist all manifestations of antidemocratic action, it is above all necessary to uproot their causes. The best defense of democracy is the most powerful mass offensive for workers' power and socialism.

This requires the implementation of a revolutionary program, perspective and strategy. The pivot of such a program is the reliance of the working masses upon their own organizations and independent mobilizations to protect democratic rights and extend them. Capitalism in its decadence strives to snatch away from the people even those freedoms they have won through previous struggles.

Liberals beseech the people to put their trust in capitalist politicians and stay within the two-party system in order to keep America democratic and at peace with other countries. Yet all the Democratic presidents they have endorsed from Roosevelt, who signed the Smith Act, to Johnson, who escalated the intervention in Vietnam despite his campaign promises, have supported legislation cutting down the rights of the people.

The only efficacious way to defend democracy is through independent political organization and mass action directed against the representatives of capitalism. The prospects of democracy are inseparably linked with the struggle for the socialist revolution which will bring the masses to power.

Liberals have an extremely straitened conception of the exercise of democratic processes. Making a fetish of purely parliamentary procedures, they wish to limit the registration of popular opinion to the regularly elected representative bodies. They reprobate mass actions which take place outside of conventional channels as illegitimate pressures upon the temporary officeholders.

Street demonstrations, sit-downs and sit-ins, strikes and other forms of direct mass action appear to them as violations rather than expressions of the popular will. When these forms of protest are resorted to, they call for strict adherence to normal constitutional methods.

Marxists, on the other hand, encourage and organize popular protests. Direct action by the masses is as vital to the practice of democracy as voting on election day. In the Middle Ages the right "to convoke a multitude" was the exclusive prerogative of the public power. According to Saint Thomas Aquinas, it could not be undertaken on the initiative of a private person, any more than a declaration of war could.

Under police states, as under feudalism, mass demonstrations are forbidden and their participants subjected to severe penalties. The rights of free assembly and public demonstration had to be torn from the ruling powers before they became incorporated into constitutional law. The propertied classes have ever since sought to hold their exercise to the minimum because such interventions change the relationship of forces to the advantage of the masses rather than the masters. And they can culminate in upsurges, general strikes and uprisings which shake the foundations of the established order.

In the preface to *The History of the Russian Revolution,* Trotsky emphasized the revolutionary impact of direct action by the oppressed masses. "The most indubitable feature of a revolution is the direct interference of the masses into historic events. In ordinary times the state, be it monarchical or democratic, elevates itself above the nation, and history is made by specialists in that line of business — kings, ministers, bureaucrats, parliamentarians, journalists. But at those crucial moments when the old order becomes no longer endurable to the masses, they break over the barriers excluding them from the political arena, sweep aside their traditional representatives, and create by their own interference the initial groundwork for a new regime. . . . The history of a revolution is for us first of all a history of the forcible entrance of the masses into the realm of rulership over their own destiny." [1]

Moderate liberals sense this subversive potential of mass action, even when they do not articulate their fear of it so forthrightly as the conservatives. In their exhortations to the unruly plebeians not to transgress the limits of the parliamentary system, they conveniently forget that the parliaments themselves resulted from such insurgency.

The conflict between the diametrically opposite programs for defending and extending democracy under capitalism proposed by liberalism and Marxism has been reflected within the labor and socialist movements. Revolutionists have been divided from reformists on this issue ever since the French Socialist deputy Alexandre Millerand entered a coalition cabinet in 1898. He took a seat as minister of commerce alongside General Galliffet, butcher of the Paris Commune, to save, so Millerand said, republican institutions from the monarchists and nationalists.

This was by no means the last time that, under the pretext of defending democratic institutions and the welfare of the working class, reformist socialists (and then the Stalinists) turned into passive accomplices of the liberal bourgeoisie and pursued a reactionary course.

In criticism of Jaurès's original support to Millerand's ministerialism, Rosa Luxemburg wrote: "Instead of making the independent political struggle of the Socialist Party the *permanent, fundamental* element and unity with the bourgeois radicals the *varying* and *incidental* element, this principle caused Jaurès to adopt the opposite tactic: the alliance with the bourgeois democrats became the *constant,* and the independent political struggles the *accidental* element." [2]

This has been the political essence of all the Democratic and Popular Fronts and electoral combinations that the Social Democrats and Stalinists have participated in since Millerand's betrayal. Under the slogan of saving democracy from reaction, they have sacrificed the political independence and subordinated the struggles of the working class for the sake of maintaining an alliance with this or that political agency of the liberal bourgeoisie. The German Socialists supported President Hindenberg on this basis, helping Hitler come to power in the prewar period; the Communist Party rallied to de Gaulle from 1944 to 1946, enabling French capitalism to restabilize itself. The same policy of "the lesser evil" led the right-wing socialists and Stalinists in the United States to back Roosevelt, Truman, Kennedy and Johnson as shielders of democracy and peace against the dangers of war and reaction represented by the Republican candidates.

Though the rhetoric may change from one occasion to the

next, the line of policy remains constant: the political independence and industrial action of the workers is sabotaged or suspended in order to support one wing of the capitalist ruling class against another. The inevitable and predictable result has been the weakening of democracy and the reinforcement of capitalist reaction.

As against this substitution of class collaboration for revolutionary policy, Marxists contend that democracy is doomed unless the workers and their allies come to the fore in the course of the struggle against reaction. Despite the notorious deficiencies of organized labor as it is presently constituted and led, the working class remains the social bulwark of American democracy. The sheer existence of powerful unions restrains the state from proceeding too fast and too far with repressive measures.

The working class alone has the potential power to head off the worst onslaughts upon democracy and turn political development in the most progressive direction. As the laboring force and the producers of wealth, the workers can start and stop industry, communications, transport and commerce, as any big strike indicates. Their numbers, their organization, their ties on the job, in addition to their strategic economic situation, can make them the most formidable of fighting forces. Together with the oppressed national minorities, the millions of students, young rebels and other allies, the wage workers would constitute an invincible social and political power that the handful of capitalists — and even the fascist hordes they might muster — would be unable to withstand. That is why the assertion of their independent action strikes such terror in the breasts of the ruling minority.

The workers and their families compose the vast majority of the nation; they have every right to rule. Whatever its merits, bourgeois democracy has to be exposed and opposed because it does not give the decision-making powers to the majority but functions as a screen for the domination of the enemies of the people. The final authority which the masses have claimed and democracy proclaimed is denied them by the master-class structure of capitalism.

The existing system has to be replaced by a superior type of democracy which will enable the producers of wealth to control their lives and livelihoods and expand their freedoms. That can only be a socialist democracy.

SECTION IV

PROBLEMS AND PROSPECTS

OF POSTCAPITALIST

DEMOCRACY

13

SOCIALISM AND BUREAUCRACY

Twentieth-century developments demonstrated that both the bourgeois and petty-bourgeois democratic movements had run up against inherent limits and largely exhausted their potentialities. This did not halt the advance of democracy but shifted it onto an essentially different socioeconomic basis. As the capitalist owners become more and more hostile to democracy and seek salvation in some form of police state, the historical responsibility for preserving and promoting democracy devolves upon the working class.

Since mass political consciousness usually lags behind the pace of economic development and changes in class alignments, most people have been slow to recognize the import of these fundamental historical facts and even slower to act in accord with them. Socialist theory seeks to explain the leading part played by the working class in lifting the struggle for democracy to a higher plateau.

Labor's independent role in furthering democracy began early in its career as a distinct social formation since the new class had to fight for the elementary right to act as an organized force. The workers waged hard battles to win the rights to unionize, strike, picket, bargain collectively and set up the closed shop. Even after these rights of labor were recognized by law, it took prodigious efforts to have them realized in fact. The industrial organization drives which broke down the open shop in the major American corporations during the 1930s culminated in sit-down strikes and factory occupations, which at times verged on virtual civil warfare.

The labor movement under capitalism has been the strongest proponent of progressive social legislation in areas ranging from free public schooling and abolition of imprisonment for debt to the eight-hour day and an end to child labor. It has championed electoral reform and the widening of the franchise. Its parties have provided a challenge and, in Great Britain and Western Europe, alternative governments to the direct agencies of the ruling class.

The barriers that the existence and activity of working-class organizations raise against encroachments upon the liberties of the people are one reason why reactionaries resist any extension of the power of the labor movement and strive to diminish its rights and influence.

With the advent of scientific socialism in the mid-nineteenth century, the movement for democracy transcended the horizon of bourgeois society in program and outlook. Thenceforward the struggle for democracy passed beyond the limited aims of improving the conditions and expanding the liberties of the working masses within the framework of private property. It was ever more consciously bound up with the perspective of overthrowing the capitalist state and bourgeois property relations. Political democracy was to be supplemented and strengthened by the acquisition of economic and social democracy.

From the publication of *The Communist Manifesto* in 1848 to the First World War, this avowed revolutionary goal was no more than a statement of intentions providing a guide to action for international socialism. With the victory of the Bolsheviks in 1917, the struggle for a new type of democracy along socialist lines passed from theoretical prevision to political actuality. Those democratic tasks which had been carried out under bourgeois auspices in the older revolutions, such as the overthrow of the aristocratic monarchy, the state church and landed nobility, distribution of the land to its plebeian cultivators, the independence of oppressed nationalities and the creation of representative political institutions, were for the first time undertaken under the leadership of the industrial proletariat heading the popular masses.

The solution of the long-postponed tasks of democratization in those backward countries which had not experienced a bourgeois revolution, initiated by the Russians toward the close of the First World War, was duplicated by the Yugoslavs, Chinese, Vietnamese and Cubans after the Second World War. All these twentieth-century revolutions had a special combined character, which is the key to their highly contradictory development.

They embodied the merging of a peasant insurrection, characteristic of the bourgeois revolution, with the proletarian conquest of power, which is the essence of a socialist revolution. This fusion of the bourgeois and socialist components of revolutionary change involved skipping over the stage of parliamentary democracy which had issued from the consolidation of the gains of the class struggles in the advanced capitalisms of the preceding centuries. Political democracy thereupon assumed essentially different traits and prospects. In form it brought forward a new type of representation — councils or soviets of workers, peasants and soldiers — and it was based on postcapitalist economic foundations.

When the workers and their plebeian partners succeeded in dismantling the political structures of landlord and bourgeois rule, demolishing the old forms of the capitalist state through revolutionary mass action, casting off the bondage of imperialism and taking over the national economy, the problem was immediately posed: what kind of state should replace the regimes which upheld the old society?

Before discussing the actual political developments during the half-century of anticapitalist world revolution since 1917, it is indispensable to review the teachings of Marxism on the subjects of democracy, the rule of the working class and socialism. The founders of scientific socialism, Marx and Engels, took it for granted that the working class would utilize the institutions of democracy to get rid of the power and property of the exploiters.

Engels wrote in his *Principles of Communism* (1847), the first rough draft of *The Communist Manifesto:* "Democracy will be of no use to the proletariat unless it serves as the means for a direct attack upon private property and for safeguarding the existence of the proletariat." [1] This conception has ever since been the dividing line between revolutionists and reformists within the labor and socialist movements: the one viewing democracy as a means of disposing of capitalism, the other as an excuse for maintaining it indefinitely.

Marx and Engels anticipated that the abolition of capitalism and landlordism would at once bring about an immense expansion of democracy. The new revolutionary regime would be the outcome of the victory of the masses over a minority of wealthy proprietors and would carry out the mandates of that majority. "The first step in the revolution of the working class," they wrote in *The Communist Manifesto,* "is to raise the proletariat to the position of ruling class, to establish democracy. The proletariat will use its political supremacy to wrest, by degrees, all capital from the bourgeoisie, to centralize all instruments of production in the hands of the state, i. e., of the proletariat organized as the ruling class; and to increase the total of the productive forces as rapidly as possible." [2]

Marxism proclaimed that the elevation of the proletariat to the status of the ruling class through the destruction of the old state machinery, the creation of a new power and the measures of expropriation would make possible a genuine democracy of the working masses for the first time since the establishment of class society. All other freedoms depended upon securing the right to life and labor and the socialist revolution would provide that material groundwork of democracy. The inalienable right of all workers to a livelihood would be assured by the nationalization of the means of production and the monopoly of foreign trade and their democratic control over the government and the publicly owned economy.

Marx, Engels and their successors also took into account the realities of the revolutionary struggle for the overthrow of the old order and the installation of a new regime. It would be preferable, they believed, if the replacement of the capitalists by the workers as the supreme power could take place peacefully and by mutual consent. But it would be extremely unrealistic and unwise to count on so favorable a variant of development. The whole history of social struggle records that, while it is conceivable, and even possible under extraordinary circumstances, for such an event to occur, it is a rare exception, not the rule.

The transfer of power from one ruling class to another, and even more, the supplanting of one social system by another, has almost always taken place through severe class conflicts and prolonged civil war. That has been the lesson of the democratic revolutions in the past and of all the socialist revolutions since 1917. That was the way national independence was wrested from Great Britain and slavery crushed in the United States.

On what empirical evidence and analytic grounds could it therefore be expected that the imperialist plutocracy which has unparalleled wealth and power to lose would relinquish these in a peaceful manner to the democratic decisions of the people? Precisely because the possessing classes will put up vindictive resistance to their expropriation and to any radical transformation of the social and political order, only a proletarian revolution can clear the road to socialism and a superior form of democracy.

The struggle for power would impose upon the progressive

forces the obligation of taking appropriate measures to defend themselves and their gains against the aggressions and attacks of the counterrevolution, as the American people were compelled to do in 1775-76 and again in 1861. When the battle was joined, the toilers and their leaders would have every justification for such action, whatever the constitutional niceties of the situation, since they would be representing the rights and interests of the majority of the people and implementing the most urgent tasks and tendencies of social progress. Today they would be the hope of the future in the most literal sense, since one of their aims would be to defuse the peril of nuclear or bacteriological extermination of the human species.

During the revolutionary period of the transfer of supremacy and ownership from the plutocracy to the people, the political regime would inescapably have a twofold character. It would be substantially democratic in its social base, its enactments, its program. At the same time it would have to take repressive measures against those active counterrevolutionaries who would be fighting against the democratic and socialist changes arms in hand, trying to overturn the power and institutions of the working masses, annul the achievements of the revolution and bring back the old order, as the slaveholders and supporters of the Confederacy sought to do in the Civil War.

Since 1917, wherever the working masses have set out to create their own power, the possessing classes have tried to stop them by force. This happened in the Soviet republic, which took power in Petrograd with fewer than a hundred casualties and then had to fight for three frightful years on twenty-one fronts against the internal counterrevolution and foreign interventionists. This combat between the revolutionary and counterrevolutionary camps was later repeated in Yugoslavia, China, Vietnam and Cuba.

From the Paris Commune of 1871 through the aborted German Revolution of 1918 and the strangled Chinese Revolution of 1925-27 to the slaughter of half a million Communists in the Indonesia of 1965, the bourgeoisie on all continents have displayed the utmost ruthlessness and disregard of democratic norms in forestalling and crushing the uprisings of the oppressed.

The harsh military measures and abridgments of freedom instituted during the period of civil warfare were a stern but unavoidable necessity if the means of abolishing class society and protecting the new-found democracy of the people were to be effectively safeguarded. These dictatorial enactments were directed exclusively against the class enemies of the revolution.

They were to be eased and eliminated as soon as the restoration of social peace under the new regime allowed. It was not to be considered the permanent and normal state of affairs throughout the period of the transition to a classless society, as Stalinism and Maoism later preached and practiced.

From the very beginning, the rule of the working class together with all the oppressed would bring far more democracy to the masses than they had ever known in the past. The revolution was to be made for their benefit and through their organized action. The toilers would exercise democratic control over the state, make the decisions on all vital matters and enforce them through their freely constituted organs of power.

In *The State and Revolution,* his classical though unfinished work on the subject, Lenin explained, in refutation of the anarchists, that the working class needs its own state when it takes power. Society cannot function without a state so long as classes and social conflicts exist and the economy cannot cover everyone's needs, although the ultimate aim of socialism is to do away with the state as an agency of coercion. The proletarian regime has to defend itself and the gains of the revolution against the resistance of the exploiters at home or abroad, as well as guiding the masses of the population in the tasks of economic, social and cultural construction. If the first obligations require military and police agencies and forcible measures which have a dictatorial edge, the second set of tasks has a democratic character. Whether coercive or constructive, the administration and execution of both functions should rely upon the mobilization and enthusiastic support of the popular masses.

Lenin discussed the measures that could keep the new regime genuinely democratic, under the control of the workers, responsible to them and responsive to their demands. He was keenly aware of the dangers of reversion to a militarized, bureaucratized and authoritarian state apparatus like those which had arisen during the recoil against previous revolutionary upheavals. The principal bodies which arrogated exorbitant authority to themselves in oppressing the people were the standing army and its officer corps, the professional bureaucracy, the police, the judiciary and the clergy.

Lenin proposed to curb the repressive and reactionary role of these parasitic organs of the old state by handing over their functions to the people themselves or at least, for the interim period, placing them under the unremitting surveillance of the masses. The professional army was to be replaced by a popular militia, the people in arms. The police were to be stripped of all political functions and made responsible for their conduct to the workers' councils. All state support to the clergy would be withdrawn, though believers of any denomination would have full right to voluntarily support their churches and pastors. Judges appointed for long terms or life would be replaced by elected judges. Juries and courts would be staffed and surveyed by neighbors of individuals accused of criminal offenses. Full-time officials at all levels were to be the real servants of the people and not act like imperious bigshots heedless of popular feelings and problems.

The objective was to give the workers constant control over all elements of the state apparatus until such time as the development of socialism enabled the functions performed by full-time professionals to be assumed by rotation among the citizen body, as had been done on a much smaller scale and in a more restricted and primitive way under Athenian democracy.

Lenin proposed numerous safeguards against the estrangement of the officialdom from the people and their elevation above them. All public officials were to be elected and subject to recall periodically or in emergency for any ill-performance of their duties, just as shop stewards stand liable to revocation today where rank-and-file workers have a democratic shop union. To cut down careerism and corruption, no officeholder was to receive more than the highest paid worker. More and more of the functionaries were to be selected from the working masses and, when their special assignments in the state apparatus were completed, would return to their previous occupations and statuses.

Lenin urged as thoroughgoing a reformation of political representation as of everyday administration of the government. The proletarian power would have to make a conscious break with the evils of parliamentarism, "the congressional racket," as it is called in the United States, by narrowing as far as possible the gap between the legislative and executive powers. All representative institutions were to be transformed from debating societies, designed to dupe the people while carrying out the dictates of the rich, into working bodies. The deputies of the toilers would not simply pass laws and proclaim edicts but personally check to see that their purposes were implemented in practice. They should not be sequestered in a national or state capital, or city hall, fussing over legislation which does not take account of the actual conditions or most pressing demands of their constituents. They should hold themselves responsible for the results of the application of their enactments.

The type of organization needed for instituting and executing such measures was foreshadowed by the Paris Commune of 1871. It was first created during the Russian Revolution of 1905 and revived in more extensive form in 1917. These were the Workers', Peasants' and Soldiers' Councils, known under their Russian name of soviets. These directly elected organs did not originate through the prevision or prescription of any political party. They were spontaneously improvised by the insurgent masses as instruments to register their will, organize their forces and carry forward their struggles against the czarist, landlord and bourgeois authorities.

These democratic bodies furnished the foundation and framework of the new state apparatus of the Soviet republic after the October 1917 triumph. It is significant that, in many of the subsequent revolutionary upsurges of our era that have expressed the demands and aspirations of the oppressed, councils of this type have sprung up as democratic organs of power. This was the case in the German Revolution of 1918, the second Chinese Revolution of 1925-27, at the start of the Spanish civil war in 1936, and, more recently, during the antibureaucratic revolt of the Hungarian workers in 1956. Such councils are anathema to the possessing classes and to all bureaucratic formations, precisely because they give independent political expression and executive power to the most advanced elements of the working class and are the most flexible means for mobilizing the broadest layers of the masses for revolutionary objectives.

The constitution, consolidation and democratic operation of a system of workers' councils or committees of action is the best antidote for bureaucratism. The councils are not to be simply administrative organs for carrying out directions from above. To serve the interests of a popular democracy, they must provide an arena where all revolutionary tendencies and shades of opinion in the working class have representation according to their strength through delegates freely elected from the workplaces and neighborhoods who can present and argue for the adoption of their proposals. The forum of the councils, which retain and exercise the supreme power and make decisions on all vital issues, can provide the surest guarantee for political democracy during the period of transition from capitalism to socialism.

It is notorious that this program for a democratic workers' state, envisaged by the founders of Marxism and attempted after 1917 by the Bolsheviks led by Lenin and Trotsky, could not be realized under the given historical circumstances. The democratic initiatives and institutions of the Russian Revolution of the early years of the Soviet republic were extinguished after Lenin's death and the suppression of the Communist Left Opposition. Soviet, party and trade-union democracy, already curtailed by the imperatives of civil war and the first years of economic reconstruction, was totally extirpated by the Stalinist machine.

The host of enemies of socialism point to this defeat of the first experiment in proletarian political democracy as proof positive that anticapitalist revolution inevitably ends in despotism and servitude. They contend that the forecasts of Marx, Lenin and their cothinkers of a more bountiful democracy after the workers conquer power are, if not the deliberate deceit of power-hungry elitists and unscrupulous intellectuals, a Utopian dream. Once the Bolsheviks seized and wielded the power, they argue, the hard facts compelled them to jettison these illusions, although the myths they succored remained useful to buttress their authority and console the masses.

The unexpected and paradoxical political evolution of the Russian Revolution from democracy to autocracy does pose a problem of the first magnitude which cannot be brushed aside as insignificant, as so many supporters and sympathizers of Moscow have so long sought to do. How did it come about that the first workers' regime not only failed to fulfill the expectations of its heralds and architects, and the masses themselves, but led to the one-man rule of Stalin?

In his famous speech at the Twentieth Congress of the Russian Communist Party in 1956, and again at the Twenty-Second Congress in October 1961, Khrushchev condemned the dreadful consequences of Stalin's tyranny. But he failed to give any historical materialist explanation of this phenomenon, which dominated and disfigured Soviet life for three stormy decades and in which he and his associates took a prominent part.

To cover up their own tracks, Stalin's heirs have been driven to the silly subterfuge of attributing what they call "the personality cult" to Stalin's pathological traits or mistakes. There are three faults in their explanation. It violates the method of Marxism. It is circular reasoning to ascribe the cult of an individual who subjugated an entire people to the acts and influence of that single individual. And it leaves unanswered the basic question: how could such a superstition and its appalling practices have arisen and fastened themselves upon a nation that had just succeeded in overwhelming capitalism, swore by the teachings of Marx and Lenin, and was on the way to socialism?

The main reasons for this abhorrent aberration in Soviet development were set forth in a series of writings during the 1920s and 1930s by one of the two leaders of the Bolshevik party who were most instrumental in the creation, the defense and the primary accomplishments of the Soviet Union. That was Leon Trotsky. He and his associates in the Left Opposition not only followed the growth of Russian bureaucratism step by step but also fought its consequences all along the way and paid for their fidelity to the ideals of socialist democracy with the loss of their liberties and lives.

Trotsky explained that the political structure of the first post-capitalist society had undergone a pathological degeneration as the result of a specific configuration of historical circumstances outside and inside the Soviet Union which disoriented the Bolshevik party, derailed the revolution and transferred sovereign power from the workers and peasants to a privileged bureaucratic caste.

Here an analogy may be helpful. A child stricken by rickets because of defective nutrition may grow up stunted, with curvature of the spine, bowlegs and bulky head, if he lacks those vital dietary ingredients which produce a normal stature, well-proportioned organs and agreeable features. But the disease can be prevented by proper nutrition and treated with adequate amounts of calcium, phosphorus and vitamin D.

Analogous rules of growth apply to social organizations and their political regimes. The young Soviet republic became a victim of ugly malformations because its society and state were deprived of the conditions and elements needed for normal development during the most formative years.

The Soviet Union was not the first or only country that has suffered in this way. Because of its economic backwardness and historical peculiarities, the budding bourgeois civilization of North America likewise witnessed a revival of antiquated social relations and institutions. American society was disfigured for three hundred years by chattel slavery, an anachronistic mode of production that had largely disappeared from Europe before it was reborn and revitalized across the Atlantic under the spur of the need of commercial capitalism for staple crops like sugar and tobacco. The first American revolution failed to uproot it, and a second was required to rid the United States of the slave power. The ongoing struggle for black liberation testifies to the persistence of its evil effects to this very day. This precedent from American history should be conducive to taking a more objective approach to the problems connected with the vicissitudes of the Russian Revolution and the stages through which its political life has been compelled to pass.

The primordial causes of the enfeeblement of workers' democracy and the triumph of bureaucratic domination were lodged in the international context after 1917. Uninterrupted reverses and inadequate leadership of the working class from 1918 on prevented the socialist revolution from being victorious in the highly industrialized metropolises of Western Europe, Germany in particular. This kept the beleaguered Soviet Union for decades in the vise of imperialist encirclement, cut off from access to the world market and assistance from the more advanced countries. Russia was thrown back upon its own inadequate resources.

The adverse effects of this prolonged isolation were reinforced by unfavorable internal factors which kept pulling back the progress of the revolution. The Russian people had to go through three years of imperialist bloodletting, two revolutions in one year and three years of civil war. After having given so much, they sank back in a collective exhaustion of their energies. The decimation of the revolutionary cadres, the weariness of the Soviet masses, the overwhelming preponderance of the peasantry over a small, fragmented proletariat involved in a shattered industry, led to a loss of faith in immediate relief from outside and in the original perspectives of international revolution.

These objective conditions facilitated the bureaucratization of the Soviet state apparatus and the gradual conservatizing of the Communist cadres at its head. The decline and destruction of Soviet and party democracy, the crushing of the Leninist wing of the party and the replacement of socialist internationalism by nationalist considerations and conceptions, formulated in the theory of building socialism in a single country, further promoted the arbitrary rule of a new aristocracy of functionaries.

Stalin's tyranny was the outgrowth of special economic as well as historical conditions. Soviet democracy was laid low by the meager productivity of Russian industry and agriculture and the terrible poverty and misery it engendered. It has been pointed out that, even under capitalism, a flourishing democracy has largely been the privilege of wealthy nations and that, even where poor countries have set up democratic institutions, as in the colonial and semicolonial world, they are not very sturdy and stable.

The same rule applies to the Soviet Union and other countries with a socialist economic base. The poorer and more backward they are, the more powerful are the tendencies toward bureaucratism and the more likely are the materially, politically and culturally privileged elements and antidemocratic forces within the revolutionary camp to become masters of the situation at the expense of the rights and powers of the masses.

It is indispensable to expropriate the capitalist exploiters, nationalize the means of production and exchange and centralize the planned economy. But these essential measures of the socialist revolution are by themselves insufficient to assure a virile political democracy for the working people. They provide the foundation of the house that has to be built.

The exercise and expansion of democracy depends upon the prevalence of a high and steadily improving standard of living. Unless the economy can provide the necessities and comforts of life for everyone in satisfactory measure, the rat race for food, clothing, shelter and the other means of personal consumption which has marked class society from its birth will be reduplicated to one or another degree under postcapitalist conditions.

In a speech before the Convention, February 5, 1794, Robespierre said: "Democracy is that state in which the people, guided by laws that are its own work, executed for itself all that it can well do, and, by its delegates, all that it cannot do itself." This is still a good definition of a revolutionary democracy. But a great deal hinges upon how much the people can actually do for itself and that depends on the amount of free time it has available for civic duties.

If the masses have to devote most of their working and waking hours to securing the basic material necessities, they cannot find time for political activity, for participating in public affairs, for discussing and deciding questions of policy. The tasks of administration must then be vested in a narrow group of professional functionaries, specialists in managing the affairs of state, the military, the economy, the educational system, the arts and sciences, whose mode of life tends to alienate them from the ranks of the nation.

The first victories over capitalism were achieved in backward countries which did not possess the powers of production to take care of the basic and growing needs of their populations. Soviet economic capacities fell far below the requirements of a socialist abundance and equality, and even the levels attained by the richest capitalisms. The system could supply

enough consumer goods to give more to the few, but not enough
to raise the living standards of the many fast or fairly enough.
Amidst these conditions of scarcity and inequality, some supreme power had to determine who would get what and how
much.

Once the institutions of democratic control by the masses
in the soviets, unions and party had been gutted by the bosses
of the monolithic party, these representatives of the more privileged layers of Soviet society, merged with the state administration, monopolized all the decision-making powers and wielded the means of coercion to enforce their edicts.

This avid caste of upstarts themselves needed an arbiter
as unchallengeable as themselves who could settle all internal
disputes while upholding their sovereign sway. The bureaucracy created this omnipotent, omniscient defender of its interests in its own image. The dictator Stalin was lifted to the
top and stayed there for three decades because he most ably
represented the collective demands and aspirations of the new
elite.

An inescapable question is posed in view of these developments: is an ultrabureaucratic state the predestined product
of any anticapitalist revolution? Yes, categorically assert the
opponents of socialism; nationalized property and totalitarian government form an inseparable partnership.

Marxism analyzes this problem by another method and
reaches an altogether different conclusion. It acknowledges
that certain tendencies toward bureaucratism would necessarily
manifest themselves in the passage from capitalism to socialism. This is no longer a hypothesis but a palpable fact, verified
by the experience of all the existing workers' states, as it had
earlier been foreshadowed by the bureaucratism of the workers' movement in the capitalist lands.

As Lenin wrote in *The State and Revolution*: "There can be
no thought of abolishing the bureaucracy at once everywhere
and completely. That is a Utopia. But to begin to *smash* the
old bureaucratic machine at once and to begin immediately
to construct a new one that will permit all bureaucracy to be
gradually abolished, that is *not* Utopia, this is the experience
of the Commune, this is the direct and immediate task of the
revolutionary proletariat."[3]

The essence of the Marxist position is that such bureaucratic
forces and tendencies need not stamp out democracy, become
all-powerful and organized into a total system of domination,
as happened under Stalinism. They could and should be combated and contained by a conscious political leadership and

the vigilant masses equipped with the necessary means of control.

Two interacting factors contribute to the hypertrophy of bureaucratism. One, which is decisive in the long run, consists of all those objective circumstances unfavorable to the growth of democracy; the other, the subjective element in the process, is the nature and intervention of the conscious political agency, the party. The revolutionary workers and their leadership can take timely steps to counteract the bureaucratic pest and its breeders and beneficiaries. They must be held in check until further victories of the world revolution, along with the raising of the economic and cultural level of the population, reduce the role of the bureaucracy to harmless proportions.

Only a government based upon councils of worker representatives freely elected by those who labor in any capacity can protect and promote democracy within the nation and keep the abuses of bureaucratism within bounds. All those parties which accept the revolutionary regime and work loyally within it should be entitled to function without hindrance and seek support for their program, proposals and perspectives.

Stalinism has so perverted Communist thought that many of the pernicious practices this counterrevolutionary current introduced into the workers' movement are wrongly regarded as part of Marxist principles. One is the false idea that there must be a single party regime throughout the postcapitalist era. Though this institution may be characteristic of totalitarianism, it is alien to Marxist tradition, the intentions of Lenin and the Bolsheviks or the program of Trotskyism which carries them forward. The Bolsheviks, for example, formed their first revolutionary government in 1917 together with the Left Social Revolutionaries and subsequently hoped to bring other democratic parties of the left, such as the Mensheviks, into political legality.

These desires were dashed by the involvement of the Social Revolutionaries and right-wing Mensheviks in counterrevolutionary conspiracies or activities during the civil war and the habits of military command in all spheres that that atmosphere inculcated. This course of events helped deal fatal blows to Soviet democracy, which requires the leaven of multiparty contention to make it genuinely representative of the diverse layers of the population.

In violation of the demands of democracy and the tenets of Marxism, Stalin converted an exceptional emergency situation into a rigid unbreakable dogma in order to serve the needs of his bureaucratic clique. Like all elites, bureaucrats fear to present their ideas in free and open debate before the masses, preferring the methods of maneuver, deceit and compulsion to those of persuasion and conviction.

It may sometimes be unavoidable, especially under conditions of severe and protracted civil conflict in backward countries, for a single revolutionary party to monopolize the political field for a period, as in Cuba. But this should be regarded as a temporary expedient, an exception, a deviation from the normal political life of a healthy workers' state. And even where one party governs, it should not be monolithic in the Stalinist mode, forbidding the expression of divergent views or stigmatizing and punishing dissidents as "counterrevolutionaries" and "agents of imperialism."

There need not be any inevitable progression or downward slide from the prohibition of other parties to the suppression of factions to the omnipotence of the dictator, as the metaphysical critics of Bolshevism allege. But once such tendencies are set into motion, there are strong impulsions to move from one step to the next. The extended rule of a single party is not the expression of strength in a workers' state but a symptom of underlying economic, social and political weaknesses which should not be embellished or waved aside.

A plurality of parties is not only most favorable to the political vitality of the state in the transitional period but also useful to the ruling party as well. The existence of competition and criticism, the presentation of alternative policies and courses, the direct confrontation of differing orientations act as a prod to keep the party from becoming insensitive, complacent and sluggish and deviating too far from the correct course. They can prepare a peaceful and legal replacement if the vanguard should degenerate to the point of failing to fulfill its role as the best representative of the forward march to socialism.

The Stalinist model also fails to make any separation or draw any distinction between the government and the ruling party. The two must be interconnected but they ought not to be identical. The party is entitled to its autonomous internal life and the government should have no right to intervene in its discussions and decisions, or those of any other political organization for that matter. The state should be forbidden by law to take police actions against any of its groupings and members for their dissident views, as is customary in the Stalinized police states.

The vanguard of the toilers, which has presumably earned the confidence of the masses during the struggle for power and maintained their allegiance during the reconstruction of the old order and the building of a new one, must itself preserve an impeccably democratic inner life. All levels of leadership should be elected, subject to recall and their acts periodically submitted to critical review. Its congresses must be regularly held. (In defiance of its own constitution, the Chinese Communist Party held no national congresses for eleven years, from 1958 to 1969.) Party members should have the right to form tendencies and factions and should not be penalized for holding minority opinions, criticizing leaders, official policies or deeds.

The trade unions must not merely be an instrument to echo and execute state policy in industry or for raising productivity and sweating the work force. This "transmission belt" conception of their functions is essentially totalitarian. They should have a certain autonomy in respect to the state and the ruling party so that they can, if necessity dictates, put forward and fight for the unsatisfied grievances of their members and act to protect the income, working conditions and social welfare of their members against injustices or the arbitrariness of the office-holders.

Workers should have the legal right to strike without reprisals if they decide to exercise that right. In most cases, if workers do take such drastic action under a revolutionary regime, this is a signal warning that something has gone wrong in the relations between the government and the class which warrants careful, self-critical investigation by the officialdom to remedy the situation.

Factories and industries should be administered under a system of workers' self-management by councils of representatives elected by everyone in the departments, plants and industrial sector. The national council of worker delegates should have its experts draw up overall plans for the economy, whatever their duration, adopt them after adequate discussion and oversee the fulfillment of their directives.

The system of workers' councils, the separation of state and party, multiparty representation, inner-party democracy, workers' self-management and union rights can be the keystones of a healthy postcapitalist state and the best curatives for the diseases of bureaucratism.

In the light of the experience of the Soviet Union and the first half-century of the world revolution, these institutions have to be supplemented and reinforced by a broad range of other democratic measures. Maximum information and publicity should be made available on all controversial questions in the state institutions, the leading economic bodies and the ruling party. This means full freedom of the press and of assembly along with all other democratic rights accorded in the most enlightened modern constitutions. To safeguard collective as well as individual rights of expression, every political party and tendency should have time to present their ideas and speak their minds over radio and TV, congregate in meeting halls, have headquarters, printshops and periodicals and whatever facilities are required for carrying on their political activity and soliciting support for their proposals.

As Lenin recommended, functionaries should be elected, subject to recall and earning no more than a skilled worker. There should be no permanent appointees or irremovable office-holders.

All elementary judicial safeguards should be accorded accused and arrested persons: the right of *habeas corpus,* which prevents people from being locked up in jail before trial; the right to counsel of their own choice; to specific charges in indictments; to a speedy trial; the right not to be subjected to cruel or unusual punishment; an end to the death penalty; and whatever other provisions have been devised to protect the individual from unjust treatment at the hands of the state.

No secret police will be permitted to pry into the private lives of citizens, keep dossiers upon them, as the FBI and KGB do, or persecute them. The workers shall control the armed forces and police and both shall be kept under the watchful eyes of the representatives of the people.

Thought control of any kind will not be tolerated. There shall be no imposition of uniformity nor official regimentation of cultural, artistic, scientific and educational activities. Cultural freedom is as essential to democracy as political freedom. The lack of it in the stifling atmosphere of the Soviet Union and elsewhere is one of the worst abominations of bureaucratic despotism.

The central aim of all such measures is to draw the greatest number of workers into political activity, make them active, not passive, citizens of the state in its manifold functions and give them a determining role in making the decisions in all vital issues affecting their lives and welfare. That is what the workers' democracy promised by Marxism must strive to do.

The uprooting of women's oppression is bound up with the transformation of the economic forms of family life from a petty individual to a communal basis, above all in the areas of feeding, child care and education. The early Soviet government introduced highly progressive legislation on marriage and the family and instituted a series of deep-going reforms, including the liberalization of divorce laws, legalization of abortions and the establishment of community kitchens and nurseries.

Under Stalin most of these reforms were abolished. Marriage and divorce laws were tightened up, abortions were again illegalized, the cult of the petty-bourgeois family was revived and the Order of Heroine of Motherhood was created for the breeders of large families. A regenerated regime, inspired by a socialist attitude, would reverse this reactionary trend and restore democratic rights to women. It would allot the necessary resources to release women from household servitude and equalize the conditions and opportunities of the sexes.

The attitude of the workers' state toward weak, poor, oppressed and underdeveloped nationalities has turned out to be no less important for the world socialist revolution than it was for the bourgeois state in its democratic forms. There are two main sides to this problem. The first concerns national minorities situated within the boundaries of the given state.

In view of the deprivations and indignities they have suffered from chauvinist governing powers in the past and their apprehensions that the new regime may perpetuate such mistreatment, these sections of the population are entitled to special consideration and concessions. Discrimination or abuse against any grouping or person because of their ethnic origin, race or color will be a serious crime in a workers' state. Such acts will meet with especially severe penalties if committed by official sources or government jobholders. One of the functions of education and culture in the new society will be the creation of a public opinion designed to forestall and quarantine such manifestations.

The second aspect involves the relations between independent workers' states. Socialist policy and morality demands more than formal acknowledgment of respect for the rights and integrity of all nations and peoples. Even capitalist states profess to abide by that rule of equality, however much they disregard it in actuality.

A big, rich and powerful workers' state has special obligations. It must lean over backwards in all dealings with small nations and weaker peoples to give them complete assurance that it is not misusing its superiority and authority to their detriment. The Stalinized Soviet Union has had an abominable record in both respects. Moscow's maltreatment of its own national minorities, such as the Volga Germans, the Crimean Tartars and the Jews, its vilification of the Yugoslavs after the Stalin-Tito split, its vassalization and attempted Russification of the East European peoples, the withdrawal of economic aid from the People's Republic of China, the suppression of the Hungarians in 1956 and the invasion and occupation of Czechoslovakia in 1968 have been criminal transgressions of the spirit of Leninist policy on the national question. The haughty attitudes and infamous actions of the Soviet rulers in this domain befit oriental potentates rather than socialists or democrats.

The right of a people to self-determination is hollow unless it can separate from its oppressor and form its own sovereign state. Though this democratic right was guaranteed by the Bolsheviks and is still acknowledged in the Soviet constitution, the slightest hint of it from any abused nationality under the Kremlin's jurisdiction is treated as treason. Revolutionary Marxists support the demand of any nationality to be free and independent of both the Soviet bureaucracy and imperialism.

Injustices can be perpetrated in the economic as well as the political relationships of the postcapitalist countries. Those less developed lands that are exclusively or largely exporters of raw materials and have a below average level of labor productivity are forced to sell their staples at the low prices set by the world market. At the same time they must buy manufactured goods and machinery at high prices.

Because of their industrialization, the Soviet Union and several other of the advanced workers' states are in a position to reap advantages from these international conditions of unequal exchange in trade with the more backward countries. The terms of trade on the world market enable them to drain toward their own economy a part of the surplus labor from the poorer peoples, to get more than they give.

In a speech to the Afro-Asian economic seminar in Algeria in 1965, Che Guevara protested against this sort of exploitation arising from a tacit complicity with world capitalism. "There should not be any more talk," he said, "about developing mutually beneficial trade based on prices rigged against underdeveloped countries by the law of value and the inequitable relations of international trade brought about by that law. How can we apply the term 'mutual benefit' to the selling at world-market prices of raw materials costing limitless sweat and suffering in the underdeveloped countries and the buying of machinery produced by today's big automated factories?

If we establish that kind of relation between the two groups of nations, we must agree that the socialist countries are, in a way, accomplices of imperialist exploitation." [4]

Pending the progressive integration, unification and coordination of their economies, the technologically superior states should have an unselfish and fraternal policy toward the weaker ones that reduces the harmful consequences of the discrepancies in their levels of development.

Scrupulous as a workers' regime may be in observing the rights of the people, its democratic functioning will be vitiated in the long run unless and until two fundamental tasks are solved. The productivity of labor must be developed to the point where enough goods are available for everyone's needs, there are no sharp divisions between the haves and have-nots, and penury, misery and gross inequality are overcome.

The second prerequisite is a series of victories for the working class over capitalism in the industrialized metropolises where the greatest powers of production are concentrated and the greatest enemies of socialism are located. The rapid and balanced growth of the national economy and the concomitant increase in its social wealth must go hand in hand with drawing the workers of the West into the mainstream of the world revolution.

However, these two factors do not have equivalent weight in fortifying the processes of democratization. The history of the Soviet Union during its first fifty years indicates that the retarding or advancing of the international revolution is more decisive in affecting the course of political democracy and the cause of socialism than improvements in the national economy. It is important to understand why, since the Stalinist theory of socialism in one country and its corollary foreign policy of "peaceful coexistence" reverse these relative values.

As a form of life and a mode of labor, socialism must be superior in all vital respects to the most advanced capitalisms. Socialism cannot be built in a single country or in a constellation of backward countries. It must be constructed on an international basis with the participation of the working classes in the highly industrialized centers who can lend indispensable aid to the majority of mankind handicapped by inherited backwardnesses. The conquest of socialist power in Western Europe, Japan and above all in North America would give maximum impetus to the struggle for democracy in all three major sectors of the world revolution: the imperialist strongholds, the colonial countries and the bureaucratized workers' states. It would especially encourage the progressive forces already at work in the noncapitalist countries to take actions aimed at removing the uncontrolled bureaucracies who block the road to socialist democracy.

The antidemocratic formations which have usurped power in the workers' states are not a logical expression of the laws of political development in the transition from capitalism to socialism, as the anti-Marxists of all sorts claim. They represent deformations produced by the peculiar course of development of the international anticapitalist revolution which has taken a temporary detour through the backward nations, the weakest links in the imperialist system, before arriving at the more advanced ones. Marx and Engels did not expect the socialist revolution to begin in the underdeveloped countries, which were least propitious for the creation of socialism, nor did Lenin and his associates anticipate that the Russian Revolution and the fledgling Soviet republic would have to fight for survival alone and unassisted for a quarter of a century in a hostile environment.

The aberrations in the Russian and world revolutions did not come about because of any original sin or lust for power in human nature nor from any totalitarian proclivities of Marxism or inherent vices of Bolshevism (the alleged dictatorial tendencies lodged in its democratic-centralist method of party organization, etc.), as its opponents contend. They arose as the outgrowth and culmination of the specific set of historical circumstances which have marked and marred the first steps of humanity in crossing over from class society to socialism.

On March 7, 1939, Leon Trotsky gave the following answer to those critics who proclaimed the bankruptcy of Marxism and Leninism because the October Revolution had led to the vicious dictatorship of the bureaucracy. "But the Great French Revolution also terminated with the restoration of the monarchy. Generally speaking, the universe is poorly built: youth leads to age, birth to death, 'all things that are born must perish.'

"These gentlemen forget with remarkable ease that man has been cutting his path from a semi-simian condition to a harmonious society without any guide; that the task is a difficult one; that for every step or two forward there follows half a step, a step, and sometimes even two steps back. They forget that the path is strewn with the greatest obstacles and that no one has invented or could have invented a secret method whereby an uninterrupted rise on the escalator of history would be rendered secure." [5]

The degeneration of the Russian Revolution and the political deformation of the Stalinized workers' states are only one part of the story and by no means its latest or last chapter. If the recession of the world revolution and the low income and cultural level of the postcapitalist societies have accounted for the diminution and destruction of democracy, it should logically follow that significant changes in these international and internal factors should serve to revive the antibureaucratic tendencies within the camp of the world revolution. There have in fact been increasing evidences of such a redirection of political development in recent years.

Every attempt by the workers to take power in the West or the East was beaten back or betrayed for a quarter of a century after the October 1917 triumph. This succession of defeats, which culminated in the 1930s with the fascist victories and the Second World War, formed the background and basis for the rise and consolidation of the Soviet bureaucracy and its grip upon the world Communist movement.

The undermining of the objective supports for Stalinist bureaucratism in the world arena began in the midst of that war. Three great events in 1943 marked the turning point in the process: the deposing of Mussolini and the repulse of the Nazi armies at Stalingrad, which heralded the downfall of fascism, and the struggle of the Yugoslav partisans, which signaled the resurgence of anticapitalist revolt. In class terms, the workers and peasants had resumed the offensive against the capitalists and landlords.

The tottering of European capitalism, the entry of the Soviet armies into East Europe and Tito's triumph broke the isolation of the Soviet Union and immensely extended its influence on that key continent. The first workers' state became the second world power.

The subsequent abolition of capitalist relations in East Europe coincided with a resurgence of the colonial revolution which not only gave political independence to many of the imperialist possessions in Asia, Africa and the Middle East but resulted in the overthrow of capitalism and imperialism in China, North Korea and North Vietnam. The victory for socialism in the most populous country on earth and the dominant one in East Asia further tilted the balance of class forces on a world scale in favor of the anticapitalist camp.

At the same time the conquest of power by indigenous popular revolutionary movements in Yugoslavia and China altered the relations between the conservative and the progressive forces within the Stalinist orbit. The overt breaches between Moscow and Belgrade in 1948 and between Moscow and Peking in 1961 demonstrated the fundamental incompatibility between the selfish designs of the Kremlin oligarchy and any independent national revolution. The Kremlin's stranglehold has been further weakened by the uprisings in the satellite states of East Europe, the assertion of independence by Albania and Romania and the mounting criticisms of its policies among the Communist Parties.

Castro's socialist revolution in Cuba created the first workers' state in the Western hemisphere. It was also the first in the second wave of victory for the world revolution which came to power without any previous connection with or contamination by Stalinism. This fact was made manifest in the more vigorous internationalism and democratism which has characterized its course to date.

The Soviet bureaucracy, which was the prime beneficiary of the defeats suffered by the masses during the counterrevolutionary decades from 1923 to 1943, has increasingly become the target of the advances made by the workers' and peasants' revolution in the quarter of a century since. The monopoly of power Moscow exercised during Stalin's time can never be reestablished.

Meanwhile, the positions and power held by the Soviet bureaucracy have also been sapped by the economic, social and cultural progress of the Soviet Union. Thanks to the means placed at its disposal by the October Revolution, the Soviet Union has risen from one of the more backward European states to rival the American colossus in industrial, military and diplomatic might. Despite the lopsided development of its economy, the USSR has spectacular achievements to its credit in heavy industry, science, education and social services. It has a highly qualified intelligentsia and technical personnel and its sixty-million-strong proletariat is no longer a small minority but the principal social force in the country.

These changes in Soviet society first expressed themselves in the de-Stalinization processes, which loosened the straitjacket of bureaucratization which had become absurd and intolerable at the time Stalin died in 1953. All segments of Soviet society from the most highly placed officials to the outlying nationalities yearned for relief and release from the senseless terror of his tyranny.

The reforms introduced by Stalin's successors under the

pressure of these feelings have had an ambiguous character. Some of the most abominable features of Stalin's despotism (the concentration camps, the universal terror, the mass purges, the frame-ups, the labor penalties, the uncurbed activities of the secret police) have been abandoned or moderated while living conditions have much improved.

But this liberalization has had very strict limits. The concessions granted to the various categories of citizens — intellectuals, workers and collective farmers — represent defensive measures on the part of the entrenched Soviet bureaucracy, which is determined to retain the substance of its supremacy come what may.

Some observers abroad, and assuredly many Soviet citizens, nourished the hope during the "thaw" and the Khrushchev interregnum that the new leaders would reform themselves, dismantle the dictatorship step by step and bestow democratic rights upon the people. However, the meager balance sheet of the internal reforms, the recent tightening of the screws by the regime, the cruel treatment of its political prisoners and the Kremlin's conduct toward the other workers' states have shattered these illusions about a "revolution from above." The crushing of the Hungarian revolution, the abusive dealings with China and the occupation of Czechoslovakia have confirmed the incorrigibly counterrevolutionary nature of the Moscow oligarchy, which, like all bureaucratic formations, does not intend to voluntarily relinquish its privileged positions.

If the ruling power in the USSR cannot be reformed, what is to be done? The solution to which a growing number of oppositionists are being driven has been prefigured by the dissident bimonthly journal, the *Chronicle of Current Events,* which has been published secretly in the Soviet Union since 1968. The fifth issue of this underground magazine summarizes a letter from a group of Estonian natural scientists and technicians that criticizes Andrei Sakharov, the Soviet nuclear scientist, who sees the paths of the United States and the Soviet Union converging and favors deepening peaceful coexistence with Western capitalism.

The Estonian scientists counterpose to this perspective the demand for "a thoroughgoing democratization of Soviet society." According to Paul Wohl in the December 24, 1969, *Christian Science Monitor,* their program called for the following: "Minorities were to be given the right to form an opposition; the administration was to become a free forum of discussion; there should be several parties; an amnesty for all dissenters; the non-Russian peoples were to govern themselves freely.

"One passage said: 'We ask our government for reforms. We are ready to keep asking for some time and to wait. But ultimately we shall demand and act. And then it may be necessary to deploy tank divisions, not in Prague and Bratislava, but in Moscow and Leningrad.'"

These sentiments voiced by the most enlightened and intransigent elements in literary and scientific circles are among the first rumblings of the volcano of dissidence engendered by the rebirth of the world revolution and the transformation of Soviet life. Many groups wronged by the Soviet authorities are demanding the rights to which they are entitled by law.

The document also discloses the dynamics of the incipient struggle against "enlightened absolutism." What has begun with a cry for reforms must sooner or later culminate in a direct test of strength with the possessors of power. Such a showdown lurks below the surface of conflicts between the defenders of the privileged social layers of the bureaucratized workers' states and the spokesmen for the interests of the workers, peasants and the oppositional intellectuals arrayed against them. As the struggle for more reforms runs up against adamant resistance from the regime, it inexorably tends to become converted into a revolutionary mass uprising, as happened in Hungary in 1956 and came close to being repeated in Czechoslovakia in 1968.

This emergent phase of political development in the Soviet Union was anticipated by Leon Trotsky in his analysis of the Soviet regime and its prospects in the decade before his assassination. He stated that, however oppressive, the bureaucracy did not constitute a new class of exploiters, of state capitalists or bureaucratic collectivists, as some thought. It was a tumorous growth upon the social organism of the USSR, a dangerously malignant but yet a transitory product of the Soviet Union's international isolation and inherited poverty and backwardness.

Though the planned economy had achieved unexampled successes, it was still very far from socialism. The USSR was a society in transition from capitalism to socialism with an unbalanced, inharmonious structure which was torn by tense contradictions and, above all, by the irreconcilable antagonism between the bureaucratic caste and the working masses. To clear the way for the march toward socialism, the Soviet workers would have to overcome and clean out the bureaucratic oligarchy and they would have to do this by way of a new political revolution.

Trotsky pointed out that the reaction to the Russian Revolution embodied in the dictatorship of the bureaucracy had essentially consisted of a political counterrevolution. Although it had deprived the masses of all political rights, the bureaucracy had in its own self-interests preserved the principal social conquests of the October Revolution, that is, the nationalized property and planning principle, and, in its costly, crude and nationalistic manner, had developed part of their potential. Accordingly, a consistent struggle of the people against the bureaucracy did not have to change the economic foundations of Soviet society. These constituted an immeasurable advance over any other system of production, an advance which every socialist was duty-bound to defend against all enemies, internal or external. What was to be replaced was the state superstructure, its methods of rule and its possessors of supreme power.

The objective of the antibureaucratic revolution would be to transfer control of the state and the economy from the privileged upper crust to the direct producers. The dictatorship of the bureaucracy would have to give way to a socialist democracy. As the power of the bureaucracy was eliminated, the government they commanded would be democratized from top to bottom through the measures recommended by Lenin, incorporated in the program of the Fourth International and amplified by the bitter lessons of the past half-century.

This salutary overturn would have a predominantly political rather than socioeconomic character. A political revolution or counterrevolution changes the methods of rule in a country; a social revolution is far more thoroughgoing and transforms the prevailing relations of production and property forms. The Belgian Marxist Ernest Mandel has illuminated the difference between the two in his introduction to *Fifty Years of World Revolution*:

"Simplistic minds who have assimilated only a mechanistic and vulgarized version of Marxism suppose that all revolutions and counterrevolutions mean the passage of power from one social class to another," he wrote. "The historical reality, however, is more complex. Neither the advent of absolute monarchy nor the French revolutions of 1830 and 1848 were social revolutions. In all these revolutions, power passed from one faction to another of the same ruling class: in the case of absolute monarchy, from the nobility of the manors to the court nobility; in the case of the nineteenth-century French revolutions, from the landowning bourgeoisie to the financial bourgeoisie and from the financial bourgeoisie to the industrial bourgeoisie. Marxism thus also encompasses the concept of *political* revolutions and counterrevolutions which do not alter the basic mode of production. Even the restoration of Louis XVIII was, in short, a political and not a social counterrevolution, since, while the nobility received financial compensation, it did not recover any of the class privileges it had enjoyed under the *ancien régime*. It was in no way reestablished as a ruling class."[6]

To date, none of the states which have abolished capitalism have reverted to that older economic system. And the overwhelming thrust of all the antibureaucratic movements that have shaken the postcapitalist regimes has been, not to reestablish private property and bring back the bankers, industrialists and landlords, but rather to defend and develop the collectivist economy by moving toward a more humane and freer system, "socialism with a human face." The Kremlin sent its troops and tanks into Czechoslovakia, not because the progressive Communists there were plotting to smuggle in capitalism, but because the spectacle of a socialist democracy in that country would have been altogether too contagious for the workers of the Soviet bloc and too dangerous for the Kremlin's own power.

The removal of the parasitic bureaucracy and the flowering of democracy in one or more of the existing workers' states would have two immensely important international repercussions. It would confirm the fact that the deformities that defiled and disgraced the postcapitalist regimes during the first and formative period of the world revolution were not inherent and ineradicable stigmas of the new society but rather relics and revivals of the old, which further advances on the road to socialism would eliminate.

The development of a thriving socialist democracy in opposition to bureaucratic domination and Stalinism in all its variants would be the most valuable contribution that any workers' state could make to the cause of world socialism. For decades the greatest political and moral obstacle to the progress of socialism in Western Europe and North America has been the treacherous role played by leaderships vassalized to Moscow and, in particular, the totalitarian image imposed on socialism and communism by the practices of Stalin, his heirs and his disciples from Poland to China. They have not only debased and distorted the program of socialism but also violated certain elementary principles of democracy gained through the bourgeois revolutions.

Such horrors as the purges, the frame-up trials, the forced confessions, the deportations, the labor camps, the liquidation of all political opposition, the suppression of free thought in politics, education, art, sociology and history and even in some of the natural sciences became common knowledge despite the Soviet censorship. They have made the task of building an honest revolutionary socialist movement in the advanced capitalist sectors excruciatingly difficult and almost insuperable up to recent years.

What is most needed now, in view of the deepening discontent in the imperialist lands, is to dispel this confusion and identification of socialism with Stalinist despotism. A political revolution enabling the working masses to reappropriate the state power taken from them by the bureaucratic usurpers would clear the way for a renovated regime in which the essence of socialism could be seen for what it really is: the most direct, all-encompassing democracy for the mass of producers.

14

THE COLONIAL STRUGGLE
FOR DEMOCRACY

The struggle for political democracy in postfeudal times falls into two distinctly different historical stages depending upon the conditions of world capitalist development. The upswing of capitalism from the sixteenth through the nineteenth centuries witnessed the emergence and establishment of democratic or liberal constitutional regimes under bourgeois auspices in Western Europe and North America. During this period they failed to appear elsewhere.

Their presence in the major capitalist countries was organically interconnected with their absence in the colonies. The immense disparity in the development of democratic forms of rule between the advanced countries and the historically retarded peoples on other continents was the political expression of the extremely disproportionate economic development in the two sectors of the world. The global expansion of capitalist relations, which fostered democratic movements in the one sphere, inhibited their growth in the other.

The Rise of Bourgeois Democracy

The ascending forces of bourgeois society in their classical stronghold in maritime Europe succeeded in abolishing feudalism, shattering the power of the absolute monarchy and the Church, transforming archaic agrarian relations and clearing the way for the full and free expansion of capitalist activities. The blows delivered by these bourgeois revolutions to the forces upholding the old order plus the further economic and social advances bound up with the Industrial Revolution resulted in the constitution of relatively stable parliamentary democracies in the principal centers of the capitalist system by the last quarter of the nineteenth century.

A heavy payment was exacted for the economic, political and cultural progress registered by the most advanced capitalist nations. Their gains were made possible not only through the suppression of the precapitalist formations and forces in their own domains but largely at the expense of the rest of the world's population.

The seizure of colonies and the plunder and exploitation of their inhabitants went hand in hand with the accumulation of capital and the extension of its world market. The selfsame international relations which stunted and distorted the economic and political development of the colonial lands were vital conditions for the expansion and enrichment of the Western capitalisms and the installation of stable forms of democracy within them. The subjugation of the colonial peoples and the implantation of diverse types of servitude among them were as essential to the making and maintenance of the European democracies as the raw materials extracted from the colonies were indispensable for their trade and manufactures.

The great merchants who opposed and overthrew King Charles I's government sought to shift the commercial center of the world from Amsterdam to London and corner the colonial trade through an aggressive foreign policy against all rivals. The French Revolution was interlaced with the conflict between the French and British bourgeoisie over possession of the West Indies and India. The outcome of these revolutions decided not only who should rule at home — and how — but equally who should rule over which colonies and command their resources.

However much the citizens of the Western democracies preferred to shut their eyes to the fact, the rights and freedoms they enjoyed were in no small degree based upon the denial of these to the more backward peoples of the planet. Only the most privileged and wealthy powers could afford the luxury of democracy, even in restricted bourgeois forms. Just as ancient Greek democracy rested upon slavery, capitalist democracy was based on the spoliation of colonies.

The colonial system, which was the cornerstone of commercial and industrial capitalism, was irreconcilable with the most limited modes of self-government. Colonialism was founded upon conquest and persisted in violation of the elementary right of national self-determination. The existence of democratic rights and institutions would have impeded the outright robbery and intensified exploitation of the subject peoples by their overseas masters.

The antidemocratic nature of the colonial system was dramatically disclosed during the era of commercial capitalism by the relations of the American people to the mother country of Great Britain. Unlike the inhabitants of India, the settlers on the Atlantic seaboard (apart from the black slaves) were not a conquered people; they prided themselves on possessing the rights of "true-born Englishmen." Nonetheless, when conditions had ripened for assuming self-government, the rulers in London adamantly refused to recognize that fact and grant them independence. The thirteen colonies had to tear that right from the British crown through seven years of armed combat. The American War of Independence was the first successful colonial revolt of the capitalist era.

The North Americans were enabled to win national sovereignty and set up a democratic republic, thanks to the high level of their socioeconomic development which, in contrast to India and other anciently inhabited lands, had from the beginning been largely based upon bourgeois relations. Except for the triumphant slave uprising in Santo Domingo touched off by the French Revolution, similar mass movements were not manifested during the eighteenth century in Canada, Mexico or the Caribbean Islands, whose economic and social structures remained in a far more backward state.

The path of liberation taken by the United States was exceptional for an overseas people in bondage to a European power. Most of the other components of the colonial system remained subject to subordination and oppression up to the twentieth century.

The Colonial Liberation Movements of the Twentieth Century

The second stage in the global struggle for democracy has been centered in the colonial and semicolonial countries and takes place not during the rise but the decline of world capitalism. It is directed against the peculiar combination of precapitalist and capitalist property and production relations which characterizes Asian, African and Latin American society.

The salient feature of this phase of democracy has been its belated historical appearance. The bourgeois-democratic movements against outdated forms of sovereignty, which had already been carried to conclusion in the plutocratic lands, were postponed until the twentieth century in the greater part of the colonial world. Exception must be made for a cluster of Latin American peoples who had thrown off the weakened clutch of Spain and Portugal in the preceding century. But almost all their indigenous governments, based on semifeudal landownership and under the yoke of foreign capital, remained oligarchic and dictatorial.

Many naive and unhistorical-minded people believed and hoped that the continents and countries which still had to be modernized would follow in the footsteps of their predecessors in the West. But neither in their economic nor political development was it possible for the latecomers to reproduce, with some delay and minor variations, the models provided by the advanced capitalisms.

When Ho Chi Minh launched the Vietnam revolution in August 1945, he could model the republic's declaration of independence from France after Jefferson's declaration of 1776. But the movement he headed could not repeat the pattern of the American colonial revolt. Politically, socially, economically and ideologically, the twentieth-century struggle for liberation had to go far beyond it.

In the dialectical processes of universal history, the accomplishments of an earlier time can be the biggest deterrent to progress at the next stage. The monopoly capitalists whose economic and strategic interests shaped the foreign policies of the Western democracies were as reluctant to extend the blessings of democracy to their possessions as their commercial and industrial predecessors. Their colonial governments might institute certain sanitary improvements and restricted educational facilities and lay down some elements of a new economic infrastructure (railroads, roads, ports, power stations, etc.) needed for the enterprises of the foreigners. What the imperialists would not do was to voluntarily accord freedom to the peoples under their dominion. They had to be forced to relinquish their rule.

None of the important democracies of the bourgeois era had come into existence by purely peaceful, legal and gradual means. Every one was the offspring of prolonged class struggle which culminated in civil war, coupled in some cases (Holland, the United States) with a war of national liberation. Bourgeois democracy was actually installed as the accepted method of progressive government through the mobilization of the masses in a fight to the death against the monarchical-clerical structures rooted in the precapitalist past. No country had won independence except by fighting for it and no society had become democratized by appealing to the sense of justice of the master classes.

When the hour sounded for the liquidation of the colonial system after the First and Second World Wars, the native bourgeoisie in Asia, Africa, the Middle East and Latin America was presented with the opportunity to organize and lead two-thirds of humanity in antiimperialist struggle to achieve national independence and internal democracy, as the commercial and industrial classes of the United States had done in their two great revolutionary wars.

However, the changes in class relations produced by the march of history and the baneful heritage of the colonial past restrained the national bourgeoisie from shouldering and carrying through the tasks of self-determination, redistribution of the land to the peasant cultivators and the creation of a hardy democratic regime which belonged historically to the bourgeois epoch.

It has been pointed out that the older and more monopolistic and imperialistic the bourgeoisie in the most developed countries became, the less democratically inclined its representatives were in their own habitats. The German, Japanese and Russian capitalists proved to be far less liberal than their English, French and American counterparts. This same rule applied with still greater force to the far more belated and backward bourgeois classes in the colonial world.

The colonial bourgeoisie had to grow up and make their way squeezed between stagnant and archaic economic and social conditions around them and the humiliations of alien economic and political control above them. However much they aspired to play an independent role in the political development of their countries, they were too weak economically, too subservient to foreign capital, too much in complicity with the semifeudal system of rural exploitation and, above all, too fearful of the claims of the peasants and workers to muster and head a revolutionary movement of the masses for national and social liberation which could thoroughly reorganize and democratize their society.

The first major testing ground of the new correlation of class forces in the struggle for democracy that marked the imperialist epoch was provided by the Russian Revolution. As early as 1906, Leon Trotsky had outlined his celebrated theory of the permanent revolution, which asserted that the stunted and feeble bourgeoisie in the more backward countries had become too timid and reactionary and too vassalized to imperialism to carry through the indicated democratic tasks of the bourgeois revolution.

The execution of these historical functions, which the bourgeois forces had fulfilled in the democratic revolutions of the West, was transferred to the revolutionary proletariat, which was called upon to lead the peasantry in a combined fight for democracy and socialism against both the native possessing classes and their foreign overlords. The strategy of distrust and conflict in place of collaboration with and subordination to the bourgeoisie in the struggle for democratization was one of the dividing lines which separated Bolshevism from Menshevism and later Trotskyism from Stalinism.

The theoretical conclusions derived from the experience of the Russian Revolution which blazed the trail toward socialism were to prove decisive in the subsequent history of the colonial liberation movements wherever nations subjected to the Great Powers strained to break the chains of their servitude. The conquest of democracy, which had formerly been identified with capitalist liberalism, was henceforward bound up with intransigent struggle to overthrow capitalist property and power. Those colonial and semicolonial peoples who have acted in accordance with this anticapitalist line have proved able to achieve both economic and political independence of imperialism; those that have followed a different course have yet to attain such autonomy.

Internal democratization was impossible without the acquisition of genuine national independence which involved the destruction of both direct and indirect dependence upon imperialism. In all those places in Asia, the Middle East, Africa and Latin America where national liberation movements have unfolded in the half-century since the October 1917 revolution, the question was posed whether or not the native bourgeoisie could do that job. What has been the balance sheet of these experiments?

1. The utmost that the big and little bourgeoisie in the colonial world have been able to attain has been a formal political independence from one or another of the Great Powers.

2. None of the neocolonial countries have taken complete command of their own economic destinies; they all remain or have relapsed into subjection to the rich metropolitan powers. The neocolonial bourgeoisie may head the state but foreign capital is the paramount factor in the shaping of the development of the economy. The most conspicuous proof of this state of affairs is given by Latin America where U. S. capital investments now total more than eleven billion dollars and all twenty of its republics are prey to the economic domination, political pressure and threatened military intervention of the colossus of the north.

3. Even where constitutional regimes or parliamentary democracies have been set up under bourgeois auspices, they remain brittle and unstable. At the first signs of serious social tension

and acute class conflict, the democratic rights of the people are curtailed or abrogated and the parliamentary regimes readily displaced by military or strong-man methods of rule. Bourgeois nationalisms in the underdeveloped countries in the imperialist epoch tend toward dictatorial rather than democratic forms of governing since, despite desires for greater autonomy, the colonial bourgeoisie is compelled to act as a junior partner of the metropolitan capitalists in the joint exploitation of their countries. Thus Panama's foreign minister, whose own country is run by the National Guard, told the Organization of American States meeting in June 1970: "Formal democracy has become an instrument of inefficiency, incapable of resolving fundamental problems in Latin America." [1]

The strength of this inherent tendency toward authoritarianism is visible not only in the recent military takeovers in Argentina and Brazil but, more tellingly, in the political evolution of Uruguay, "the Switzerland of Latin America." This small nation of 2.7 million people had the most deeply rooted and long-lasting bourgeois-democratic traditions and institutions and its freedoms had seldom been threatened by the military coups so common elsewhere on the continent.

In the early years of this century, Uruguay underwent a peaceful "revolution from above" which made it the most enlightened and progressive regime in Latin America. Its welfare state gave the maximum in democratic rights and social services that can be delivered to the people under a free enterprise system preserving a landed oligarchy.

By the end of the 1960s, there was little left of parliamentary democracy in Uruguay. Gripped by economic and social crisis, this model liberal democracy promulgated a new constitution on March 1, 1967, which vested the diffuse executive power of a governing National Council in the president. Two and a half years later, as class conflicts sharpened, the country was plunged into disarray. The president, backed by the army, ruled by decree with no effective checks by the Congress. A highly repressive press censorship was imposed; union activity was repressed by the army; oppositional political figures and strikers were arrested by the hundreds, with no trial or civil guarantees; the right of free assembly was virtually abrogated; the police were accused of torturing political prisoners. Meanwhile, through its participation in the Organization of American States, Uruguay has had to fall into line with the mandates of Washington.

The extreme fragility of democratic forms under the best bourgeois auspices is attributable to four main factors: continued economic dependence upon the metropolitan industrial powers, gross material inequalities, failure to transform the anachronistic rural economy where the majority of the people live, and fright of the upper crust before the anticapitalist potential of the masses. The combination of an undeveloped industry and a semifeudal agrarian structure permeated by capitalist interests makes the situation of the peasant population unbearable. The democratic path is rendered impassable or cut off completely where the country and the countryside live in a perpetual stage of siege and every manifestation of protest by the students, peasants or workers is repressed by force.

The alienation of democracy from capitalism in the political consciousness of the colonial peoples is demonstrated in the paradoxical fact that nowadays almost all the left bourgeois leaders of the emerging nations, regardless of the capitalist nature of their economy and government, paste the honorific label of socialism upon their professed democracy. This was true of the "guided democracy" of Indonesia's late President Sukarno, the "popular democracy" of Nasser and not least, the crisis-torn government of the bourgeois Congress Party of India, which deceptively proclaims itself to be as much socialist as democratic.

The Anticapitalist Struggle for Democracy

The inexorable demands for social change and democratization in the colonial world could not be halted by the default of the national bourgeoisie paralyzed by fear of the revolutionary masses and imperialist retaliation. To the contrary, these aims have had to be pursued against them and despite them.

The major tasks of the democratic revolution, such as national independence and unification, agrarian reform, secularization, freedom for oppressed nationalities and equal rights for women, the creation of a democratic state and modernization and industrialization, have had to be undertaken by a new constellation of class forces in which the revolutionary proletariat in league with the insurgent peasant masses conducts a war to the death against both the indigenous bourgeoisie and their imperialist protectors. Thus the struggle for democracy in this century has become inseparably connected with the revolution for socialism.

Such was the course actually taken by the Chinese, Vietnamese, North Korean and Cuban revolutions. The world historical significance of these victorious colonial revolutions consists in the demonstration that the movement for popular democracy has to break through the framework of bourgeois private property in order to realize its objectives. If the national revolution brought democracy to the first-born countries of capitalism, participation in the process of international socialist revolution is required to give democracy to the backward peoples. Only along this road could they succeed in freeing themselves from direct or indirect imperialist domination, win national sovereignty, uproot the remnants of feudalism, transform the lives and labor relations of the rural population, build adequate roads, housing, hospitals, schools, mobilize and plan the country's resources to overcome economic underdevelopment and speed industrialization by planned methods.

The striking contrasts over the past twenty years between revolutionized China and bourgeoisified India in the spheres of agriculture, industry, removal of colonial inferiority and stimulation of the initiative of the masses, as well as between Cuba and other Latin American nations in these respects during the past decade, testify to the weightiness of this rule now governing developments in the "Third World."

The Struggle for Socialist Democracy

However, this is merely the first and by no means the last word to be said about the struggle for democracy in the existing postcapitalist countries. If the experience of the past fifty years has essentially validated the proposition that the gateway to democracy in the underdeveloped societies must pass through the socialist revolution, it has likewise demonstrated that the conquest of power by the workers and peasants and the nationalization of the means of production do not suffice to settle the problem of instituting a stable form of socialist democracy superior in all respects to the freest bourgeois parliamentarism.

Indeed, the problem of democracy has been most acutely posed on a higher level following the expropriation of the capitalists. The organizers of the young Soviet republic aspired to set up a democracy broadly based upon freely elected workers' and peasants' councils. But the specifications which Lenin projected in his *State and Revolution* for such a rule of the masses and which his government tried to consolidate in the early years of the USSR were negated by the usurpation of power by the privileged bureaucratic caste under Stalin after his death. Since then ultrabureaucratic regimes of the same sort have fastened themselves upon other countries with a socialist economic base.

Thus the first and formative phase of the international anticapitalist revolution has exhibited a type of political development analogous to the pristine period of the antifeudal revolutions in Europe. The victorious bourgeois revolutions did not all at once and immediately establish durable popular democratic forms of rule in their countries. Cromwell's dictatorial republic was supplanted by a restored Stuart dynasty which was in turn displaced by the House of Orange. England was governed by an aristocratic oligarchy well into the nineteenth century. The "emergency republic" of Robespierre, which represented the fullest embodiment of popular self-action at the height of the French Revolution, was succeeded by the Directorate, the Napoleonic Empire and the Bourbon Restoration. France did not adopt a liberal parliamentary system until after the crushing of the Paris Commune in 1871. Even the Dutch republic, the first-born antimonarchical child of the bourgeois epoch, slipped back into a kingdom at the end of the eighteenth century.

As late as 1848, monarchy, either absolute or constitutional, remained the predominant mode of governing states. A firm democratic system under bourgeois hegemony had to have not only a powerful thrust of the insurgent masses to bring it into being but also a vigorous and thriving national capitalism to keep it going. Otherwise, political democracy could not sustain itself for long.

Unlike the bourgeois revolutions which took power under the most advanced capitalist conditions of their time, the first socialist revolutions have unfolded within the most retarded situations. All the peoples from Russia through China to Cuba that have driven out the possessing classes, nationalized their economies and established a revolutionary state power of a socialist type had not previously gone through any renovation of their social and political organizations along bourgeois-democratic lines. They suffered from the double handicaps of quasi-feudal stagnation and capitalist underdevelopment.

When these peoples embarked upon their revolutions, they were obliged to undertake the solution of such onerous presocialist tasks as combating imperialism for national sovereignty and unification, uprooting feudalism, satisfying the peasant hunger for land and democratizing their political life simultaneously with the socialist tasks of abolishing capitalist ownership, collectivizing agriculture, operating a planned economy, building up a competitive industry and creating a new ensemble of social relations.

So colossal a conjuncture of chores would have taxed the capacities of the finest leadership and been immensely difficult under the most auspicious circumstances. However, the post-capitalist countries have encountered extremely adverse internal and international conditions that have been most disadvantageous to their harmonious development. In addition to natural calamities, they have been plagued by their inherited economic and cultural backwardness, by imperialist encirclement, hostility, embargo and military aggression and by the confinement of the proletarian power to the poorest lands. The new socialist relations of production have had the misfortune to be inaugurated in a socioeconomic setting which was ill-prepared and least suited to nourish them.

The democratic tendencies of socialist development demand a high level of technological, scientific, industrial and agricultural development, a preponderant and cultured working class in control of the economy and the government, an abundance of consumer goods and the amenities of contemporary civilization, a peaceful environment and, above all, a broad international basis. The first group of states which broke loose from capitalism lacked these fundamental advantages. They have had to try and create a new society at top speed and largely from scratch at the cost of intolerably heavy material sacrifices by the working population.

The same set of factors — the pauper inheritance from the preceding centuries, the isolation of the revolution and its confinement to the more backward countries, the pressures of the imperialist powers, the deficient development of the productive forces and the insufficiency of consumer goods, the inadequate cultural level of the laboring masses — have been the prime causes for the malignant growth of the bureaucratic deformations that have curbed, crippled and in the most flagrant cases extirpated all traces of workers' democracy in the country and the ruling party.

Certain theorists have deduced from these aberrations that the postcapitalist societies in the "Third World" are doomed to pass through two separate stages in their evolution. They must first undergo a protracted and tormenting period of primitive socialist accumulation with a stinted consumption in which economic advancement proceeds under the harsh authoritarian direction of a privileged elite. Then, when the proper degree of industrialization and productive power yielding a capacious social surplus has been reached, this will ineluctably bring with it a relaxation of totalitarianism and the gradual introduction of democracy from above.

Such a schema may serve as a comforting apology for the tyranny of a bureaucratic caste or for lauding by contrast the virtues of bourgeois democracy. However, the theory errs in two cardinal respects from the standpoint of Marxism. It is predicated upon a crude and mechanical economic determinism which leaves out of account the conscious political activity of a vigilant revolutionary leadership sensitive to the needs of the people. More fundamentally, it encloses the long-term evolution of the workers' states within narrow national limits and disregards the decisive weight of the international factors in fashioning the revolutionary processes of our time.

The history of the workers' states that have emerged over the past half-century demonstrates how terribly real the danger of bureaucratic degeneration, disfigurement and domination is. Lenin was well aware of the danger in the Soviet Union and paid special attention to checking and containing this phenomenon in the last years of his life. He and his associates rejected the contention of the critics and opponents of the Bolsheviks that the seizure of power had been premature because of the backwardness of the country or that it was unwarranted because the very structure of nationalized economy inevitably gave rise to authoritarian methods of political rule and bureaucratic management of industry.

They assigned to the vanguard party, as a free association of revolutionists, the special role of spurring the creative initiative of the masses in order to prevent the growth of a privileged stratum that would come to lord it over the rest of the population. The intervention of the subjective political agency of the party was essential to counteract the exceedingly unfavorable objective conditions confronting a harassed, impoverished and isolated workers' state with a predominantly peasant population.

According to the original Bolshevik program, the revolutionary party of the proletariat and its regime should strive to ward off the proliferation of bureaucratism to monstrous proportions and reinforce a socialist democracy along two interlinked lines. They must enact and enforce all the measures required to ensure that the working masses, in whose name the revolution had been made, really exercise a democratic control over the state and the economy through their freely-elected institutions and that democracy is practiced within the vanguard party itself. The party and the trade unions should be independent of the state apparatus. The presentation of alternative programs by competing parties loyal to the revolution should be encouraged. Through such a policy, the productive forces could be promoted under optimum political conditions.

At the same time, they recognized the limited efficacy of the best internal measures and methods of administration in curing the ills of bureaucratism and getting at its underlying material sources. As socialist internationalists, they believed that the twin curses of backwardness and bureaucratism could not ultimately be disposed of unless and until the proletarian revolution went beyond the poorer areas of the earth and encompassed a number of the advanced industrial countries. The spread of the revolution to the centers of capitalist power and wealth would remove the ever-present threat of imperialist aggression, reduce the costly burden of military preparations and place vastly greater supplies of fraternal economic aid at the disposal of the poorer countries. The consequent increase in their capacities of production and rise in the standard of living would lessen material inequalities, strengthen social solidarity, reduce the scope and strength of bureaucratism and clear the way for the flourishing of democratic methods in all fields of national life.

This beneficent perspective has yet to be realized primarily because of the delayed emergence of the socialist revolution in the advanced capitalisms. Instead, bureaucracy has grown apace. It consequently appears likely that a supplementary political revolution is on the agenda in those postcapitalist countries where a commanding social stratum has succeeded in depriving the masses of all participation in decision-making and monopolizes political power. The limitations of the de-Stalinization from above in the Soviet Union and the Kremlin's brutal suppression of the Czechoslovak efforts to give socialism "a human face" serve to emphasize the stern necessity for such a drastic course of action.

The antibureaucratic revolution from below would not challenge or change the foundations of the nationalized and planned system of production but would free it of distortions. Its principal objective would be to debureaucratize the nation from top to bottom, maximize the initiative and power of the masses and establish the extensive workers' democracy promised in the socialist program.

Such a revolution would not be unprecedented. The forward-moving forces of bourgeois society had to do the same in their day. Decades after its "Great Rebellion," the British bourgeoisie changed dynasties to guarantee the supremacy of Parliament in 1688. In order to consummate the work of 1789-93 and meet the demands of economic progress, the French threw out a used-up monarchy and ruling upper crust in 1830 and again

in 1848. These political overturns did not entail any reversion
to feudalism but rather a reinforcement of bourgeois forms
of property.

Similarly, the antibureaucratic offensive of the masses would
not lead back to the restoration of capitalism, as some fear
and others contend. It would press forward to a more efficient
mode of planned production within a genuinely democratic
socialist framework.

The prospect of a supplementary political revolution against
bureaucratic usurpation and despotism is today not so startling
and audacious an innovation in Marxist theory as it appeared
when the idea was first broached by Leon Trotsky in the
1930s in connection with the struggle against the Stalinist
dictatorship in the Soviet Union.

According to Fidel Castro, a workers' state has to defend
itself against the internal menace of bureaucratism, as well
as against the aggressions of imperialism. Ever since 1965,
the Cubans have been conducting a persistent campaign against
the scourge of bureaucratism, though they have yet to develop
the proper forms of institutionalizing workers' democracy.

Mao Tse-tung has called upon the Russian people to overthrow the post-Stalin "revisionists" at the head of the Soviet
Union. He has further defined "the great proletarian cultural
revolution," which convulsed China for three years, as "in
essence a great political revolution" intended to expand the
democratic power of the people. This exorbitant claim cannot
be substantiated. An intraparty, interbureaucratic conflict for
power, in which the opposition headed by Liu Shao-chi was
denied the simple right of publicly expressing its views and
criticisms, can hardly be taken as a sterling example of an
enhanced proletarian democracy. It is not possible to sweep
out bureaucratism through the bureaucratic methods employed
by the Peking regime.

It must be acknowledged that the achievement of a virile
political and social democracy in that part of the world where
the bulk of humankind is concentrated has been and remains
exceedingly difficult and complicated. Imperialism and bureaucratism, backwardness and poverty stand as mighty obstacles
thwarting its progress. Yet there is no other way to overcome
these obstacles to democratization than through the expansion
and deepening of the international socialist revolution.

15

DEMOCRATIC PROSPECTS

FOR A SOCIALIST AMERICA

The right of revolution is the supreme right of any people and the ultimate safeguard of its democracy. It was twice exercised by Englishmen of the seventeenth century. It was the cornerstone of the political theory of the American Declaration of Independence and the doctrinal justification for the uprising against crown rule. If government must rest on "the consent of the governed," the majority of the people have the authority, and even the obligation when it becomes intolerably tyrannical, to alter or abolish it and replace it with a better and freer form of government which "to them shall seem most likely to effect their safety and happiness." Although revolution is not to be lightly resorted to, it is an inalienable right, asserts the birth certificate of the American nation.

The right of revolution became a permanent part of the heritage of progressive mankind during the ascent of bourgeois society. The thirty-fifth and final article of the Declaration of the Rights of Man and the Citizen of 1793, which was drawn up by Robespierre and passed by the French Convention, paraphrased that passage in Jefferson's Declaration as follows: "When the government violates the rights of the people, insurrection is the most sacred right, and the absolutely irremissible duty of the people as a whole and of each of its sections."

Abraham Lincoln explicitly reaffirmed this democratic right. In 1848, in a speech to the House of Representatives opposing war on Mexico, he declared: "Any people anywhere being inclined and having the power, have the right to rise up and shake off the existing government, and form a new one that suits them better. This is a most valuable, a most sacred right

— a right which we hope and believe is to liberate the world."
Later, in his first inaugural address as president, March 4,
1861, Lincoln reiterated: "This country, with its institutions,
belongs to the people who inhabit it. Whenever they shall grow
weary of the existing Government, they can exercise their constitutional right of amending it, or their revolutionary right
to dismember or overthrow it."

Americans retain the constitutional right to urge revolutionary change in the United States today. However, state and
federal authorities continually seek to curb this right of ad-
vocacy by enacting and applying sedition statutes. The monopolist minority they represent will certainly resist to the
death any attempts by the masses or their leadership to organize and engage in revolutionary struggle against their rule.

Their opposition and repression will not prevent more and
more of the discontented from considering the desirability of
revolutionary action as the only way forward for this country.
For a long time in this century, most Americans believed that
revolution had nothing to do with their lives. Such convulsions might occur and even be justified in more backward
and less fortunate lands, but there appeared no need for a
revolution in the affluent "land of the free."

That complacent outlook has begun to change with the rise
of the Afro-American and Third World liberation struggles, the
student militancy, the massive antiwar protests and women's
liberation movement during the 1960s. The need for a fundamental transformation of American society is now recognized
by millions of black, brown, red and white Americans whose
numbers should grow as the crisis of the imperialist system
intensifies.

Certain questions about the prospects of democracy in the
event of a socialist revolution inevitably arise in the mind of
thoughtful rebels. What assurance is there, they ask, that with
the changeover from monopolist to working-class rule, Americans will have more freedom and not less? Won't we be liable
to the same dangers of totalitarian tyranny after capitalism
is eliminated here as happened in the Soviet Union under
Stalin and his successors? What are the chances that a bureaucratic minority will take power from the people and hold despotic sway over their lives and thoughts? We certainly won't
fight to risk all that.

Such doubts are comprehensible in view of the lack of democracy and limitations upon the sovereignty of the masses
in existing postcapitalist societies. It is impossible to evade
coming to grips with these issues if only because they are

pushed to the fore by opponents of the socialist revolution from the ultraconservatives to reformists and anarchists. The categorical prediction that socialist revolution must lead to a loss of liberty is the trump card played by defenders of the status quo in arguments against Marxism.

Considerations of this kind may carry less weight among the Afro-American and Third World peoples who bear the brunt of the oppression and exploitation of the existing system than among white Americans who enjoy more rights and privileges, just as they have less ideological and political influence among the masses in the underdeveloped countries than in the industrialized metropolises. The former feel they have little to lose and much more to gain.

In any case, these questions deserve serious treatment because they constitute stumbling blocks to the progress of the socialist movement and raise problems of the utmost importance to political theory and practice in the transition from capitalism to socialism.

Only a historical and materialist approach can provide a satisfactory answer to these questions. It is necessary to begin by reviewing the specific factors responsible for stunting and stifling workers' democracy after the heroic first years of the Soviet revolution and which have impeded the development of democratic institutions and norms in the workers' states established since then. This can lay the basis for inquiring whether and to what extent these same causes would be operative in a postrevolutionary America. The real outlook for democracy can be clarified and gauged by this method of contrasts.

The preceding chapters analyzed the principal deterrents to the flourishing of democracy and the circumstances facilitating the capture of power by the bureaucratic formations in the Soviet Union and other postcapitalist regimes. They can be summarized in the following list: the failure of the revolution to be extended into the most highly industrialized countries; the consequent isolation of the first regime of workers and peasants in a world of capitalist states and its encirclement by imperialism; the low level and deficient productive powers of the economy; the preponderance of the peasantry over the working class in the population; cultural backwardness; the absence of a prior democratic revolution, which first acted as a propellant to the conquest of proletarian power and thereafter became a brake upon the development of the revolution; inadequate agricultural productivity; the exhaustion of civil war and the necessity to maintain extensive armed forces and incur huge military expenditures; continued scarcity of consumer goods and services which generated gross and growing inequalities and privileges and made the uncontrolled state into an all-powerful arbiter in the domain of distribution. The crucial political element in this process was the defeat or the absence of a sufficiently conscious leadership able to alert and mobilize the masses to combat the pernicious effects of the adverse objective circumstances in which the national and world revolution had to develop for an extended period.

The fact that the first victories of the anticapitalist revolution and the earliest experiments in constructing a base for socialism took place in the countries least prepared for the new methods of production and politics imposed such immense handicaps and hardships upon their revolutions that they had to sacrifice political democracy as the price of the survival of their socioeconomic conquests.

If we turn to the current situation of the United States and the most likely set of circumstances attending the struggle for workers' power, not a single one of the deleterious factors that have thwarted the harmonious development of the antecedent revolutions and engendered such cruel bureaucratic malformations will exert an equivalent influence on the coming American revolution. Indeed, the basic national and international conditions governing the class struggle and its outcome on American soil should have a very different weight and impact.

Let us analyze these formative forces one by one.

The place occupied by the United States in the sequence of world socialist revolutions will be very different from that of the original participants in this process. As the first to break loose from capitalism and imperialism, the Soviet Union had to incur the heavy penalties of pioneering in almost all fields of socialist endeavor. This has held true for the other revolutionized states in the backward countries.

The third American revolution, on the other hand, will unfold, not in the initial and most onerous period of socialist pathfinding, but at its climactic phase. It will emerge at a far more matured point in the progress of the world socialist movement and will be able to take full advantage, not only of its own more highly developed forces and resources, but also of the support and achievements of its predecessors. Just as the French Revolution occurred at the height of the democratic upsurge and shattered European feudalism, so the overturn of imperialism in its last stronghold will deliver the decisive blows to world capitalism.

The American socialist revolution will not stand alone in a

hostile world, nor can it be ringed about and quarantined by menacing imperialist powers, as the Soviet Union, China, Vietnam and Cuba have been. What power on earth could challenge it?

The addition of this newcomer to the socialist family would be joyously welcomed by the countries which had already broken their bondage to capitalism. The existing workers' states would not contend against a socialist America, as Washington today combats Cuba and China, but fraternally solidarize with it.

Moreover, other countries in the Western hemisphere would soon follow the example of the colossus of the north in ousting their capitalists and orienting toward socialism in a federated fashion, if, indeed, they have not previously set foot on that road.

Unlike the Soviet Union of 1917-21, China and similar lands, the United States will possess the most efficient and developed productive facilities at anyone's command at the time of the revolution's triumph. Its science, technology and industry already lead the world. Rationally reorganized and planned, the American economy is capable of an astounding forward leap in productive capacity. Even while working hours can be appreciably shortened, its output would provide an increasing margin to go for the improvement of the less developed economies elsewhere.

The Soviet Union, China and other countries embarked on the task of socialist construction with tens and hundreds of millions of illiterate peasant families bogged down in precapitalist barbarism. Even today these governments have been unable to overcome the immense difficulties in transforming the countryside and attaining an adequate level of agricultural output.

The population of the United States has an altogether different social composition and economic structure. Small family farmers represent only a small slice of the American nation and account for only a fraction of agricultural commodities. The fact that the most mechanized and monopolized agriculture of advanced capitalism has already solved the vexing problems of productivity and modernization of rural life will be of tremendous advantage to American socialism. Whereas the Soviet Union and China are plagued by agricultural underproduction, capitalist agriculture in the United States suffers from overproduction, as the piling up of surpluses in the warehouses and the periodic destruction of foodstuffs testify. A socialist economy, which produced for use and not for profit and would be morally obliged to equalize food and fiber consumption at home and abroad, could easily dispose of that otherwise insoluble problem.

Unlike the earlier workers' states, the bulk of Americans consist of wage workers, not peasants or small proprietors. They have excellent capacities and a colossal untapped potential for achievement. While the American working class is politically and ideologically more retarded than its counterparts in other countries, it is well educated, technically qualified, strongly organized and disciplined, combative and extremely productive.

There are no insuperable obstacles to preparing, training and equipping them to challenge and confront the capitalists and take over the functions of directing the state and reorganizing society that the revolution will demand of them. What they do not know at first, they can learn fast and acquire in the process of their revolutionization. Democracy will remain a fraud unless and until the working masses have the decisive voice in the government and economy, because they and their families constitute the overwhelming majority of the American people.

One of the most powerful and persistent causes of bureaucratism in the Stalinized regimes has been the scarcity of goods which led to inequalities and a fierce scramble among the diverse categories of the population for the available means of consumption. Such a paucity of goods and services and the need for an arbitrary authority to ration them is unlikely to reappear in any very strong way in the United States. The unparalleled productive power of the economy can provide enough of the necessities and comforts of life to satisfy everyone's requirements and leave enough surplus to lift up the rest of humanity in cooperative endeavor.

The revolutionary regimes from Russia to China were obliged to carry out the tasks of both the democratic and socialist revolutions at one and the same time. They had to undertake such presocialist tasks as the abolition of feudal relations and relics, agrarian reform, national independence and unification and the democratization of political life along with the overthrow of imperialist domination, capitalist property and the construction of a new social order. These backward countries, which had to bear the combination of historical tasks belonging to different epochs on their too weak shoulders, found the double burden too much to sustain. Their democracy collapsed under the strains of the overload.

The United States long ago passed through its democratic revolutions. Except for the liberation of the Afro-American and other oppressed nationalities and the oppressed women — the major presocialist problems handed down from the second American revolution — the Americans can apply all their energies to the solution of such purely socialist chores as organizing and operating a planned economy, eliminating inequalities and discriminations of all kinds, overcoming the differences between mental and manual labor through automation and education, creating unalienated human relations, enhancing the functions of the self-acting masses and diminishing the powers of the state.

If the achievements and institutions bequeathed by our earlier democratic revolutions fostered illusions which have considerably delayed the development of the socialist forces and the advent of the third American revolution, they have prepared the American people for creative participation in political and cultural activity which will prove of immense benefit to socialism in the long run.

It appears as though the socialist revolution in the United States will be less fortunate than its forerunners in at least one highly important respect. The greater weakness of the colonial and semicolonial possessing classes makes it easier to win power in those lands, whereas their underdevelopment creates tremendous problems for the political and economic consolidation of the revolution.

The anticapitalist forces in the United States will confront the wealthiest, most highly centralized, powerfully organized and well equipped of all ruling classes. These fanatics of private property are convinced that God and history have delegated them to defend their antiquated social system to the death. They will stop at nothing to preserve their privileges and power. Their capacities for ruthlessness in defense of their possessions have been displayed in the genocidal war against the Vietnamese and at home in the brutal repressions of rebellious blacks. Their partisans will no more be inhibited by scruples in putting down any threat to revolution than were the southern slaveholders or the German, Spanish and Indonesian bourgeoisie.

Just as the preparatory period of the coming American revolution has been stretched out for a long time, so it can be anticipated that the direct struggle for power between the armed camps will be exceedingly ferocious, hard-fought and protracted. It will require extraordinary efforts, tenacity and discipline to dislodge and dispossess the monopolist masters of America.

There will be some compensation later for this cost. If it will be far more difficult to overcome the opposition of the class enemy, the wealth and productivity of the country will greatly facilitate the rapid progress of the new regime once the wounds of civil strife have been healed and its damages repaired.

Another aspect to be considered is the changes which the revolutionary struggle will effect in the consciousness of the working class. In order to meet and defeat their adversaries, the revolutionary workers and their allies will have to perform prodigious feats of organization and administration which should sharpen their intelligence, understanding and ingenuity. They should come out of the ordeal not exhausted amidst a devastated land (unless atomic weapons are loosed against them) but trained, tempered and exhilarated by the vistas of a new world opened up before the people.

Would it be realistic to expect that, after such a transformation in their psychological outlook, the insurgent American masses, which have bested the mightiest array of counterrevolutionary forces ever assembled, will thereupon permit a new breed of bureaucrat to put a saddle and bridle upon them in the name of socialism, as happened in the poorer workers' states? One of the strongest spurs to revolutionary action would be the drive of the workers and oppressed nationalities to take command of their own destinies. This thirst for democracy will make it all the harder for any aspirants to bureaucratic domination to take away from the masses the decision-making powers their revolution has given them.

The reduced chances of such an eventuality would not come from any innately democratic or independent traits of the American people and its working class. The main assurance against its recurrence will be the lack of strong economic compulsions and social incentives for a relapse into despotism.

The streams of wealth can flow so abundantly in this rich country that every member of the postrevolutionary society can be provisioned with whatever basic necessities they require while the masses can enjoy more improvements in their conditions of life than they have ever known. Residual inequalities will be a minor rather than a major feature of society and should steadily be reduced as the new economy and way of life assert their potential. Meanwhile, the education of the younger generation in moral incentives and social solidarity and the assumption of more and more public functions by the workers with the shortening of their working hours can add a growing guarantee against usurpations by officeholders.

The socialist revolution will do more than enlarge the democratic freedoms of the American peoples. It will accelerate democratization for the rest of mankind. This may well be its foremost boon in the transitional period.

Other peoples will have ample reason to rejoice at the demise of the monster of American imperialism and the end of its death-dealing machinery. They would be relieved of the terrible tensions arising from fear of aggression, intervention and war by Washington and its satellites. Their governments could stop the arms race which consumes so much of the national resources and devote these revenues to public welfare, raising living standards and other useful social purposes. The dread shadow of the mushroom cloud portending nuclear annihilation in the course of imperialist expansion would be banished.

The socialist victory in the United States would give tremendous impetus to the processes of democratization in the bureaucratically degenerated and deformed workers' states. It would encourage their peoples to throw the detested tyrants off their backs and assume the sovereign power to which they are entitled and which socialism promises and can give. They would no longer hesitate to do so for fear that the imperialists and their agents would take advantage of their internal divisions for reactionary ends. Nor could the apologists for the bureaucracies brandish that argument as an excuse for perpetuating their dictatorial rule or perpetrating aggressions against other nationalities.

In addition to the more propitious circumstances within the United States, significant recent events in the international socialist movement and the workers' states presage a more favorable path of development for democracy in the later stages of the world revolution. At the height of Stalin's terror many people were so mesmerized by the phenomenon that they mistook that transitory totalitarianism for the essence of communism. The insistence that this was the permanent structural feature of any form of socialism was the theme of Orwell's fantasy of 1984, Professor Popper's contraposition of "the open society" to "the closed society" and the stock-in-trade of the anticommunist propaganda offensives sounded in all keys by the Western imperialists.

Since that time the de-Stalinization reforms in the Soviet Union, the decomposition of Stalinist monolithism, the more democratic features of the Cuban Revolution (the first since the October 1917 revolution under a leadership not trained in the Stalinist school), the resistance to regimentation shown by the intellectuals in the Soviet bloc, the Hungarian revolt of 1956 and finally the drive for democratization in Czechoslovakia in 1968, which was cut short and crushed by the Soviet invasion, have cast a new light upon the situation.

The antibureaucratic campaigns of the Cubans, the Yugoslav experiment in workers' self-management as well as the left communist oppositions which have sprung up throughout the postcapitalist sector, signify that, far from being an inherent and irremovable curse of communism, bureaucratism is fundamentally at odds with the growing momentum of its inner tendencies. As the postcapitalist societies move ahead, the urge to extrude such excrescences becomes ever stronger. The increasing degree of democratization which will result from the advances of the debureaucratization movements of the masses in the workers' states betokens that, when the American revolution comes to fruition, the forces of democratization in the two sectors of struggle can reciprocally reinforce each other.

The workers' states which have arisen from the socialist revolutions in the half-century since the founding of the Soviet Union have been the battleground for two polar types of rule. One is more or less democratic in character, expressing the power and guarding the welfare of the toiling mases in whose name the revolution was made. The other is despotic and Bonapartist, bent on defending the privileged positions of a commanding caste which has succeeded in usurping the decision-making powers from the masses.

The second form of political development prevailed during the recession of the world revolution from 1923 to 1943 as the other went into decline. Since then a reversal has been taking place. The first type of political development is now on the rise while its opposite is waning in strength. As the center of revolution shifts from the more backward to the more advanced areas of the world and as the revolution embraces more and more peoples, the democratic option is bound to gain strength.

Just as democracy was stunted and short-lived in the period of the antifeudal revolutions and then bloomed with the maturing of bourgeois relations, so the political democracy which has had such hard sledding in the first stage of anticapitalist revolution will have far better chances of prospering as the international revolution spreads and socialism grows. This is especially true for the United States.

The prevalence of diametrically opposite conditions in the domestic and world contexts in which the American socialist struggle will unfold should favor a quite different line of political development and an opposing outcome here. Once the supremacy of the workers has been won and the publicly-owned economy is operated in a planned manner, our people should see democracy flourish on a scale never before experienced by any nation, our own included.

In addition to the more propitious objective setting, the nature of the leadership it must have should be further assurance that the democratic character of the American revolution will be maintained and enhanced. Our exposition of the deterrents to bureaucratic deformation stressed the crucial role that the intervention and guidance of the revolutionary party can play in the process.

The vanguard party with a clear understanding of the sources of bureaucratism and the ways to counteract its vices and which is determined to combat them, can help curb the dangers by promoting workers' democracy to the maximum. The cadres of the revolutionary party must be imbued with full knowledge of the harm done to the progress of world socialism by the scourge of bureaucratism and Stalinism in all their variants and impart these lessons to the insurgent masses. The Fourth International and its cothinkers in the United States, the Socialist Workers Party and Young Socialist Alliance, have incorporated these lessons in their traditions, programs and practices. They intend to see that they are put into effect within their own organizations and extended to all spheres of their activity and influence.

Granted that the party which leads the working class and its state can do much to obstruct and hold down the growth of bureaucratism in the transitional period, what guarantees the good faith and conduct of that party itself? Its internal democracy, the plurality of parties and the system of workers' councils can serve to keep it on the right road. All the same, there is no inviolable guarantee in any party, government, union or council system that the principles of democracy will be observed in the customs of everyday life.

The final surety must reside in the vigilance and consciousness of the people themselves. This is the heart of democracy. As a genuinely democratic creed and movement, socialism does not fear the independent activities and initiatives of the masses; it trusts and solicits their potential for growth and learns from their creative activity. Marxism has full faith in the latent capacities of the people to find out its own best interests. They can be deluded and make wrong judgments at times. But mankind has progressed politically in no other way than through the mistakes of the masses — and their correction of these mistakes.

The crux of political democracy is posed in the question:

who will watch the watchmen? In the final analysis, only the different sections of the oppressed can fulfill this function for themselves. To do so, they must retain all democratic rights, including the right of revolutionary action if they feel compelled to engage in it. The Afro-American and other oppressed nationalities, the women, the workers and whoever suffers discrimination must watch out for any insensitivity to or slighting of their rights, needs and welfare and take the necessary measures to guard them, not only in the course of the revolution but after its victory. The full emancipation of humanity can come about only through the self-conscious action of a socialist-minded populace against all forms and forces of oppression.

Reactionaries and liberals alike contend against the Marxists that a new revolution, socialist in nature and working-class in composition and leadership, would inevitably result in a loss of liberty and retrogression all along the line. Such warnings were once heard from the upholders of the British crown and the apologists for the slaveholders. The last-ditch defenders of capitalism merely echo their apprehensions — and for the same selfish class reasons.

Such a conclusion cannot find support in the facts of American development. The course of American history in the eighteenth and nineteenth centuries proves that each of the bourgeois revolutions was the gateway to immense progress in our national life. Each in its own way and measure spurred the expansion of democracy. Why should only earlier bourgeois and not contemporary socialist revolutions bring benefit to mankind?

Indeed, the third American revolution promises to solve many more problems and do far more good than its predecessors. It offers the only way to save mankind from nuclear incineration, rescue the American nation from the menace of reactionary dictatorship and release the potentialities of science, technology and industry for the common good. Far from reducing or destroying democratic rights, the abolition of capitalism and the introduction of socialist relations will bring about, in the words of Abraham Lincoln, "a new birth of freedom" for this country and the rest of the world.

NOTES

Foreword

1. Gabriel, Ralph Henry, *The Course of American Democratic Thought*, p. 13.

1. Success in Greece

1. Hobhouse, L. T., *Sociology and Philosophy*, p. 195.
2. Barker, Ernest, *The Political Thought of Plato and Aristotle*, p. 4.
3. Glotz, Gustave, *The Greek City*, p. 129.
4. Leveque, Pierre, *The Greek Adventure*, p. 251.
5. Durant, Will, *The Life of Greece*, p. 266.

3. The Democracy of the Medieval Commune

1. Thompson, James W., *Economic and Social History of the Middle Ages*, vol. II, p. 780.
2. Pirenne, Henri, *Belgian Democracy*, p. 110.
3. Cheyney, E. P., *The Dawn of a New Era: 1250-1453*, p. 111.

5. Achievements and Limitations of the Bourgeois Revolutions

1. Motley, John Lothrop, *The Rise of the Dutch Republic*, p. 1581.
2. Abernathy, George L., ed., *The Idea of Equality*, pp. 100-15.
3. Rude, George, *The Crowd in the French Revolution*, p. 9.
4. Lefebvre, Georges, *The Coming of the French Revolution*, p. 178.
5. Thompson, J. M., *The French Revolution*, p. 431.
6. Guerin, Daniel, *La Lutte de Classes Sous La Premiere Republique*, vol. 1, p. 233 (translation by George Novack).
7. Fried, Albert and Sanders, Ronald, ed., *Socialist Thought*, pp. 52.
8. Ibid., pp. 67-68.
9. Cobban, Alfred, *Aspects of the French Revolution*, p. 12.

10. Holborn, Hajo, *A History of Modern Germany 1840-1945*, p. 811.

6. Bourgeois Democratic Ideology

1. Becker, Howard and Barnes, Harry Elmer, *Social Thought from Lore to Science*, vol. 1., p. 379.
2. Palmer, Robert R., *The Age of the Democratic Revolution*, vol. 1, pp. 14-15.
3. Parrington, Vernon, *Main Currents in American Thought*, vol. 1, p. 189.
4. Marx, Karl, *Capital*, translation by Eden and Cedar Paul, p. 104.
5. Hobbes, Thomas, *Leviathan*, p. 97.
6. Lilburne, John, *A Whip for the Present House of Lords;* as cited in MacPherson, C. B., *The Political Theory of Possessive Individualism: Hobbes to Locke*, p. 137.
7. Wallace, Malcolm W., ed., *Milton's Prose*, p. 378; as cited in Kohn, Hans, *The Idea of Nationalism*, p. 172.
8. See Novack, George, *Empiricism and Its Evolution*, chapter 1 for an explanation of the class origin of Locke's contradictions.

7. The Evolution of Parliamentarism

1. Locke, John, *Two Treatises on Government*, section 240.
2. Koch, Adrienne and Peden, William, ed., *The Life and Selected Writings of Thomas Jefferson*, p. 166.
3. Deutscher, Isaac and Novack, George, ed., *The Age of Permanent Revolution*, p. 364.

8. Parliamentary Liberalism in Crisis

1. Bevan, Aneurin, *In Place of Fear*, pp. 3-4.
2. Trotsky, Leon, *The Only Road for Germany,* p. 21.

9. Bonapartism, Military Dictatorship and Fascism

1. Bevan, Aneurin, *In Place of Fear*, p. 6.
2. Trotsky, Leon, *Whither France?*, pp. 18-19.
3. Trotsky, Leon, *Fascism: What It Is, How to Fight It*, pp. 28-29.
4. Trotsky, Leon, *What Next?*, p. 29.
5. Ibid, pp. 12-13.

10. Two Traditions of American Democracy

1. Commager, Henry S., *Living Ideas in America*, p. 209.

2. Ibid., p. 216.
3. Mills, C. Wright, *The Power Elite,* pp. 229-30.
4. Hartz, Louis, *The Liberal Tradition in America,* p. 6.
5. Dewey, John, *Freedom and Culture,* p. 155.
6. Koch, Adrienne and Peden, William, ed., *The Life and Selected Writings of Thomas Jefferson,* p. 413.
7. Ibid.
8. Dewey, John, *Freedom and Culture,* p. 162.

11. The Realities of American Democracy

1. Berle, A. A., *Economic Power and the Free Society,* p. 14.
2. Johnson, Sam Houston, *My Brother Lyndon,* pp. 104-105.
3. Huberman, Leo, "Freedom Under Capitalism and Socialism," *Monthly Review,* October 1965.
4. *New York Times,* November 13, 1969.
5. Mills, C. Wright, *The Sociological Imagination,* p. 188.
6. *New York Times,* November 8, 1969.
7. Parkinson, C. Northcote, *The Evolution of Political Thought,* p. 180.
8. Hitler, Adolf, *Mein Kampf,* vol. 1, p. 78.
9. McDonald, Forrest, *E Pluribus Unum,* pp. 235-36.
10. Douglas, William O., *Points of Rebellion,* pp. 6-7, 41, 95, 97.

12. How Can Our Democracy Be Defended and Extended?

1. Trotsky, Leon, *The History of the Russian Revolution,* p. xvii.
2. Luxemburg, Rosa, *Rosa Luxemburg Speaks,* p. 101.

13. Socialism and Bureaucracy

1. Ryazanoff, D., *The Communist Manifesto of Marx and Engels,* p. 331.
2. Ibid., p. 52.
3. Lenin, V. I., *The State and Revolution,* chapter 3, section 3.
4. Guevara, Che, *Che Guevara Speaks,* p. 108.
5. Trotsky, Leon, *The New International,* May 1939, p. 134.
6. Mandel, Ernest, ed., *Fifty Years of World Revolution (1917-1967),* pp. 25-26.

14. The Colonial Struggle for Democracy

1. *New York Post,* August 19, 1970.

BIBLIOGRAPHY

There is no lack of books in English about both democracy and revolution in their various aspects. The following list consists, not of all those works consulted in connection with this book, but only of those volumes which are referred to or cited in the text.

I have been especially indebted throughout to the writings of Leon Trotsky on these topics, in chapter 7 to Professor C. B. MacPherson's incisive study of *The Political Theory of Possessive Individualism*, and in chapters 6 and 10 to Daniel Guerin's two books: *Fascism and Big Business* and *La Lutte de Classes Sous La Premiere Republique*.

Abernathy, George L., ed., *The Idea of Equality,* Richmond, 1959.
Adams, Henry, *The Degradation of the Democratic Dogma,* New York, 1958.
Adams, John A., *A Defence of the Constitutions of Government of the United States of America Against the Attack of M. Turgot,* London, 1794.
Barker, E., *The Political Thought of Plato and Aristotle,* New York, 1959.
Becker, Howard and Barnes, Harry Elmer, *Social Thought from Lore to Science,* New York, 1961.
Berle, A. A., *Economic Power and the Free Society,* New York, 1957.
Bevan, Aneurin, *In Place of Fear,* London, 1952.
Buonarroti, *Conspiration Pour L'Egalite Dite De Babeuf,* Paris, 1957.
Cheyney, E. P., *The Dawn of a New Era: 1250-1453,* New York, 1936.
Cobban, Alfred, *Aspects of the French Revolution,* New York, 1968.
Commager, Henry S., *Living Ideas in America,* New York, 1951.
Curti, Merle, *Probing Our Past,* New York, 1955.
De Bertier de Sauvigny, Guillaume, *The Bourbon Restoration,* Philadelphia, 1966.

De Ruggiero, Guido, *The History of European Liberalism,* Boston, 1966.

Deutscher, Isaac and Novack, George, ed., *The Age of Permanent Revolution,* New York, 1964.

Dewey, John, *Freedom and Culture,* New York, 1939.

Domhoff, G. William, *Who Rules America?,* Englewood Cliffs, 1967.

Douglas, William O., *Points of Rebellion,* New York, 1970.

Durant, Will, *The Life of Greece,* New York, 1939.

Epstein, Leon D., *Political Parties in Western Democracies,* New York, 1967.

Fried, Albert and Sanders, Ronald, ed., *Socialist Thought,* New York, 1964.

Gabriel, Ralph Henry, *The Course of American Democratic Thought,* New York, 1956.

Glotz, Gustave, *The Greek City,* New York, 1929.

Guerin, Daniel, *Fascism and Big Business,* New York, 1939.

Guerin, Daniel, *La Lutte de Classes Sous La Premiere Republique,* Paris, 1946.

Guevara, Che, *Che Guevara Speaks,* New York, 1967.

Hartz, Louis, *The Liberal Tradition in America,* New York, 1955.

Hitler, Adolf, *Mein Kampf,* New York, 1939.

Hobhouse, L. T., *Sociology and Philosophy,* London, 1966.

Hobsbawm, E. J., *The Age of Revolution: 1789-1848,* New York, 1964.

Holborn, Hajo, *A History of Modern Germany 1840-1945,* New York, 1969.

Huberman, Leo, "Freedom Under Capitalism and Socialism," *Monthly Review,* October 1965.

Johnson, Sam Houston, *My Brother Lyndon,* New York, 1970.

Koch, Adrienne and Peden, William, ed., *The Life and Selected Writings of Thomas Jefferson,* New York, 1944.

Kohn, Hans, *The Idea of Nationalism,* New York, 1951.

Laslett, Peter, ed., *Locke's Two Treatises of Government,* Cambridge, 1967.

Lefebvre, Georges, *The Coming of the French Revolution,* New York, 1961.

Lefebvre, Georges, *The French Revolution, From Its Origins to 1793,* New York, 1965.

Lenin, V. I., *The State and Revolution,* New York, 1929.

Leveque, Pierre, *The Greek Adventure,* Cleveland, 1968.

Luxemburg, Rosa, *Rosa Luxemburg Speaks,* New York, 1970.

McDonald, Forrest, *E Pluribus Unum,* Boston, 1965.

MacPherson, C. B., *The Political Theory of Possessive Individualism: Hobbes to Locke,* Oxford, 1962.

Mandel, Ernest, ed., *Fifty Years of World Revolution (1917-1967),* New York, 1968.

Marx, Karl, *Capital,* Trans. by Eden and Cedar Paul, London, 1930.

Mills, C. Wright, *The Power Elite,* New York, 1959.

Mills, C. Wright, *The Sociological Imagination*, New York, 1959.

Moore, Barrington, Jr., *Social Origins of Dictatorship and Democracy*, Boston, 1966.

Moore, Stanley W., *The Critique of Capitalist Democracy*, New York, 1956.

Motley, John Lothrop, *The Rise of the Dutch Republic*, London, 1907.

Pablo, Michel, *Dictature du Proletariat, Democratie, Socialisme*, Paris, 1957.

Paine, Thomas, *Writings*, vol. 1, New York, 1894.

Palmer, Robert R., *The Age of the Democratic Revolution*, 2 vols., Princeton, 1959, 1964.

Parkinson, C. Northcote, *The Evolution of Political Thought*, London, 1958.

Parrington, Vernon, *Main Currents in American Thought*, New York, 1930.

Pirenne, Henri, *Belgian Democracy*, New York, 1915.

Pirenne, Henri, *Early Democracies in the Low Countries*, New York, 1963.

Rude, George, *Revolutionary Europe, 1783-1815*, New York, 1964.

Rude, George, *The Crowd in the French Revolution*, London, 1959.

Ryazanoff, D., *The Communist Manifesto of Marx and Engels*, New York, 1930.

Sabine, George H., *A History of Political Theory*, New York, 1961.

Schilpp, Paul A., ed., *The Philosophy of John Dewey*, New York, 1951.

Thompson, James Westphall, *Economic and Social History of the Middle Ages*, New York, 1959.

Thompson, J. M., *The French Revolution*, London, 1966.

Trotsky, Leon, *Fascism: What It Is, How to Fight It*, New York, 1969.

Trotsky, Leon, *The History of the Russian Revolution*, New York, 1936.

Trotsky, Leon, *The Only Road for Germany*, New York, 1933.

Trotsky, Leon, *The Revolution Betrayed*, Garden City, 1937.

Trotsky, Leon, *What Next?*, New York, 1932.

Trotsky, Leon, *Whither France?*, New York, 1936.

INDEX

Adams, Brooks, 143
Adams, Henry, 143
Adams, John, 181
Adams, Sam, 184
Adams, Sherman, 195
Alexander II, 92
Alexander the Great, 21
Alfonso XIII, 151
Antipater, 22
Aquinas, Thomas, 218
Aristotle, 18, 21, 27, 31
Augustus, 34

Babeuf, Gracchus, 81, 83-86, 104
Baltzell, E. Digby, 192
Bancroft, George, 126
Barker, Ernest, 21
Barnes, Harry Elmer, 103
Becker, Howard, 103
Ben Bella, Ahmad, 80
Bentham, Jeremy, 111, 121
Berle, A. A., 191
Bevan, Aneurin, 144, 156
Blum, Leon, 151
Bruening, Heinrich, 160, 172
Buonarotti, Filippo, 83

Caesar, Julius, 34, 36, 159
Capital (Karl Marx), 111
Castro, Fidel, 264
Charles I, 61-62, 65, 69, 252

Charles II, 70, 109, 131
Chateaubriand, Francois, 120
Cheyney, E. P., 42
Christian Science Monitor, 246
Chronicle of Current Events, 246
Churchill, Winston, 150
Colonial Mind (Vernon Parrington), 110
Common Sense (Thomas Paine), 11, 12, 105, 205
Communist Manifesto (Karl Marx and Friedrich Engels), 94, 224, 225
Cromwell, Oliver, 61-69, 80, 81, 116, 131, 260

Daladier, Edouardo, 171
Danton, Georges, 76, 78, 83
David, 20
de Gaulle, Charles, 19, 135, 161, 171, 219
Dewey, John, 122, 183-87, 188
Domhoff, G. William, 192
Douglas, William, 205
Doumergue, Gaston, 171
Dulles, John Foster, 198
Dupont de Nemours, Pierre, 75
Durant, Will, 31

Eisenhower, Dwight, 161, 194, 195, 198, 203

Engels, Friedrich, 84, 94, 225, 226, 243
Evolution of Political Thought (C. Northcote Parkinson), 204

Fifty Years of World Revolution (Ernest Mandel, ed.), 248
Franco, Francisco, 163, 165, 169
Franklin, Benjamin, 113
Freedom and Culture (John Dewey), 183, 185-86
Fulbright, William, 152, 198

Gabriel, Ralph, 10
Galliffet, Gaston, 219
Gandri, 41
Gentile, Giovanni, 165
George III, 11, 102, 188, 205
Gracchi, 35-36
Guevara, Che, 199, 241

Hamilton, Alexander, 52
Harrington, James, 56
Hartz, Louis, 183
Hebert, Jacques, 82, 84
Henry VIII, 130
Hindenburg, Paul von, 167, 219
History of the Russian Revolution, (Leon Trotsky), 218
Hitler, Adolf, 118, 135, 147, 160, 163, 165, 166, 167, 169, 170, 173, 204, 219
Hobbes, Thomas, 108, 114, 115, 116
Hobhouse, L. T., 19
Ho Chi Minh, 254
Holborn, Hajo, 100
Homer, 21
Huberman, Leo, 197

In Place of Fear (Aneurin Bevan), 144, 156
Ireton, Henry, 64, 65

James I, 61
Jaures, Jean, 219
Jefferson, Thomas, 103, 126, 135-36, 137, 182, 183, 184, 186, 187, 188, 189, 209, 254, 265
Johnson, Lyndon B., 193, 194, 198, 202, 205, 209, 217, 219
Johnson, Sam Houston, 193

Kapp, Wolfgang, 162
Kennedy, John, 194, 198, 209, 219
Kennedy, Robert, 193, 198
Kent, James, 181
Kleisthenes, 25, 27
Krushchev, Nikita, 231, 246

Laslett, Peter, 125
Laud, William, 62
Leclerc, Eugene, 82
Lefebvre, Georges, 75
Leipart, Theodor, 168
Lenin, V. I., 72, 140, 148, 183, 228, 229, 230, 231, 232, 235, 236, 239, 243, 248, 259
Leveque, Pierre, 30
Leviathan (Thomas Hobbes), 114-15
Liberal Tradition in America (Louis Hartz), 183
Lilburne, John, 66, 109, 115
Lincoln, Abraham, 97, 183, 184, 186, 189, 204, 209, 265-66, 276
Liu Shao-chi, 264
Locke, John, 102, 108-10, 115, 116, 124-25, 128-29, 132, 133, 183
Louis XVI, 74, 86, 88, 103
Louis XVIII, 249
Louis Philippe, 75, 94
Luxemburg, Rosa, 219
Lycurgus, 22

Mably, Gabriel, 103
McDonald, Forrest, 204
Madison, James, 186
Malcolm X, 200
Mandel, Ernest, 248
Manifesto of the Equals (Sylvain Marechal), 84
Mao Tse-tung, 264
Marat, Jean Paul, 76
Marechal, Sylvain, 84

Marx, Karl, 84, 94, 111, 183, 225, 226, 231, 232, 243
Medici family, 44
Mein Kampf (Adopf Hitler), 204
Memoirs (Sherman Adams), 195
Mill, James, 155
Mill, John, 121
Mill, John Stewart, 121, 122
Millerand, Alexandre, 139, 219
Mills, C. Wright, 182-83, 192, 199
Milton, John, 119
Montesquieu, Charles, 103, 133
Motley, John L., 60
Mussolini, Benito, 149, 154, 163, 165, 166, 167, 169, 244
My Brother Lyndon (Sam Houston Johnson), 193

Napoleon I, 68, 73, 74, 80, 87-88, 117, 159, 205
Napoleon III, 94, 160, 161
Nasser, Gamal Abdel, 258
Nixon, Richard, 209

Observations on Civil Liberty (Richard Price), 105
Only Road for Germany (Leon Trotsky), 147
Orwell, George, 273
Ovando, Alfredo, 162
Overton, Richard, 64, 66, 109

Paine, Thomas, 11-12, 13, 103, 105, 119-20, 129, 188
Palmer, R. R., 69, 103
Parkinson, C. Northcote, 204
Parrington, Vernon, 110
Pericles, 18, 27, 28, 31
Petain, Henri, 135, 171
Petty, William, 64
Philip II, 56
Phillips, Wendell, 184
Philosophy of John Dewey (John Dewey), 185
Pirenne, Henri, 41, 43, 45
Plekhanov, Georgi, 101
Points of Rebellion (William Douglas), 205

Politics (Aristotle), 21
Polybius, 35
Pompidou, Georges, 161
Popper, Karl, 273
Price, Richard, 105
Principles of Communism (Friedrich Engels), 225
Proxmire, William, 203

Rainborough, 64
Ricardo, David, 121
Rise of the Dutch Republic (John Motley), 60
Robespierre, Maximilien, 72-84, 234, 260, 265
Roehm, Ernst, 169
Ronsin, 82
Roosevelt, Franklin D., 150, 198, 209, 217, 219
Roosevelt, Theodore, 198
Rousseau, Jean, 103, 108, 129, 132
Roux, Jacques, 82
Rude, George, 73

Saint Just, Louis, 80
Sakharov, Andrei, 246
Santayana, George, 183
Saul, 20
Schleicher, Kurt von, 160, 172
Seward, William, 188
Siles, Luis, 162
Smith, Adam, 121
Social Contract (John Locke), 103
Spartacus, 35, 36
Spencer, Herbert, 121
Stalin, Joseph, 172, 231, 233, 235, 240, 241, 245, 246, 249, 259, 273
State and Revolution (V. I. Lenin), 228, 235, 236, 259
Strachey, John, 55
Strasser, Gregor, 169
Suharto, 163
Sukarno, Achmed, 258
Sweezy, Paul, 192

Tito (Joseph Broz), 241, 244

Tribune of the People (Gracchus Babeuf), 83

Trotsky, Leon, 72, 84, 136, 140, 147, 159, 166, 167, 172, 218, 230, 232, 243, 247, 255, 264

Truman, Harry, 198, 205, 209, 219

Turgot, Anne Robert, 180

Two Treatises of Government (John Locke), 109, 110, 124, 128

Van Aersens, Francois, 60

Vane, Henry, 128

Varlet, Jean, 82

Victor Emmanuel III, 167

von Papen, Franz, 160, 172

Waldeck-Rousseau, Pierre, 139

Walwyn, William, 66, 109

Washington, George, 68

Westminster Review, 155

What Next? (Leon Trotsky), 172-73

Whither France? (Leon Trotsky), 166

Who Rules America? (G. William Domhoff), 192

William of Nassau, 60

William of Orange, 55

William the Silent, 68

Williams, Roger, 70

Wilson, Woodrow, 150, 198, 209

Wohl, Paul, 246

For further reading

REVOLUTIONARY CONTINUITY
Marxist Leadership in the United States
by Farrell Dobbs
How successive generations of fighters took part in the struggles of the U.S. labor movement, seeking to build a leadership that could advance the interests of workers and small farmers. 2 volumes, $16.95 each

TRADE UNIONS IN THE EPOCH OF IMPERIALIST DECAY
by Leon Trotsky, Karl Marx
What are the tasks of trade unions under capitalism? What is their relationship to workers' fight for economic justice and political power? Includes "Trade Unions: Their Past, Present, and Future," by Karl Marx. $14.95

LABOR'S GIANT STEP
The First Twenty Years of the CIO: 1936-1955
by Art Preis
How the political struggle of major currents in the workers' movement marked the rise of the Congress of Industrial Organizations (CIO) in the 1930s. And how it continues to pose the issues that must be resolved today by the labor movement as it is transformed by its struggles with the employers. $26.95

LEON TROTSKY SPEAKS
The major political questions of the twentieth century are discussed in this book by an outstanding communist leader. Includes a defense of the right to revolution, made in 1906 in the prisoner's dock of the tsar's court; speeches as a leader of the revolutionary government following the Bolshevik-led revolution; and "I Stake My Life," Trotsky's 1937 defense of his twenty-year Bolshevik course and challenge to the organizers of Joseph Stalin's frame-up trials. $23.95

THE JEWISH QUESTION
A Marxist Interpretation
by Abram Leon
Explains the historical roots of anti-Semitism and how in times of social crisis it is used by the capitalists to mobilize reactionary forces against the labor movement and divide working people in face of their common exploiters. $17.95

FASCISM AND BIG BUSINESS
by Daniel Guerin
Examines the development of fascism in Germany and Italy and its relationship with the ruling capitalist families there. $19.95

THE STRUGGLE AGAINST FASCISM IN GERMANY
by Leon Trotsky
Writing in the heat of struggle against the rising fascist movement, the Russian revolutionary leader examines the origin and nature of fascism and advances a working-class strategy to combat it. $28.95

THE SPANISH REVOLUTION (1931-39)
by Leon Trotsky
Analyzes the revolutionary upsurge on the land and in the factories leading to the Spanish civil war and discusses the causes of the fascist victory. $27.95

REVOLUTION AND COUNTER-REVOLUTION IN SPAIN
by Felix Morrow
A contemporary account of the revolution and civil war in Spain in the 1930s in which the proletariat, betrayed by its anarchist, social democratic, and Stalinist leaderships, went down to defeat under the blows of an armed fascist movement. $17.95

FASCISM: WHAT IT IS AND HOW TO FIGHT IT
by Leon Trotsky
Fascism, Trotsky explains, has been able to conquer only in those countries where conservative workers' parties blocked the proletariat from utilizing a revolutionary situation to seize power. Booklet. $3.00

THE FIGHT AGAINST FASCISM IN THE U.S.A.
by James P. Cannon and others
Forty years of struggle described by participants. $8.00

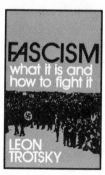

WHAT IS AMERICAN FASCISM?
Writings on Coughlin, Hague, and McCarthy
by James P. Cannon and Joseph Hansen
$8.00

WRITE FOR A FREE CATALOG.

Works by George Novack

UNDERSTANDING HISTORY
Marxist Essays
How capitalism arose, why this
exploitative system is historically
outdated, and how revolutionary
change in society and human
development is fundamental to
social and cultural progress. $15.95

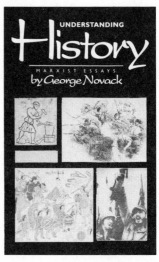

AMERICA'S REVOLUTIONARY HERITAGE
Marxist Essays
Explanatory essays on Native
Americans, the first American
revolution, the Civil War, the rise
of industrial capitalism, and the
first wave of the fight for women's
rights. $21.95

THE ORIGINS OF MATERIALISM
The rise of a scientific world outlook in
ancient Greece, concurrent with the
development of agriculture, manufacturing,
and trade that prepared the way for it. $19.95

EMPIRICISM AND ITS EVOLUTION
A Marxist View
Traces the evolution and contradictions of
the philosophical outlook of empiricism as
an ideological expression of the social
system of capitalism. $13.95

GENOCIDE AGAINST THE INDIANS
"The conflict between the red man and the
white is usually represented as essentially racial
in character. But their war to the death was at
bottom a social struggle," Novack explains. "The
scramble for wealth was at its root. In this case,
the chief prize was individual ownership of the
land." Booklet. $3.00

AN INTRODUCTION TO THE LOGIC OF MARXISM

Marxism is dialectical, Novack explains. It considers all phenomena in their development, in their transition from one state to another. And it is materialist, explaining the world as matter in motion that exists prior to and independently of human consciousness. $12.95

HUMANISM AND SOCIALISM

The relationship between humanism—the rational, secular expression of the ideals of the democratic revolution—and scientific socialism. $13.95

POLEMICS IN MARXIST PHILOSOPHY

Essays on Sartre, Plekhanov, Lukács, Engels, Kolakowski, Trotsky, Timpanaro, and Colletti. $19.95

PRAGMATISM VERSUS MARXISM

An Appraisal of John Dewey's Philosophy

A defense of Marxism against the pragmatism of John Dewey, chief theoretical spokesman in the 1930s of the middle-class democratic movement in the United States. $19.95

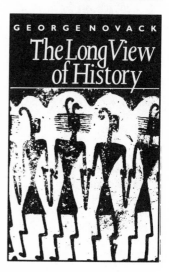

THE LONG VIEW OF HISTORY

Why the struggle of working people for an end to oppression and exploitation is a realistic perspective built on sound scientific foundations, and why revolutionary change is fundamental to social and cultural progress. Booklet. $3.50

Also from Pathfinder

NELSON MANDELA SPEAKS
Forging a Democratic, Nonracial South Africa

Tells the story of the revolutionary struggles that have brought South Africa to the threshold of a political and social transformation. $18.95

TO SEE THE DAWN
Baku 1920—First Congress of the Peoples of the East

How can peasants and workers in the colonial world achieve freedom from imperialist exploitation? How can working people overcome the divisions incited by their national ruling classes and act together for common class interests? These questions were addressed by 2,000 delegates to the Baku congress, meeting at a time when the young workers' and peasants' republic in Russia gave hope of a new dawn for the world's toilers. Complete proceedings. Part of the series, The Communist International in Lenin's Time. $19.95

THE TRUTH ABOUT YUGOSLAVIA
Why Working People Should Oppose Intervention

George Fyson, Argiris Malapanis, and Jonathan Silberman

The carnage in Yugoslavia is a product of the crisis-ridden world capitalist system. Rival gangs of aspiring capitalists— fragments of the former Yugoslav Stalinist regime—are fighting a war for territory and resources. Far from displaying humanitarian concern, Washington and its competitors in Europe are intervening militarily to protect and advance their respective interests. $8.95

TO SPEAK THE TRUTH
Why Washington's 'Cold War' against Cuba Doesn't End

Fidel Castro and Che Guevara

Castro and Guevara explain why the U.S. government remains determined to destroy the example set by the Cuban revolution and why its effort will fail. With an introduction by Mary-Alice Waters. $16.95

FEBRUARY 1965: THE FINAL SPEECHES
Malcolm X

Speeches from the last three weeks of Malcolm X's life, presenting the still accelerating evolution of his political views. A large part is material previously unavailable, with some in print for the first time. First volume in the chronological series. $17.95

COSMETICS, FASHIONS, AND THE EXPLOITATION OF WOMEN
Joseph Hansen, Evelyn Reed, and Mary-Alice Waters

How big business uses women's second-class status to generate profits for a few and perpetuate the oppression of the female sex and the exploitation of working people. $12.95

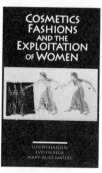

THE COMMUNIST MANIFESTO
Karl Marx and Frederick Engels

Founding document, written in 1847, of the modern working-class movement. Explains how capitalism arose as a specific stage in the economic development of class society and how it will be superseded through the revolutionary action on a world scale of the working class. Booklet. $2.50

THE REVOLUTION BETRAYED
What Is the Soviet Union and Where Is It Going?
Leon Trotsky

Classic study of the degeneration of the Soviet workers' state under the domination of the privileged social caste whose spokesman was Stalin. Illuminates the roots of the crisis of the 1990s. $19.95

FARMERS FACE THE CRISIS OF THE 1990s
Doug Jenness

Examines the deepening economic and social crisis in the capitalist world and explains how farmers and workers can unite internationally against the mounting assaults from the billionaire bankers, industrialists, and merchants. Booklet. $3.50

SEE FRONT OF BOOK FOR ADDRESSES.

New International

A MAGAZINE OF MARXIST POLITICS AND THEORY

IN ISSUE 7

Opening Guns of World War III:

WASHINGTON'S ASSAULT ON IRAQ

BY JACK BARNES

The U.S. government's murderous blockade, bombardment, and invasion of Iraq heralded increasingly sharp conflicts among imperialist powers, more wars, and growing instability of international capitalism. 333 pp., $12.00

New International

Washington's assault on Iraq

OPENING GUNS OF WORLD WAR III

— by Jack Barnes —

1945: WHEN U.S. TROOPS SAID 'NO!' — by Mary-Alice Waters

— 7 —

SPECIAL WAR ISSUE

IN ISSUE 5

The Coming Revolution in South Africa

BY JACK BARNES

The world importance of the struggle to overthrow the apartheid system and the vanguard role of the African National Congress, which is committed to lead the national, democratic revolution in South Africa to a successful conclusion. 198 pp., $9.00

New International

THE COMING REVOLUTION IN SOUTH AFRICA

by Jack Barnes

The future belongs to the majority

by Oliver Tambo

Why Cuban volunteers are in Angola

speeches by Fidel Castro

— 5 —

IN ISSUE 8

Che Guevara, Cuba, and the Road to Socialism

Exchanges from both the early 1960s and today on the relevance and historical importance of the political and economic perspectives defended by Ernesto Che Guevara. 204 pp., $10.00

New International

CHE GUEVARA CUBA AND THE ROAD TO SOCIALISM

Articles by Che Guevara, Carlos Rafael Rodríguez, Carlos Tablada, Jack Barnes, Steve Clark, Mary-Alice Waters

8

IN ISSUE 6

The Second Assassination of Maurice Bishop

BY STEVE CLARK

The accomplishments and lessons of the Grenada revolution, 1979-83, and how it was overthrown from within by the Stalinist gang that murdered Maurice Bishop. 272 pp., $10.00

DISTRIBUTED BY PATHFINDER